HEALING

Francis MacNutt, o.p.

HEALING

Ave Maria Press / Notre Dame / Indiana 46556

First printing, June, 1974
Sixth printing, September, 1976
141,000 copies in print.

ACKNOWLEDGMENT
   Excerpts from the *Jerusalem Bible,* copyright © 1966 by Darton,
   Longman & Todd, Ltd., and Doubleday and Company, Inc. Used by
   permission of the publisher.

Library of Congress Catalog Card No.: 74-81446
International Standard Book Number: 0-87793-074-0

Art by Sister Joan Marie Scheet, O.S.B.

Calligraphy by Sister Susan Scheet, O.S.B.

Printed in the United States of America

Contents

The Spirit of the Lord
has been given to me
for He has anointed me
He has sent me to bring
the good news to the poor,
to heal the broken hearted,
give sight to the blind,
and freedom to the
downtrodden.

LUKE 4:18

Preface

IN THE PAST few years an extraordinary change has been going on in the Roman Catholic Church—all the way from the grass-roots level to the most official pronouncements: the healing ministry is being renewed.

On the part of official pronouncements the most far-reaching of all the changes in understanding the sacraments went into effect January 1, 1974. The "Anointing of the Sick" is now for the professed purpose of healing the whole man and is no longer primarily a preparation of the soul for death. In line with this reorientation of the sacrament's purpose, it is to be administered not just to those in danger of death, but to anyone suffering from a serious illness.[1] These changes represent a return to an earlier view of the Anointing of the Sick prevalent in the Church until the time of the Middle Ages.

At the same time, at the grass-roots level we are seeing prayer groups rediscovering the power of praying for the sick.

1. *Study Text II: Anointing and Pastoral Care of the Sick* (Washington, D.C.: Publications Office, U.S. Catholic Conference, 1973).

This is not just a theoretical change; it is a change based on people's experience who have seen the sick healed through prayer. On a typical Pentecostal retreat now when I ask for a show of hands of those who have seen the sick healed through their prayers about half the hands go up. Similarly when I ask how many think, as far as they can judge, that any of their own illnesses have been healed through prayer, about half the hands go up.

Yet, I can remember a few short years ago when even the Catholic charismatic prayer groups had reservations about praying for physical healing.

My own involvement in the healing ministry came about in a very natural way; I never had much internal resistance to overcome—except lack of courage. My question has never really been as to its reality, but as to its wise use.

I was first prepared for this ministry by my desire to become a doctor, a desire which was nearly fulfilled in 1944 when I was accepted by Washington University Medical School after only two years of college premed. If all had gone well I would have become a doctor at the young age of 23, but that dream was blasted when I was drafted in September of 1944, just ten days before entering med school. The next two years I served in the Medical Department of the Army as a surgical technician, mostly working in the operating room of the hospital at Camp Crowder, Missouri.

Years later, when I entered the Dominican Order and read the lives of the saints with all the fervor of those novitiate days, I couldn't help but wonder why they seemed to have so much success going around healing the sick through their prayers, while we were never encouraged to pray for such things. We got the impression that praying for healing was presumptuous, like pretending to be a saint—which I certainly was not. We were not worthy of extraordinary manifestations of God's power.

How clearly I remember my Protestant friend who came and asked me to heal his son's partial blindness. This was in July, 1956, only a month after my ordination, and I didn't know how to respond to him. One thing I did know was that I was no saint, so I refused to go over to his home. I knew I was disappointing him but I felt I would disappoint him even more if I went to his home and his boy was not healed by my prayer.

But years later when I was teaching homiletics at the Aquinas Institute of Theology and was also trying to counsel many people, I felt that something was missing in my ministry. What kind of spiritual direction could I give to all these people coming for counsel—many of them sent by their psychiatrists? They were depressed—some to the point of attempting suicide; some were alcoholic, some homosexual, some hopelessly confused, feeling worthless and unlovable. They were the "not O.K." people, the "frogs." Their emotional problems could not be separated from their "spiritual" lives; as human beings they were being dragged down by sadness and guilt. Yet they could not overcome their problems by willpower. Some priests, brothers and sisters were among them—people who had dedicated their lives to Christ, but found that they were not able to live happily in community in spite of all their good will. I could not honestly say to myself—or to them—that all this destructive suffering was redemptive. I could not sincerely tell the mentally depressed patient, who was going through shock therapy, that his anxiety state was God's will and was a cross specially chosen by God for him. Clearly, there was a mystery involved in this, but it was the mystery of evil, of original sin; I could not believe that it was the mystery of God's direct will for man.

When I heard that Rev. Alfred Price, one of the Episcopalian founders of the Order of St. Luke (for the healing ministry), was going to speak at the Presbyterian Seminary of

Dubuque, I took the then bold step of going over to a Protestant seminary to hear him (this was around 1960). Everything he said made sense; especially that Jesus Christ has given his apostles as much a commission to heal as to teach. On the basis of New Testament evidence that seemed irrefutable. So, if the Church still claimed Christ's commission to teach, what had happened to the allied commission to heal and cast out demons? After the talk a group gathered for discussion and compared notes on how they prayed for the sick. They described some of the phenomena they had experienced, such as feeling heat in the hands, followed by swelling if the prayer went on too long. What really astonished me was that some of these ministers were not bothering to discuss a theory about whether or not healings took place; they were discussing a ministry they were sure of. For them there was no problem: healings took place. For me a whole new world had opened up. But I didn't know what to do about it; there was no one to encourage me to launch out.

The next time I heard about healing was in 1966, at the annual convention of the Speech Association of America (which I was attending as Executive Director of the Christian Preaching Conference). There in Chicago I was introduced by some friends to Mrs. Jo Kimmel, a speech professor at Manchester College, who I was told had remarkable success in praying for the sick. Upon meeting her and finding that she really did have some unusual—and to me almost unbelievable—experiences in praying for the sick, I called a priest friend of mine and together we spent a whole day pumping her for information about all this prayer for healing. I remember expressing surprise at her belief that these extraordinary healings would really take place. Her response was to ask why I thought healing should be extraordinary. She plainly considered healing an ordinary part of Christian life, and said that there were hundreds of people with experiences like her own. Where have they been, I thought. I've never met anyone like this; it's a whole new world—except that I had read about things like this in those saints' lives, back in novitiate days.

She offered to introduce me to some of these people by arranging for me to attend a retreat (a Camp Farthest Out for 800 people) in Maryville, Tennessee, in August, 1967. There I met two of the main speakers, Mrs. Agnes Sanford and Rev. Tommy Tyson, and learned still more about praying for healing. A year later, at a School for Pastoral Care held in Whitinsville, Massachusetts, I learned still more from Agnes, Tommy and Rev. John Sanford.

These schools (really five-day workshops) were instituted by Rev. Ted Sanford and his wife, Agnes, to help convince ministers that the healing ministry should be part of the normal work of any Christian minister. Although her husband died some years ago, Mrs. Sanford has carried on the work of teaching and is perhaps more responsible than anyone else for renewing the healing ministry in the main-line churches.

I was the first Roman Catholic priest to attend one of these Schools of Pastoral Care and immediately saw that the basic teachings on healing were very much in line with the Roman Catholic tradition. In fact, healing is probably easier for Catholics to understand than for most Protestants, since we have grown up with a tradition of saints blessed with extraordinary gifts, including healing, the one that is still used as a test for canonization. Consequently, most traditional Catholics have little difficulty in believing in divine healing. What is difficult is to believe that healing can be an ordinary, common activity of Christian life. When I discovered, though, that healing was common in the lives of people like Agnes Sanford it all seemed to make sense; if it were true, it meant I would no longer have to tell people whose sicknesses were disintegrating their personalities that their illness was a God-sent cross, but I could hold up the hope that God wanted them well, even when medical science could not help.

A short time after coming to believe in the reality of healing in the lives of these friends I had grown to love and respect, Jo Kimmel, Tommy Tyson, and Agnes Sanford, I realized I could not treat this good news as if it were some abstract theorem but would have to put it into practice.

The first person I prayed for was a sister who had been through shock treatment for mental depression and had been taken as far as psychiatry could take her. I knew she had nothing to lose by my praying with her. And I had nothing to lose, except a certain false humility, by offering to pray for her healing. To my surprise (at least partly) she was healed. This encouraged me to believe that if *I* prayed for people they might be healed. (Somehow it was much easier to believe that God could heal the sick *through prayer* than to believe that he would heal *through my prayer.*)

Since then I have seen many people healed—especially when I have prayed with a team or in a loving community. Although I travel too much to be able to follow up and estimate accurately, I would make a rough estimate that about half those we pray for are healed (or are notably improved) of physical sickness and about three-fourths of those we pray for are healed of emotional or spiritual problems. I say this as an encouragement for others to consider the possibility that God might use their prayers someday to heal the sick.

In no way do I conceive prayer for healing as a negation of the need for doctors, nurses, counselors, psychiatrists or pharmacists. God works in all these ways to heal the sick; the ideal is a team effort to get the sick well through every possible means.

Nevertheless, although I am aware that some prayer can have a psychological effect through the power of suggestion,

I am convinced through my own experience that prayer for healing brings into play forces far beyond what our own unaided humanity contributes. The results of prayer have been extraordinary—so much so that what once would have astonished our retreat team we now take almost for granted. The extraordinary has become ordinary.

And that's the way I think the healing ministry should be: an ordinary, normal part of the life of every Christian community.[2]

In gaining the experience to write this book I have learned a great deal giving team retreats, working with such gifted friends as Mrs. Barbara Shlemon, Sister Jeanne Hill, O.P., Mrs. Ruth Stapleton, Father Michael Scanlan, T.O.R., Rev. Howard Ervin, and Father Bob DeGrandis.

The beginnings of this book were encouraged by Ms. Dolores Cooper, while Ms. Mary DesRoches contributed a great deal to the writing of the early chapters, especially in commenting on their scriptural aspects. (Discussions with Sister Dorothy Dawes, O.P., also helped me deepen some of my own spiritual understanding of healing.) In editing the manuscript Sister Jane Marie Dempsey, V.H.M., has been a helpful critic, while Sister Aimee Marie Spahn, O.S.F., and Mrs. Pat Brimberry have helped in typing the manuscript. Last but not least, Mr. and Mrs. William Callaghan have provided me a place to escape and write undisturbed at their hermitage in Clearwater, Florida.

In working out my ideas of healing I have had the opportunity to attend healing services and to talk to such persons as Kathryn Kuhlman and Oral Roberts, as well as to discuss the controversial ministry of exorcism with Rev. Don Basham,

---

2. Bruce Baker has made a 27-minute film based on our teaching about healing: *The Healing Ministry of the Church*, distributed by Pyramid Films, Box 1048, Santa Monica, Calif. 90406. I recommend it for groups wanting to learn more about healing.

Rev. Derek Prince, Father Richard Thomas, S.J., and Mr. Bob Cavnar.

Above all I am indebted to Sister Mary Margaret Mc-Kenzie, V.H.M., and Sister Miriam Young, O.P., the staff at Merton House, for making it possible for me to finish this book (three years in the writing) by praying with the people who come here to ask for healing and by helping me preserve some time and a place for writing.

Francis S. MacNutt, O.P.
Merton House, St. Louis, Mo.

Somebody touched me. I felt power had gone out from me.

LK. 8:46

PART ONE

The Healing Ministry---
Its Underlying Meaning and
Importance

1

Does Healing Happen?

Is it possible that God directly heals people? Does it really happen? All other questions in this ministry depend on this first question of all: is there such a thing as healing?

In the absence of direct experiential evidence, educated Christians have tended, in recent centuries, to rely upon the opinion of theologians and scripture scholars. The uneducated seem to rely more upon the devotional life of the Church, its shrines and the popular lives of saints for their belief about miraculous healings.

In the past 50 years, however, with a growing appreciation of literary forms in the bible, some theologians and scripture scholars have questioned whether we should accept the miracles of Jesus in a literal way. In a similar way, the existence of Satan, as a personal entity, has been questioned; consequently, a literal acceptance of the exorcisms of Jesus is severely called into question. (The controversy following the opening of the film *The Exorcist* is a good example.)

Yet, we are now seeing a return of the direct experience of God's healing power in such striking ways that the living tradition of the Church—what the Spirit is helping us to experience and understand *today*—is leading us again to a more lively awareness of what Jesus did in his healing ministry. If we ourselves see miracles of healing, we no longer have the difficulty of visualizing the healings in the gospels. Suddenly, everywhere I travel I discover that people are experiencing at firsthand the healing power of God. From my own hometown of St. Louis busloads of people are traveling to attend the healing services of Kathryn Kuhlman in Pittsburgh, nearly a thousand miles away. Local church authorities have heard that many Catholics, including nuns, are going on these pilgrimages and they cannot understand why. It is one sign of the times.

The climate is changing. People are hungering and thirsting to know God in a direct, experiential way. And the sick need healing, just as much as they did in Christ's day. Those needs and desires are basic to our humanity. If the risen Christ is still healing the sick, then there is no problem in making Christianity relevant to the needs of most people today. And, if you, like Jesus, could walk among the sick and heal as many as came to you, you would have some of his problems—like finding a place to hide from the pursuing multitude of the sick.

But does he still heal? The most convincing argument is always, I think, experience: "Go back and tell John what you have seen and heard: the blind see again, the lame walk . . . and happy is the man who does not lose faith in me" (Lk 7:22-23). The simple and the poor followed Jesus in crowds because they saw what happened, while the religious leaders tried to figure out what it all meant. When the apostles continued Christ's healing ministry the people continued to come in crowds, while the theologians continued to question what was going on. After the healing of the cripple at the Beautiful Gate of the Temple, the high priests, rulers, elders and scribes arrested Peter and John to question them:

They were astonished at the assurance shown by Peter and John, considering they were uneducated laymen; and they recognized them as associates of Jesus; but when they saw the man who had been cured standing by their side, they could find no answer. So they ordered them to stand outside while the Sanhedrin had a private discussion. "What are we going to do with these men?" they asked. "It is obvious to everybody in Jerusalem that a miracle has been worked through them in public, and we cannot deny it. But to stop the whole thing spreading any further among the people, let us caution them never to speak to anyone in this name again" (Acts 4:13-17).

And so the first persecution in the infant Church was occasioned not only by the apostles' preaching the resurrection, but by their power of healing in the name of Jesus. The actual experience of seeing a crippled man healed confronted the religious people of Jesus' day with two decisions to make: one theoretical—was the healing real or not? and one practical—what should they do about it? They judged that it was real. But, as for doing something, they decided to forbid it, because they felt that it was doctrinally unsound (being connected with preaching the resurrection of Jesus), and that it would undermine their authority—especially since the preaching and healing were done by "uneducated laymen." Consequently, these religious authorities tried to suppress the new movement by forbidding the apostles to preach.

Today religious leaders are again being confronted, not by theories of theologians, but by the witnessing to healing that people—many of them "uneducated laymen"—claim to have experienced. Consequently, we are faced with an opportunity not merely to discuss a theory, but to make a judgment: "Is this true?" and to make a decision: "Should we do something about it?"

My own experiences have convinced me that divine healing does happen, and commonly. Having come to that judgment, I decided that I had better learn as much as I could about this new phenomenon and start praying for the sick. For me it was no longer an option: if I could help the sick by my prayers, but would not, then I would be in danger of hearing, "Insofar as you neglected to do this to one of the least of these, you neglected to do it to me" (Mt 25:45).

If you have not yourself experienced the ministry of healing, or have not talked to a friend who has, it may be hard to accept that God does directly touch the lives of people to heal them.

As a Harvard graduate with a Ph.D. in theology I am as aware as anyone of problems of credulity and of a prevailing theological climate which questions whether God "intervenes" or "interferes" in the universe. But my own experience leads me to the conclusion that healing is the most convincing demonstration to most people that God is *with us*—that he is not "out there" beyond the reach of human compassion. Many Christians today live by a practical norm of "God helps those who help themselves" and seem quite willing to limit the present Christian ministry of healing to whatever the art of medicine can achieve. Healing by prayer, they would say, was meant for a more primitive age, but now that we understand reality better, we can achieve through medicine what used to be claimed through prayer in a prescientific society open to the powers of suggestion. I can see no point in setting medicine in opposition to healing by prayer (a point that will be developed later in this book); in fact, some doctors themselves now practice a coordinated ministry of medicine and prayer. Such books as Paul Tournier's *A Doctor's Casebook in the Light of the Bible*,[1] Dr. William Reed's *Surgery of the*

---

1. New York: Harper and Row, 1960.

Soul,[2] and *Faith Healing: Finger of God or Scientific Curiosity* (subtitled "An Unexpected Medical Look at the Role of Faith in Healing")[3] are all examples of the renewed interest of doctors in the power of prayer as related to their profession.

Other individuals object to healing by saying, why talk about healing of individuals when the great healings needed today are the healing of broken relationships, the healing of a broken society, and a healing of a world tormented by institutional injustice and the threat of war?

Again, this opposition set up between the need for the larger healing of society and individual healings is a false one. (I know of no one involved in social action work who does not himself go to a doctor or dentist when he is sick under the pretext that other, more global problems occupy his attention.) The larger issues of injustice will be helped when individuals in society are themselves made whole—when they are healed emotionally so that they can enter into healthy relationships, so that they are not acting out of prejudices or ancient hurts.[4]

Recent experience with groups in Latin America indicates to me that praying for the healing of man's inner being will help as much as anything toward the creation of a just society.

---

2. Old Tappan, N.J.: Fleming Revell Co., 1969.
3. Edited by Claude A. Frazier, M.D. (New York: Thomas Nelson, Inc., 1973).
4. One of the least publicized aspects of the healing brought by the Pentecostal movement has been the healing of relationships among whites and blacks:

"This striking interracial phenomenon occurred in the very years of America's most racist period, those between 1890 to 1920. In an age of Social Darwinism, Jim Crowism, and general White Supremacy, the fact that Negroes and whites worshipped together in virtual equality among the Pentecostals was a significant exception to prevailing racial attitudes. Even more significant is the fact that this interracial accord took place among the very groups that have traditionally been most at odds, the poor whites and the poor blacks." Vinson Synan, *The Holiness-Pentecostal Movement in the United States* (Grand Rapids; Eerdman's, 1971) p. 165.

My friends working in the ministry of social justice have experienced the failure of so many dreams of the 1960's and they wholeheartedly agree that more is needed than mere structural change. I find that many who have had the longest experience working with the oppressed are the most open to learn about prayer for inner healing. They themselves see the widest range of its applications.

This is not an either/or question. We need to work at healing on *all* levels—and by all possible means: political, economic and by prayer. (Nor would I put prayer last.)

We are beginning to see the exciting possibility of bringing a number of heretofore conflicting tendencies in the Church together: the drive for social justice together with the renewed concern for prayer and interiority. The common joining point is intercessory prayer for a definite healing effect to take place in the world of suffering humanity. In Bogota, Colombia, for instance, a conference was held in February, 1973, for 23 Catholic charismatic leaders from eight countries. (The subsequent 1974 conference drew some 250 leaders); among their points of agreement were the following:

—These leaders share a common Latin American vision;
—They find a tremendous thirst for God among the people;
—They find that this is now accompanied by visible manifestations of the power of the Spirit.

In expanding on this power of the Spirit the resume of the discussion reports that:

"Everywhere there were reports of God confirming his word and bringing people together through extraordinary manifestations of power—especially of healing. In the poor barrios of Santa Cruz, Bolivia, Father Ralph Rogawski, O.P., and Sister Helen Raycraft, O.P., estimate that about 80 percent of the sick who ask for prayers in the poorest barrios are healed. On a large scale the conversion-preaching of Julio Cesar Ruibal in Bolivia is accompanied by extraordinary miracles of healing, reported now all over Latin America in the picture sections of the newspapers. The priests and sisters at the conference reported rediscovering the power of prayer in their own lives. Several priests had felt their lives had ended in failure in their attempts to bring Christianity to the people, until they found this new power in simple presentation of the gospel message.

" 'An explosion in the Church is what I see. We have been too cautious; now we have to be positive and move out among the people,' said one participant.

"In all this common vision there was agreement that the Holy Spirit is moving in power to do three basic things:

"I. To transform *individuals* into a real personal relationship with Jesus Christ through the baptism of the Spirit;

"II. To heal relationships and *to build community*— especially in the family and the neighborhood community; and

"III. *To transform society* by healing relationships of injustice and oppression.

"In these three areas of transformation and liberation the participants found, again, certain common elements:

"I. In the transformation of *individuals:*

"A. Most of the participants had experienced a *personal conversion.* Commonly, the conversion was from attempting to promote works of justice through purely human, temporal and political means. These efforts in some instances were successful (Father Rogawski), in other instances failures (Father Talavera, Father Umana), but all sensed the inadequacy of these solutions trying to use purely human resources. When God's power to enlighten and heal was brought to bear on the same situation, new priorities emerged and true community began to form.

"B. *Inner healing* is seen to be a principal means of bringing about this interior transformation. Justice cannot be brought to a society until there are just men; and men cannot be just until they are healed of the hurts and wounds of the past. In Latin America these wounds are prevalent as a result of widespread oppression and injustice, of "machismo," and of the wounds caused by broken families and prolonged poverty.

"The priests and sisters, too, spoke of the need for inner healing in their own lives—of the failure and loneliness they have often suffered.

"Whether or not inner healing is more needed in Latin America than in the U.S. is debatable; what does seem clear is that the need for it was recognized by all participants in the conference as being of key importance in building up the people of Latin America.

"C. *Physical healing* was also seen as being vitally important—especially among the *poor,* who are almost all sick, with minimum medical care. Traditional preaching about suffering has always emphasized endurance of the Cross. This has led the people to an almost pagan view of God as handing out suffering—a God of wrath who is to be propitiated. A God of love is hard for the people to see without the kind of healing ministry Jesus himself exercised. In Cali, Colombia, where a five-day mission at the barrio parish of San Juan Battista was begun with a healing service, attendance immediately doubled and generated a desire of the people to learn more about the gospel and to learn to pray together.

"In relation to the ministry of healing, there were also many fears on the part of the participants, because of the superstition connected with healing in the minds of the people:

"i) miracle-mongering and fraudulent healers and shrines have given this whole ministry a bad name. Just two years ago in Colombia a notorious fraud took place with a young girl healer who was exploited by her parents.

"ii) increasing a fatalistic tendency among the people to let God take action without any initiative on their part to improve their lot—to create sanitary conditions and to visit the doctor. The missionaries have had a hard time encouraging the people to take action and are not about to let them use prayer as a fatalistic dependence.

"iii) confusion in the people's minds which connects healing with witch doctors, *curanderos* and other forms of superstition.

"iv) a general reaction against the old church piety which emphasized prayer, shrines, healing and relics and otherworldly attitudes and that failed to lead the people to take action against injustice in the real world in which they lived.

"Those priests and sisters, however, who have actually been working in Latin America with the healing ministry report that these problems are all more theoretical than real—that they are objections thought up by a clerical mentality and are not found among the people once they understand a true Christian concept of prayer for healing in community."[5]

In short, the opposition sometimes set up between a need for the larger healing of society and individual healing is a false one. It is not an either/or, but a both/and situation.

Typical of the growing discovery of the advantages of joining prayer to work for justice is this letter (October 24, 1973) from fellow Dominicans, Father Ralph Rogawski and Sister Helen Raycraft, who work in the poorest slums of Bolivia:

As you know, for the last seven years we've been working in the marginated areas of Santa Cruz, Bolivia. This

---

5. *First Latin-American Charismatic Leadership Conference,* reported by Francis S. MacNutt, O.P. Private printing by Thomas Merton Foundation, 4453 McPherson, St. Louis, Mo. 63108.

work developed in such a way that both of our communities now live permanently in different areas of the city, sharing something of the life of the people, promoting neighborhood organizations, cooperatives, popular education and health programs, etc. These continue, but more and more under the leadership of the people themselves. We saw that at the heart of the problem of social justice is the need of a change of heart of the people themselves, a conversion to *be* just and to create new patterns and values in living. Somehow this had to come about through a personal rediscovery of Jesus Christ. So we sought ways to bring people together in the name of Jesus Christ. There was a need of some kind of Christian community on a neighborhood or even a street basis.

In December of 1972 we tried something different. Using what we have learned and experienced in the charismatic renewal, we went into a neighborhood and began preaching Jesus Christ to any group of people interested enough to come. It was a simple program, preaching for a while, and then leading the people to pray spontaneously. We discovered more. People were very open to Jesus Christ and to reading the New Testament. With time, deep changes came about in their lives. They began to meet and pray regularly, and the seed of an explicit Christian community was born. And more, some spontaneously wanted to accompany us to other neighborhoods to preach with us! This experience has been repeated many times in Santa Cruz with similar results.

I think, then, that we can see that there can be a real correspondence between healing and the aspirations of contemporary spirituality. Theology is a reflection upon Christian revelation in the light of the experience of the Christian community. The simplest, least complicated explanation of the healings of Jesus is that they happened as described, and my own recent experience, as well as that of countless other Christians, goes to back up that explanation. In the past five years I think I can safely say that I have seen hundreds of healings take place through prayer.

Many of these healings taken individually are ambiguous as proof; they can be explained in a variety of ways. Who can say that we know all the factors of a case, so that we can say with certainty, "This remission of disease took place following prayer and therefore prayer caused it to take place"? But I do believe that anyone who would come with me on retreat after retreat would see so many blessed by healings that he would see a cumulative body of evidence all pointing in the direction of an extraordinary power being present, of a number of healings taking place well beyond the realm of chance occurrence.

Books have been written that document cases of healing[6] and, in an effort to scientifically demonstrate the power of prayer, some fascinating studies have been done on the effects of prayer upon plant growth—something that can be measured and calculated before and after prayer. Rev. Franklin Loehr, for instance, a chemist, reports in his book, *The Power of Prayer on Plants,*[7] the results of 156 persons praying in 700 unit experiments using more than 27,000 seeds and seedlings involving about 100,000 measurements and achieving up to a 52.71 percent growth advantage for prayer seedlings. Other experiments scientifically controlled include "Some Biological Effects of the 'Laying on of Hands,' " by

---

6. Kathryn Kuhlman's *I Believe in Miracles* (Englewood Cliffs, N.J.: Prentice-Hall, 1969) and Emily Gardiner Neal's *Where There's Smoke: The Mystery of Christian Healing* (New York: Morehouse-Barlow, 1967) are two such books.
7. New York: Signet, 1969, reprinted from the 1959 edition.

Dr. Bernard Grad,[8] in which he tested the speed with which wounds heal in mice, as well as a remarkable experiment in which the rate of growth of plants was measured when the plants (in this case, rye grass) were prayed for at a distance of 600 miles.[9]

While some of the experiments have an element of the bizarre—testing mice and rye grass—yet these were the most apt scientific controls and were perhaps necessary for a contemporary mentality seeking proof through scientific measurement. It would be a pity if scientists discovered persuasive evidence for the power of prayer at a very time when theologians were calling into question the value of the ancient Christian tradition of praying for the sick.[10]

I personally find most Christians (priests, in particular) very open to discussing the possibility of praying for healing and many have themselves been encouraged (Father Michael

8. From *The Journal of Pastoral Counseling,* Vol. VI, No. 2, pp. 38-41.

9. *Op. cit.,* Robert Miller, "The Effect of Thought Upon the Growth Rate of Remotely Located Plants," pp. 62-63.

10. "But the average orthodox clergyman is not much interested in practices that would convey healing. The 'orthodox' Christian, whether liberal or conservative, has little exposure to such sacramental acts and little or no interest in physical or mental healing through religious means. This fact has been brought home to me graphically on several occasions. One was the experience just a few years ago of a friend who is State Commissioner of Health for one of the large eastern states. At this instance a group of doctors and clergy were called together to discuss the whole subject of spiritual healing. While the physicians as a whole were deeply involved in the discussion, the clergy who attended hardly treated the subject as a serious one.

"At about the same time a similar meeting was called by a large western hospital which has a department of religion and health. A selected group of clergy and medical men were invited to meet together and discuss the problems. All but one of the physicians responded and 80 percent of them came, while barely 50 percent of the clergy even answered the letter and less than 30 percent of them attended the meeting." Kelsey, Morton T., *Healing and Christianity* (New York: Harper & Row, 1973) pp. 5-6.

Scanlan, for instance) to launch out and begin praying for the sick with more confidence than before. They, in turn, bring back encouraging accounts of the visible renewing of their own ministry.

> Priests today are discovering the power of intercessory prayer as part of their professional practice and spiritual counseling. This prayer is directed at physical and especially inner healing. Serious problems such as drug addiction, alcoholism, and long-seated emotional disturbances in some cases seem to have been helped by priests who recognize the appropriateness of joining prayer to the equally necessary professional counseling. They have seen the power of Christ come through them as channels of his love. As yet not many priests have experienced this power, but for those who have, the problem of discovering the relevance of their ministry has disappeared.[11]

The kind of experience we are beginning to see more and more among priests and ministers is typified by a column appearing in the *Brooklyn Tablet:*

> ". . . The one priestly gift that was particularly emphasized, explained and manifested during the days of retreat was the gift of healing.
> ". . . In prayerful presentations by all members of the team, we considered the four areas of evil wherein Jesus wishes to heal humanity through the ministry of healing: sin, inner healing, physical healing, and deliverance from evil spirits. We listened in gratitude to God while members of the

---

11. *The Spiritual Renewal of the American Priesthood,* edited by Rev. Ernest Larkin, O. Carm, and Rev. Gerald Broccolo, with seven other authors (Washington, D.C.: U.S. Catholic Conference, 1973) p. 18.

team recounted some of their successful ministrations in all
four areas of healing. . . .

"Unquestionably the highlight of each day was the
Eucharistic Liturgy celebrated in the evening. Inspired hom-
ilies were delivered amid manifest appreciation and joy on all
sides. Inner gifts of healing took place during Mass, sometimes through the ministration of brother-priests. The Holy
Spirit favored me with a deep peace and joy which I have not
previously known. It remains constant. I have experienced
a greater love of prayer, of Mary, of the scriptures and of the
Eucharist. Other priests there received these same gifts.

"In the final Eucharistic Liturgy a number of priests presented their physical ailments to Christ for healing through
the ministering hands of brother-priests. In my own case, I
was healed of a severe difficulty in swallowing food which
was due to a hiatal hernia in the esophagus, and which caused
me to regurgitate a portion of every meal I have taken in the
last few years. This difficulty disappeared immediately after
the Mass. It has not returned.

"The Spirit of Christ is manifestly with us. Alleluia!"[12]

Seeing this kind of healing take place time after time in
our own day I no longer have any difficulty in believing that
even greater things actually took place in the ministry of
Christ. He said that we would do even greater works than he
did (Jn 14:12) and I suppose I would see even more healing
take place in my own ministry if I were a fitter instrument for
God's healing love than I am. But even so, as noted in the
Preface, I would estimate that half the people for whom we
pray for physical ailments are healed or are notably improved.

For me most of the battle in learning to pray for healing
was simply to conceive that God would answer my prayers

12. "The Holy Spirit and Seventy Priests" by Father John B. Healey
in the *Brooklyn Tablet,* Sept. 13, 1973.

for physical needs in a human, physical way. But he does. He treats us as human beings, not disembodied spirits. One of the most moving testimonies to God's healing physical infirmities came to me from a doctor and his patient. The patient, Mrs. Katherine Gould of Metairie, Louisiana, had asked prayer for both an inner, emotional healing and for the cure of various internal physical complaints, including a bladder hernia. Afterwards she wrote:

May 4, 1972

Dear Father,

There was so much *lifting* for me at the Ardmore retreat that I questioned the feeling of physical (internal) lifting as perhaps being partly caused by my imagination. At the time we prayed, though, I was persuaded that healing did happen.

You remember, we also prayed for an increase of my doctor's faith. (I'm enclosing his letter.) How I wish I could share the picture of his face after making his examination. He threw his arms up, saying, "Thank you, Jesus," because what had to happen was a lifting and restoring of all the organs in my pelvic region. According to him this kind of thing is not successfully resolved without major surgery.

After the prayer for inner healing I was so occupied with knowing Jesus in a newer, deeper, closer way that physical healing had really become secondary; I had lost the fear of surgery or of being ill. So it seems even more generous of him to let me see his miracles. How precious for Jesus to love us in such close and personal ways and to demonstrate for us signs and wonders of himself.

Sincerely,

Katherine Gould

With her letter came the following enclosure from her doctor (also from Metairie, Louisiana):

May 3, 1972

Father Francis,

This is written to testify to the glorious and magnificent power and healing grace of our Lord Jesus Christ. Mrs. Katherine Gould was seen by me, a gynecologist, for treatment of a bladder hernia—which can be corrected, as far as medical science knows, only by surgery. At the time she said she would be attending a retreat, and I suggested that she might pray for healing. This morning she returned to my office, entirely asymptomatic, without any discernible evidence of a bladder hernia. This precious grace of Our Lord causes my heart and spirit to fill with joy.

In Christ,

James A. Seese, M.D., Ob.Gyn.

The healing experience of Katherine Gould and countless other people has reinforced my conviction that among those signs that will be associated with believers one will be: "They will lay hands on the sick, who will recover" (Mk 16:18).

Does healing happen? As you can see, I believe it does. I feel a small portion of the wonder St. John must have experienced when he wrote about the One who causes all this to happen:

Something which has existed since the beginning,
that we have heard,
and we have seen with our own eyes;
that we have watched
and touched with our hands:

the Word, who is life—
that is our subject.
That life was made visible:
we saw it and we are giving our testimony,
telling you of the eternal life
which was with the Father and has been made
    visible to us (I Jn 1:1-2).

2

Our Prejudices Against Healing

AT THE MEETING I attended in Bogota, Colombia, in February of 1973 (reported in Chapter 1), all the representatives agreed that the renewal of the Catholic Church in Latin America will be brought about through a renewal of the healing ministry as well as through the liberation of the peoples from oppression. These representatives were priests and sisters engaged in the charismatic renewal of the Catholic Church in Latin America, most of whom had had long and active records in working for social justice. Yet, they had discovered in prayer for healing a power for liberating people from inner problems and physical sickness that they had never known before.

At this remarkable meeting, all 23 priests and sisters reported the same phenomenon: Christ is once again at work among his people just as he was 2000 years ago, reaching out and healing the sick and wounded. One Dominican missionary reported that nearly 80 percent of the poor people who prayed for healing in the barrios of Bolivia where he works were cured or notably improved.

Despite reports like these, there remains a stout resistance in many Christians who have a hard time believing that such healings can take place. Although the gospels abound with accounts of healings, why is it that in our day many who follow Christ find it so hard to believe that healing can still take place? It is ironic that many Church leaders, disturbed by the loss of faith among their people, themselves lack a strong, active faith in Christ's power to help the sick and wounded in their flock. I have before me an article from the *St. Louis Post-Dispatch,* for instance, titled "Religious Education Agency Rejects Teaching That Jesus Is the Answer." How could I encourage a drug addict to turn in faith to Christ as Savior if I did not believe that Christ would actually free the victim from his bondage in answer to our prayer together? I believe that the ministry of healing is what lifts the central doctrine of redemption and salvation from the realm of the abstract into the reality of men's lives. One of the greatest losses the Church has suffered has been her full heritage of healing power. This loss, this unbelief, has come about, I believe, through the growth of five basic prejudices against healing, all of which I have myself faced and seen in varying degrees in the attitudes of many Christians I know.

1. *"We want nothing to do with faith healing."*

When I encourage people to pray for healing, the first obstacle I usually meet is a stereotyped connection they have made between the healing ministry and *faith healers.* Because they have never themselves prayed for healing with the laying on of hands, their idea of it is conditioned by the only times they have seen such prayer: on television programs taken at tent meetings where revivalists shout and people grow hysterical and faint, or in newspaper articles which depict the Elmer Gantry type of exploitive evangelist, photographed with up-

raised arms and glassy eyes. These real-life images are vivid
enough to blot out the picture-book image of Jesus as he
walked among the sick and touched and healed them. The
image of "faith healer" has so completely taken over that it
is hard to imagine healing in any other context, very much as
the stereotype of "Pentecostal" makes the baptism of the
Holy Spirit unacceptable to many without shedding a prejudice or two.[1]

The question might be posed, "Was Christ a faith healer?"
When we read the gospels, especially Mark, we cannot help
being struck by the constant references to Christ's healing
ministry; about half the material of the first eight chapters
is devoted to narratives of his curing the sick: "He cured so
many that all who were afflicted in any way were crowding
forward to touch him" (Mk 3:10). Can we imagine what this
scene was like? Would we demean the Lord himself by classi-
fying him as a "faith healer," with a sense of our own superiority to such a person? And if he was not a faith healer,
what descriptive word should we use?

Whether we find the right word or not ("minister of
healing" for instance), the important point is to recover the
full heritage of healing that belongs to the Christian and to
the Church. To disparage the healing ministry because of
certain excesses of snake-handling sects in Tennessee makes
no more sense than to criticize the very concept of the
Eucharist because of the excesses of some of the hunting
Masses of the Middle Ages.[2] In either case, the fault lies in

---

1. An interesting illustration of this stereotyped image was the title
of an article written on my work: "Pentecostalism Comes in from the
Tents" (*St. Louis Review,* August 29, 1969).
2. In the so-called hunting Masses, a group of nobles, eager to begin
the hunt early on Sunday morning, would have several priests or
bishops in their entourage all celebrate Mass together, each taking a
different section. In this way it could be rushed through in five or
ten minutes.

the minister or in the way the ministry is carried out, and not in the validity of the act itself.

2. *"My sickness is a cross sent from God."*

A basic attitude that completely undercuts the idea of divine healing is the conviction that God himself sends the suffering. In such a view, asking for healing is to oppose God's will and to refuse the cross he offers. Even granted that it is permissible to ask for relief, it is far *better* for the sick person to accept and bear his suffering. This endurance is more heroic, more Christlike. "If you are going to be a saint, you must expect suffering and sickness."

This undue emphasis on the cross and the benefits of suffering has largely displaced both the belief in and the desire for healing among many Christians of main-line churches.[3] Certainly it has affected preaching on the subject of suffering. Too often the preacher presents sickness as an effect of *God's chastising love* rather than as an element in the kingdom of *evil*. The traditional Christian teaching is that sickness is an effect of original sin.

Our attitude toward sickness—whether to ask God to remove it, or whether to accept it as his will—is such a key problem that an entire chapter will be devoted to it (Chapter 3). To be sure, if I believe that God has sent me a sickness to test my love, I am not going to pray to be rid of it. Rather, I will embrace my cross and refuse to avail myself of any alleviation. Yet, nowhere in the gospel do we see Christ encouraging the sick to live with their illness. On the contrary,

---

3. Dr. Morton Kelsey in his fine work, *Healing and Christianity* (cited in Chapter 1), traces the dramatic shift in belief from early Christianity, when healing was considered as God's ordinary will, to the present, when sickness is presented as God's ordinary will for man. This great shift took place between the third and fifth centuries A.D.

he everywhere treats sickness as a manifestation of the kingdom of Satan which he has come to destroy.

3. *"It takes a saint to work a miracle, and I'm no saint."*

Traditionally, Catholics have always believed in miracles.
But these cures took place not for the sick primarily, but as
signs of a further truth. For instance, if healing came about
through the prayers or the touch of a particular individual,
it was a sign that he (or she) was extraordinarily holy. If
a number of cures took place, they might be a sign that the
person was a candidate for canonization as a saint. Consequently, for an ordinary person to pray for the sick would
be a sign, surely, of presumption and pride.

The reader will recall that I spoke in the Preface of the
time when, a month after my ordination in 1956 (long before Vatican II), a Protestant friend came to visit me at St.
Albert's College, Oakland, California. He asked me to drive
with him to his home to pray for the cure of his son who had
been born partially blind. I felt both embarrassed and challenged. I knew the gospel well enough to remember, "These
are the signs that will be associated with believers: . . . they
will lay hands on the sick who will recover" (Mk 16:17-18).
But nothing in my seminary training or experience had prepared me to pray for the healing of the sick (except for one
class period devoted to the sacrament of Extreme Unction,
as it was then called, since it was reserved for those in danger
of death). From my reading of the lives of the saints, I did
believe in the possibility of healing. But only saints could do
such things. And I was no saint. What was I to do? I did
not think it right to build up my friend's hopes when I myself
did not believe my feeble prayers would help. I was trapped:
I did not think my prayer could cure his son's blindness; on
the other hand, I did not want to weaken his childlike con-

fidence in prayer. I decided to tell him how I felt: I couldn't drive to his home and pray for his son. The best I could do was to give him the phone numbers of two other Dominicans I thought were holy, who might be willing to go if I asked them. I saw his disappointment and knew that he would not call the other men; after all, I was his friend. That was the best I could do in those days.

In the 15 years since then, my ordinariness has not changed at all—I am not a saint, certainly not with a capital "S." But my attitude about praying for the sick has certainly changed. A fear of my own unworthiness would not now keep me from getting into my friend's car and going over to pray for his son's sight. What I did not at that time realize was the abundant goodness of God, who desires so much to heal his people that he uses ordinary men like myself. He does not limit himself to extraordinary figures like a St. Anthony or a Padre Pio who seem so far removed as to be almost unreal, mythological figures.

Christ's statement, as reported in the concluding section of St. Mark's Gospel, is encouraging: "These are the signs that will be associated with *believers.*" He did not say, "with saints" but with ordinary "believers." My personal problem with healing was really a false humility. In the name of this virtue, we unwittingly have emptied our lives of the very life and power that Christ came to bring. Lowering our heads and saying, "Lord, I am not worthy," we denied ourselves the joy of praying with sick friends in order that Christ might heal them.

4. *"We don't need signs and wonders anymore; we have faith."*

Another attitude, one of superiority toward healing, holds that miracles were needed in the early Church to get it started; but now that people believe, there is no further need for signs or proof. This attitude is the outcome of an overemphasis on doctrine: healing of the sick takes place, not primarily because the Father is compassionate and desires to heal broken humanity, but because he wants to make a point. Now that he has made it, it is more perfect for man to believe with naked faith without external signs. Primitive man needed props; but the mature church of today no longer needs inducements of that sort to believe. Certain Protestant groups have even made a dogma of this view ("Dispensationalism") and assert that the time for miracles has passed; any miracles reported today must be frauds. Most Roman Catholics of a traditional background are open to miracles, but tend to see them as signs of a higher truth and not to be sought for their own sake. Healing is, it is true, a sign of a higher reality, and faith does not depend on signs and wonders. But healing the sick is in itself something to be sought. Is the point of healing merely to be a proof-factor for man's intellect, or is it God's mercy reaching out to the sick? (More of this in Chapter 4.)

5. *"Miracles do not take place; they only represent a primitive way of expressing reality."*

Serious as are the four previously mentioned blocks to praying for the healing of the sick, they still do not strike at the very possibility of God's moving with direct healing power. But certain current trends of thought deny even this possibility. Along with the great advances of modern biblical scholarship, a few authors tend to view everything in the gospel in purely natural, secular terms. This exaggerated demythologizing (or taking the myths from the biblical narratives and reducing them all to simple human experience) would question the possibility of a God who acts directly in history and in our personal lives. It would deny healing through any means other than that of medical science. While not a scripture scholar himself, the popular spiritual author, Louis Evely, reflects this attitude when he states:

> Miracles are merely a holdover from the age of pre-scientific explanation, an anachronism which persists only in those moldering ivory towers which continue to exist in the real world.[4]

Once one begins to question whether Christ himself really had any power over natural forces, then clearly he must ask how his own prayer could possibly work "miracles" today. Such thinking destroys the very idea of a cure taking place other than through natural, recognizable processes, and relegates divine healing to the era of primitive religion. I have described in various discussions examples of actual healings that I have witnessed, only to hear these cures explained away as the result of psychological suggestion. Terms that prejudice the discussion from the beginning unless they are challenged, would include ones like the following:

> "I don't believe in an unpredictable God who *intervenes* in nature, who plays favorites."

> "I don't believe any more in the 'God out there,' who 'zaps in' like some pagan deity."

Remarks like these imply that those who believe in healing believe in a kind of primitive God in the heavens. My own experience has been that a person who has known God's healing love and power senses the presence of God *within* himself, the immanent God, the God who works in and through his creation. Far from imagining God as distant, I

4. Louis Evely, *The Gospels Without Myth* (New York: Doubleday, 1970), p. 25.

sense him as more present than ever before. He has many ways of acting in our lives. To limit his power by saying that he acts only through nature, does indeed make him seem distant and impersonal. In effect, to insist that God does not heal puts him "out there," makes him an impersonal force, even less involved than any compassionate human being.

The gospels state that when Jesus sent his disciples out to preach, he instructed them to cure the sick and then to say, "The kingdom of God is near at hand" (cf. Lk 9 and 10). This is precisely what I see repeated when a healing takes place: Christ seems closer; his kingdom is near at hand— now.

Nevertheless, many Christians have never seen healing occur in response to prayer, and, naturally, they exclude it from their spirituality. It is not surprising that such lack of confidence in the power of prayer leads people to wonder whether God has any power at all. "If he does have power, why doesn't he exert it? Does he really care about us? If he doesn't have any power, but simply exists as part of the human process, are we sure he even exists?"

Weeds in the Wheat

At this point I am reminded of the parable of the enemy who went out and sowed weeds in the wheat field while the farmer slept; using poetic liberty, I take the farmer to represent the leaders in the Church; the wheat is the Good News that Christ has come to proclaim liberty to the captives and healing for the whole man. Sometime in the night (the Dark Ages) the Enemy came and sowed an interlacing network of weeds that choked out even the expectation of a harvest of wheat. Instead of the Good News of healing, a multitude of interlocking arguments encourages us to return to an acceptance of suffering: the Bad News. The arguments run rather like this:

I. In relation to *God:*

God ordinarily does not want to heal. Suffering and sickness are his will for most people; the proper attitude for a Christian is *acceptance,* not prayer for alleviation. "God has sent you this Cross, especially tailored for you. Do not reject it, for it will lead to greater glory in the next life."

II. In relation to *you:*

A. Even if God should occasionally heal the sick, it would not be through your prayers, for you are *not good enough;* after all, you are not holy; you are no saint.

B. Even if it can be shown that God does occasionally heal the sick, you should be *superior to* that type of spirituality:

1. Nor do you want to be associated with an over-emotional, revivalistic type of religion associated in the popular mind with *faith healers.* Your approach is purer, more intellectual than that.

2. You do not need *signs and wonders* to believe. Your faith does not depend on the kind of evidence a less spiritual person might need.

3. You can accept suffering in preference to healing. If God offers you the alternatives of healing or suffering, you will take the higher road, the royal road of the Cross by choosing the *higher way of suffering.*

III. In relation to the very *nature of healing:*

Miracles of healing are merely a holdover from the age of prescientific explanations. It is time to forget a superstitious view of reality and get on with the real work at hand; Christianity needs to be purified of its "super-

natural" element, which is irrelevant to the present state
of man's intellectual and spiritual development.

It seems to me that all the above attitudes either obscure
or completely undercut the Good News Christ came to bring.
We are beginning to see on a wide scale a renewal of God's
gift of healing in a manner not seen in the Church since
apostolic times. This, I believe, could be the effort of a personal, loving God to counteract man's diminishing faith in
him. Healing is not on the periphery of Christianity; it is central. If we deny God's active healing power, we soon lack
evidence of his personal love for us. If we doubt whether God
really loves us, does it make any difference whether we believe
in him or not?

And, last, we may wonder if, indeed, God actually exists
at all.

3

The Basic Message of Christianity: Jesus Saves

WHEN I HEAR the phrase, "Jesus saves," I remember poorly lettered billboards on many a country road. I also remember an unpleasant incident when I was buttonholed by a street evangelist who asked, "Are you saved, brother?" But these unhappy experiences of revivalism and insensitivity cannot change what is central for me, as for every Christian: Jesus does save.

What does it really mean? How does it affect my life? "Our divine savior," "our holy redeemer," and "Behold the Lamb of God who takes away the sins of the world," can all become such familiar phrases that the words lose their power to touch us. They can become pious cliches, empty of force. What does Jesus save *me* from?

In traditional terms Jesus saves us from personal sin and from the effects of original sin which include ignorance, weakness of will, disoriented emotions, physical illness, and death.

Some of this freedom will unfold only in the deepened life that takes place after our resurrection. But even now the process has begun: "the kingdom of God is at hand." Jesus is freeing us from sin, from ignorance ("the Spirit will lead you into all truth"), from weakness of purpose, from disoriented emotions, and from physical sickness—from all the sickness, therefore, that destroys or lessens the human personality—in order to give us *new life,* a new relationship of love and union with his Father through the power of the Holy Spirit. The saving power of Jesus frees us from all those elements of evil that prevent us from entering our new life with God.

Jesus, therefore, came to do two basic things:

1) Positive: To give us a new life, a loving relationship of union with his Father and with himself, through the Holy Spirit.

2) In relation to the obstacles to new life: To heal and free (save) us from all those sick elements in the human personality that need to be transformed so that the new life may freely enter in.

This is, of course, the astounding message of the Good News. The danger is, and always has been, that we let this merely remain a doctrine, a truth to be believed: that we do not understand how to let the reality of Christ's saving power penetrate the very center of our being. Healing is simply the practical application of the basic Christian message of salvation, a belief that Jesus means to liberate us from personal sin and from emotional and physical sickness.

But does Jesus intend to heal us from these evils here in this life? Or does healing pertain only to a future life when God will "wipe away all tears from their eyes; there will be no more death, and no more mourning or sadness"? (Rv 21:4). I believe that a full understanding of the liberating, healing, saving message of Jesus Christ demands that we investigate

whether he has come to free us *even in this life* from disease
and disordered emotions which, since the creation of man,
have traditionally been considered the effects of evil—of
"original sin."

To understand a Christian view of healing let us penetrate
deeper into the meaning of "Jesus saves," into the meaning of
his mission—and ours.

The Name "Jesus"

The Hebrews attached great significance to choosing a name
for a newborn child. The name often indicated the role the
child was to play in the family or in the history of the people.
The son of Isaiah the prophet, for example, was named
"Shear-jashub," "a remnant will return," and the very name
symbolized the people who, after Isaiah's own time, would return from exile and punishment. Later, John the Baptist was
named at God's command, contrary to the inclinations of his
relatives, as a sign that this child's life was more than ordinary,
that he was specially chosen from the moment of birth to play
a unique role in the plan of salvation.

Little wonder, then, that when God came to dwell among
us he chose a name that would indicate who he was and what
his mission would be. Luke's narrative illustrates this through
the story of the annunciation: The angel Gabriel appeared to
Mary and said: "You are to conceive and bear a son, and you
must name him Jesus" (Lk 1:32).

Now, the word "Jesus," or "Yeshua" in Aramaic, means
"Yahweh is Salvation" and though it was not an uncommon
name in that day, the name here proclaimed the very message
of the one who bore it. He who was the Messiah, the "anointed
one" or "the Christ," had come to express by word and work
that "Yahweh is Salvation."

His Mission

This is precisely how Jesus conceived his mission: the time of the Messiah would be a time of healing, of liberation, of salvation. Because the Hebrews did not think of man as divided into body and soul, but as a whole person, when they spoke of healing they thought not only of *saving souls* but of *healing persons*. And man's person includes his body and his feelings.

As Jesus—"Yahweh is Salvation"—began to preach, he expressed clearly why he had come. Luke describes how Jesus in his very first sermon boldly asserted his healing mission:

> He came to Nazara where he had been brought up, and went into the synagogue on the sabbath day as he usually did. He stood up to read, and they handed him the scroll of the prophet Isaiah. Unrolling the scroll he found the place where it is written: "The spirit of the Lord has been given to me, for he has anointed me. He has sent me to bring the good news to the poor, to proclaim liberty to captives and to the blind new sight, to set the downtrodden free, to proclaim the Lord's year of favor." He then rolled up the scroll, gave it back to the assistant and sat down. And all eyes in the synagogue were fixed on him. Then he began to speak to them, "This text is being fulfilled today even as you listen" (Lk 4:16-22).

Luke goes on to say that some of his listeners were critical, not of his teachings but of what he failed to do: " 'We have heard of all that happened in Capernaum, do the same here in your own countryside' " (Lk 4:23).

Later when John the Baptist sent his disciples to ask if Jesus was the Messiah, Jesus again pointed to his own healing works as *the sign that he was the Christ:*

When the men reached Jesus they said, "John the Baptist has sent us to you to ask, 'Are you the one who is to come, or must we wait for someone else?' " It was just then that he cured many people of diseases and afflictions and of evil spirits, and gave the gift of sight to many who were blind. Then he gave the messengers their answer, "Go back and tell John what you have seen and heard: the blind see again, the lame walk, lepers are cleansed, and the deaf hear, the dead are raised to life, the Good News is proclaimed to the poor, and happy is the man who does not lose faith in me" (Lk 7:20-23).

It must be noted, too, that St. Mark, probably the earliest to set the gospel into writing, devotes much of his account to the healing episodes in the ministry of Jesus, and less to the actual teaching of Jesus. Today we no longer view the miracles of Jesus solely as "proofs" of his divinity or as "guarantees" that his teachings were correct and from God; rather we are seeing that the miracles were the very actions of God present in the life and works of Jesus. *The healing acts of Jesus were themselves the message that he had come to set men free;* they were not just to prove that his message was true. In a very basic sense, his medium was his message. The sign of salvation was that men were being saved, restored to all that they had lost.

A clear indication that Jesus himself did not stress the miraculous but the ordinary aspect of his healing ministry is seen in the fact that Jesus calls his healings "works" rather than "miracles." They were, so to speak, the normal thing for him to do; they formed an integral part of his mission. As David Stanley explains:

The most convincing indication that Jesus' miracles are not intended to impress the reader of the gospels with the merely prodigious is found in the vocabulary employed to designate these actions. There are but two, or at most three, instances of any usage which approximates to our word "miracle" . . . . If there is one aspect of Jesus' acts of healing which goes unstressed in the gospels, it is their capacity for merely arousing wonder. In the synoptic gospels they are designated as "acts of power" (*dynameis*) a term which stresses their character as manifestations of the divine power, and hence their aptness, together with his words, as a vehicle of Jesus' proclamation of the coming of God's kingdom. They are presented simply as the Good News in action.[1]

Unfortunately, in our English translations of the New Testament most versions translate the Greek word for "acts of power" as "miracles," thus implying something extraordinary and rare.

The Mission of the Disciples

Since the healing of man—his spirit, his emotions, and his body—is an essential part of the message of salvation, we can now see why Jesus gave his disciples the power to heal when he sent them out to preach. This is true both of his special group of the twelve, and of the larger group of seventy-two.

He called the twelve together and gave them power and authority over all devils and to cure diseases, and he sent them out to proclaim the kingdom of God and to heal (Lk 9:1-2).

After this the Lord appointed seventy-two others and sent them out ahead of him, in pairs, to all the towns and

1. "Salvation and Healing," *The Way,* October, 1970, pp. 302-303.

places he himself was to visit. . . . "Whenever you go into a town where they make you welcome, eat what is set before you. Cure those in it who are sick and say, 'The kingdom of God is very near to you'" (Lk 10:1, 8-9).

He was simply giving them the power to preach the same message of Good News that he himself preached. That message was not merely a doctrine; it contained the very power of God liberating man from the wretched state he was in. They were preaching as their Master preached: Jesus made the crowds welcome, "and talked to them about the kingdom of God; and he cured those who were in need of healing" (Lk 9:11).

The Early Church

The inspired account, of course, that describes the activity of the early Church is *The Acts of the Apostles*. Certainly this title does not refer merely to the acts of the twelve apostles, for this book tells far more about Paul's activities than about any of the original twelve, except for Peter. What is meant in the title is not *Apostles* but *apostles*—the deacons, Stephen and Philip, Barnabas, Silas and all the other early Christians who were sent out to preach the gospel and to heal.

Knowing that the synoptic gospels usually speak about Jesus' healings as "acts of power" rather than as miracles helps us understand the basic theme of Acts, which is to show that the early Church, the early Christians, had the same power to preach, to heal, and to cast out demons that Jesus had. The Church is the continuation of Jesus' saving power in history. The Jerusalem Church (Peter) and the gentile churches (Paul) all carry on the same preaching and healing as Jesus himself did, because Jesus is the one who is still doing it. Only now he is mutiplied in his apostles who can be his witnesses to the end of the world.

Just as Jesus connected preaching and healing in his presentation of the gospel, the early apostles carried on that tradition with no diminution of power. When these early Christians were persecuted, listen to how they prayed for help:

And now, Lord, take note of their threats and help your servants to proclaim your message with all boldness, by stretching out your hand to heal and to work miracles and marvels through the name of your holy servant Jesus (Acts 4:29-30).

Notice that they did not pray to preach *and* to heal, but to preach *by* healing. They preached the message of salvation by actually continuing the works of Jesus. A doctrine of God's salvation without the salvation actually taking place, or a concept of healing without the healing taking place, is empty rhetoric. (Perhaps this is why so much of today's preaching impresses people as abstract and irrelevant.)

As we read through Acts, we realize that the same Spirit that empowered Jesus in his life and work continued in the mission of the Church. A thoughtful reading of the text shows that there are definite parallels between the work of Peter and Paul (not, as is far too often emphasized, just conflict and controversy). Both are representatives of the Christian community which continues the saving mission of Jesus.

ACTS OF PETER	ACTS OF PAUL
Peter and John heal a lame man at the Gate Beautiful (3:1 ff.). "In the name of Jesus Christ the Nazarene, walk."	Paul cures a man, lame from birth, at Lystra (14:8 ff.). "Get to your feet—stand up."

Peter cures Aeneas, the paralytic who had been bedridden for eight years (9:32 ff.).

Paul cures the father of Publius who was in bed suffering from fever and dysentery (28:7 ff.).

Even Peter's shadow cures the sick (5:12a ff.).

Even handkerchiefs or aprons which had touched Paul cure the sick (19:11 ff.).

Crowds come and they are healed (5:16).

"The other sick people on the island came as well and were cured" (28:10).

At Jaffa Peter revives the dead woman Dorcas (9:36 ff.).

At Troas Paul raises the dead boy, Eutychus, to life (20:7 ff.).

The ordinary expectation of the apostles is shown by their direct form of prayer: "Walk," "Stand up," "Get up and fold up your sleeping mat," "Get to your feet." The apostles use the same form of prayer that Jesus had used and that the Church uses in the sacraments: a prayer that expects something to happen because we have prayed for it. Here, healing does not seem extraordinary, but the ordinary answer to prayer. And not only do we read of healings worked through Peter and Paul, but through Philip, Stephen, and Ananias of Damascus. The clear implication is that healing and liberation are part of the mission of the Church.

Consequently, a better translation for *The Acts of the Apostles* would be "Acts of Apostles" to indicate that the book contains only *some* of the noteworthy activities of *some* of the apostles. The work of the Church is not yet complete but is meant to continue with modern apostles, contemporary Chris-

tians who preach and perform the same acts of power that
Jesus—and Peter, Paul, Barnabas, Agabus, Ananias, Philip
and Stephen—did.

The Saving Mission of Jesus Today

It follows, then, that unless we hold that healing was only
meant for the early Christian community as a special grace
to get the Church established, the healings characteristic of
the early Church should somehow continue happening in our
day. We still have the sick with us and we are still standing
in the need of being made whole. All around us in the pews
on Sunday morning we see broken persons. And sometimes
those in the pulpit or at the altar are broken, too. Since the
Church is made up of people, we still need healing as much
as ever.

Significantly, St. Augustine in his early writings claimed
that healing had ceased in the Church and was no longer
necessary. But experiences in his own life changed his mind.
Notably, in his own diocese nearly 70 attested miracles took
place in two years' time. In 427, just three years before he
died, Augustine, in his book of *Retractions,* took back what he
had said in his early writings (*De Vera Religione*) about the
age of miracles being past, and described miraculous cures
which he had seen and which were enough to change his
mind.[2]

The ending of the Gospel of St. Mark[3] indicates that a
share in Christ's mission is extended to all believers:

Go out to the whole world; proclaim the Good News to

2. *Cf.* Morton T. Kelsey, *op. cit.,* p. 185.
3. This ending is not in the earliest manuscripts; many scholars believe
that Mk 16:9-20 was added by the early Christian community. If
so, it shows that the faith of the early Christians continued to expect
the power of healing as an ordinary activity of their community.

all creation. And these will be the signs that will be associated with believers: in my name they will cast out devils; they will have the gift of tongues; they will pick up snakes in their hands, and be unharmed if they drink deadly poison; they will lay their hands on the sick, who will recover (Mk 16:17-18).

There is no indication that at some time the charismatic dimension of the Church will cease or that its main purpose is to build up the institution to such a point that the structured elements can carry on under their own power.

If the work of the Christian is to carry on the same mission as Christ's it is important for us to recapture the important elements of that mission. Here is how Peter, in a thumbnail sketch, describes Jesus' public ministry:

> You must have heard about the recent happenings in Judaea; about Jesus of Nazareth and how he began in Galilee, after John had been preaching baptism. God had anointed him with the Holy Spirit and with power, and because God was with him, Jesus went about doing good and curing all who had fallen into the power of the devil (Acts 10:37-38).

Here the emphasis is on what Jesus did, rather than on what he said; for what he did was the message of the gospel. He preached salvation and healing by actually healing people and freeing them from evil.

Think of what it might mean if we could, in all honesty, describe how we had fully entered into the imitation of Christ and give as the best, most succinct description of our own lives: "God has anointed me with the Holy Spirit and with power, and because God is with me, I go around doing good and curing all who have fallen into the power of the devil."

And think of what it might mean if the entire Church

could make the claim to those who honestly inquire about her credentials: "Go back and tell the doubters what you have seen and heard: the blind see again, the lame walk, lepers are cleansed, and the deaf hear, the dead are raised to life, the Good News is proclaimed to the poor and happy is the man who does not lose faith in me."

The test of orthodoxy is not doctrine alone, for doctrine remains incomplete unless it is accompanied by the power to make the doctrine come true in our lives:

> I tell you most solemnly, whoever believes in me will perform the same works I do myself; he will perform even greater works, because I am going to the Father (Jn 14:12).

4

Wholeness Is Holiness

IF JESUS COMES to save and to heal, what is it that he saves and heals? Did he just come to save souls? Are pastors intended to study only the "cure of souls"—the *cura animarum?* Is the Divine Physician interested only in man's spirit?

I think it is only honest to say that most theologians and preachers in the Catholic Church have emphasized with great certainty Christ's desire to save souls and to take away sin, the sickness of the soul; but there has been no corresponding certainty about Christ's desire to heal the sickness of the body. In fact, quite the contrary, sickness has been often presented not as evil, but as a blessing desired by God because of the great good that comes to a person's soul as a result of suffering.

How then are we to regard sickness basically? Is God's will ordinarily sickness—or is it health? If it is health, does God heal man's body with a power beyond the natural resources of medicine and health care?

Personally, I believe that the attitude of most Christians

61

today in regard to healing is more shaped by pagan thought
than by Christianity—that most sermons on sickness and
suffering reflect more the influence of Roman stoicism than
the doctrine of the Church's Founder.

Attitude of Christ Toward Sickness

I think it is also fair to say that every time Jesus met with evil,
spiritual or physical, he treated it as an enemy. Every time a
sick person came to him in faith, Jesus healed that person. He
did not divide man, as we so often do, into a soul to be saved
and healed and a body that is to suffer and remain unhealed.
We are the ones who talk about saving souls, but nowhere in
the New Testament does it say that Christ came to "save
souls"; he came to save men—body and soul.

Jesus healed those whose spirits were sick and needed
deliverance or forgiveness; he also healed those whose bodies
were lame, blind, and leprous. In fact, there are many more
accounts of how he healed the physically sick than of how he
forgave sins. We remember how, when the paralytic was
brought in by his friends (Mt. 9:1 ff.), Jesus forgave his sins.
Since the scribes thought he was blaspheming, Jesus replied,
"Now which of these is easier to say, 'Your sins are forgiven,'
or to say, 'Get up and walk'? But to prove to you that the
Son of Man has authority on earth to forgive sins, he said to
the paralytic, 'get up and pick up your bed and go off home.' "
The authority Jesus exercises over both these forms of evil
seems to be the same, but which is easier *for us* to say: "Your
sins are forgiven," or "You are healed"? Why do we have such
faith in the words, "Your sins are forgiven" when they are said
in the sacrament of Penance, but have so little faith in the
thought that "You are healed" in the Anointing of the Sick?

Even a cursory reading of the New Testament leaves a
convincing impression that Jesus was typically Hebrew in his

view of man: he did not divide man into body and soul, but he saw him as a whole person. He came to save persons, not just souls. He came to help the suffering in whatever way they were suffering. Sickness of the body was part of that kingdom of Satan he had come to destroy.

The early Church, as we have seen in the Acts of the Apostles, acted as Christ did: the apostles proclaimed the gospel and healed the sick. The Epistle of James, traditionally used as the scriptural foundation for the Anointing of the Sick, moves back and forth between forgiveness of sins and physical healing with no discernible change of assurance or emphasis:

> If one of you is ill, he should send for the elders of the church, and they must anoint him with oil in the name of the Lord and pray over him. The prayer of faith will save the sick man and the Lord will raise him up again; and if he has committed any sins, he will be forgiven. So confess your sins to one another, and pray for one another, and this will cure you; the heartfelt prayer of a good man works very powerfully. Elijah was a human being like ourselves—he prayed hard for it not to rain, and no rain fell for three and a half years; then he prayed again and the sky gave rain and the earth gave crops (Jas 5:14-18).[1]

---

1. The understanding of this passage of St. James was much affected by the only official translation of the New Testament sanctioned by the Church for nearly 1,500 years: the Vulgate. This translation from the original Greek to the Latin was done by St. Jerome around the year 400 A.D. In it the Greek words for (1) *save* and (2) *heal* are both translated by the Latin word "salvo"—save. It makes a real difference in the understanding of the passage whether it is translated "So confess your sins to one another, and pray for one another, and this will *save* you" or ". . . and this will *cure* you."

In this way, the very texts of the bible that would encourage the faithful to pray for physical healing were translated to emphasize the spiritual aspect alone.

James here seems to give the example of Elijah to increase our readiness to pray for material needs—such as rain—and not just spiritual needs. James emphasizes that our prayer must be *heartfelt;* apparently, if we don't have faith in this kind of prayer it will not work very powerfully.

A Later Christian Tradition: the Body Should Suffer

What happened to the simple gospel view of Christ healing the whole man? The historical development can be traced from the early Fathers of the Church as they moved gradually from a wholehearted belief in healing (St. Justin Martyr and St. Irenaeus in the second century) to a view that the body's suffering is preferable for the sake of the soul (St. Gregory the Great in the fifth century).[2] What happened in all those centuries to diminish the Church's belief in Christ's healing ministry is complex; but certainly one of the main factors was that Platonic, Stoic, and Manichean thought infected Christian spirituality. These philosophies, dominant in the world of early Christianity, tended to view man's body as a prison that confines his spirit and hinders his spiritual growth. Under the influence of the Desert Fathers, severe asceticism was held up as the model of Christian perfection: man's body is to be distrusted and not just tamed; it is to be put to death through various mortifications and penances. The Christian then looks forward to a time when his soul will be released from the confines of the flesh.

An exaggerated model of the flesh warring against the spirit, the Spiritual Combat, tends to put the body in the category of an enemy to be subdued through punishment rather than an ally to be healed.

---

2. Dr. Morton T. Kelsey has a clear summary of this history in Chapter 8 ("Healing in the Victorious Church") of *Healing and Christianity.*

Today a book on spiritual growth is likely to treat of the "Art of Becoming Human," and a seminarian's room may well be filled with the finest hi-fi equipment and colorful fine-art reproductions; but many of us can remember our own training where we were even forbidden for years to read *Time* magazine in our starkly simple cells. For nearly 1,500 years a traditional spirituality emphasized severe mortification and distrust of the body. Seeing a rerun of *The Nun's Story* with its world of black habits and the putting to death of "worldly" desires one night made me realize how much times have changed. That film now seems almost unreal, as if it came from another century.

But the effects, hidden perhaps, of that older spirituality are still with us. There is much to be said for it, and in some ways we may have lost something; but it did reflect, in part, a stoic, unchristian view of the body that is still very much with many people. Recently I was asked to pray for an elderly lady who is losing her eyesight through glaucoma. She said she felt guilty about praying for healing because she felt that maybe God wanted her to endure failing sight to prepare her soul for its last passage. (Yet, she had no qualms about trying to get help from a doctor; it was only in direct relation to God, in prayer, that she felt that maybe she ought to be blind.)

She, and many other Christians like her, are affected by a basically pagan view of the universe—stemming from Platonic, Stoic, and Manichean sources which they have probably never even heard of. In these, the body is seen as an encumbrance if not an enemy to the spirit. The lady I mentioned had formed her thinking from the lives of saints she had read and retreat sermons she had heard which stressed penance and reflected an attitude of contempt for the body.

A fascinating example of this kind of spirituality that treats the body as an enemy to be subdued is the *Autobiography of*

Blessed Henry Suso, O.P. (In this writing Blessed Henry refers to himself in the third person):

> Having learned that true love for Christ Crucified demands imitation, he decided to conquer his ease-loving nature by chastising the flesh so that the soul might go free; for this purpose he wore for a long time a hair shirt and an iron chain around his body so tightly as to draw blood.
>
> He had someone make him a half-length, tight-fitting, coarse undergarment, equipped with 150 sharp brass nails, the points facing the flesh. This was his night shirt for 16 years.
>
> On simmering summer nights when the heat was almost unbearable and he was half-dead from the day's fatigue or from blood-letting, he would fret and squirm sleeplessly from side to side like a worm being pricked with sharp needles. Then there was the annoyance caused by insects. . . .
>
> But no matter how long the nights were in winter or how hot in summer, he refused to yield an inch to the Flesh's craving for comfort, even though his hands and arms became afflicted with a nervous trembling.
>
> In order to prevent himself from obtaining any relief from the pests, he fastened his belt around his neck and tied his hands in such a way that he could not move them in his sleep. He was so securely confined in this manacle that if a fire had broken out, he would have been as help-less as a handcuffed prisoner.
>
> After some time he discarded this instrument, only to encase his hands in a pair of leather gloves which he had instructed a tinsmith to stud with sharp iron nails. The purpose of this new instrument was to tear his flesh every time he tried to obtain relief from the plaguing insects. More than once when he unlocked his voluntary prison to

go to Matins, his bruised and bloody body looked as if it had come out the loser in a fight with a bear. . . .

After 16 years of these torturous practices when his whole nature was tamed and withered, an angel appeared to him on Pentecost Sunday with the welcome whisper that God wanted him to discontinue this manner of life. He lost no time in throwing his Flagella into the Rhine.[3]

Certainly, Blessed Henry's example is extreme, even for the 14th century in which he lived; but his basic attitude was typical of a spirituality which was the backdrop for the lives of some saints that strongly influenced our own ideals of perfection until quite recently. Some saints, "victim-souls," were genuinely inspired to mortify their bodies by self-inflicted penances; for most of us, choosing extraordinary penances was regarded as presumption since God might not have called us to the heights of heroic sanctity.

The least we could do was not to try to escape those sufferings that were not self-chosen but sent by God. Sickness was generally regarded as a gift from God to help men grow spiritually. To pray for healing, in such a case, would be a sign of weakness and a concession to the flesh. Consequently, one could expect God to say "No" to a prayer asking for healing.

The pervasiveness of this basic contempt for the body is perhaps most clearly evident in the negative attitude toward human love and the beauty of the physical aspects of marriage which marked much of the thinking of the early Church and largely prevailed until Vatican II. In this view, human love and its physical aspects ("the relief of concupiscence") were regarded as entirely secondary to the procreation of children. Several of the great Fathers of the Church such as St. Gregory

---

3. Blessed Henry Suso, *The Exemplar,* tr. by Sister Ann Edward, O.P. (Dubuque: Priory Press, 1962), I:37-38.

the Great (pope from 590 to 604) even went so far as to consider that any bodily pleasure taken in marriage itself was sinful:

> In his *Pastoral Rule,* Gregory provided a chapter on "How the Married and the Celibate Are To Be Admonished." The married were to be admonished that they might copulate only to produce children. This was merely Augustine. But Gregory went further. Not only is pleasure an unlawful purpose in intercourse, but if any pleasure is "mixed" with the act of intercourse, the married have "transgressed the law of marriage." Their sin, to be sure, is as small a one as the nonprocreative purpose in Augustine; it may be remitted by "frequent prayers." But sin has been committed. The guilty married have "befouled" their intercourse by their "pleasures" (*Pastoral Rule* 3.27, *PL* 77:102). . . . Miraculously a man might have intercourse without sin, as one might be in a fire without burning. But miracles did not usually attend marital intercourse; sin was to be expected.[4]

At first it might seem that these stern attitudes toward marriage had little to do with Christ's healing message, but they exemplify in dramatic fashion a harsh attitude toward the body and "the world": only man's spirit is truly worthy of unconditional prayer. Prayer to heal man's broken body, like prayer for all other material benefits, was considered of questionable spiritual benefit. Christians were taught to pray with faith only for "grace" and other spiritual gifts.

Today we no longer regard the body as an enemy, but celebrate its goodness. Scores of books are written to cele-

---

4. John T. Noonan, Jr., *Contraception* (New York: Mentor-Omega, 1967), pp. 187-188.

brate the Christian dimensions of marriage, but still our spirituality of sickness seems relatively untouched. *The New Catechism* ("The Dutch Catechism"), for example, in its brief treatment of illness and the Anointing of the Sick, repeats none of the medieval praise of sickness as an imitation of the Cross, nor does it treat the body as an enemy; yet it has very little to say about illness that is practically helpful. All that this well-known compendium of contemporary Catholic faith has to say is that: (1) people often feel abandoned by God in times of sickness; (2) this can lead to a new perspective on reality and a deepened relationship with God; (3) Christians should visit the sick. There is no suggestion that a Christian might consider praying for healing.[5]

The Anointing of the Sick

The sacrament of the Anointing of the Sick has, in its history, closely patterned itself on the changes in attitude toward healing. Originally, it was regarded basically as a sacrament intended for physical healing. Its model was the Epistle of St. James, which instructs the elders to gather around the sick man and pray for forgiveness of sins and for healing. Later, as the attitude toward sickness changed and it was seen more as a blessing than a curse, the purpose of the sacrament shifted until its primary effect was spiritual: to prepare a soul in danger of death for immediate entrance to glory. Physical healing was still prominently mentioned in the words of the sacrament (faithfully passed down and representing an earlier tradition), but this was now regarded as the secondary purpose of the sacrament, while the primary effect had to do with the soul. Its name became Extreme Unction (Last Anointing). Originally this name, Last Anointing, only referred to

---

5. *A New Catechism* (New York: Herder and Herder, 1967), pp. 468-469.

the fact that it was the last in the list of seven sacraments that used anointing with oil as part of its ritual.[6]

Later, in popular understanding, "Last" came to mean the last act the Church performed to prepare a person for death. Furthermore, regulations were made insuring that this sacrament was to be administered only in danger of death. All this emphasized that the only sure effect of Extreme Unction was a purely spiritual one: that the person was being prepared to meet God at the moment of death. The tradition that Christ also worked physical cures through this sacrament also perdured—but it was regarded as a secondary effect. Many priests can tell remarkable stories, accounts of how the sick either got well or noticeably improved after being anointed. We did believe in the possibility of an occasional physical healing, but our faith was directed almost exclusively to the spiritual preparation for death, especially since the sacrament was not to be ministered unless there was a proximate danger of death. As a result, the sight of a priest in the sickroom was often regarded by the patient as a harbinger of death. I remember being asked by a Protestant friend to visit a Catholic relative who was in the hospital to undergo an operation. I promised to go, but an hour later the friend called back, embarrassed, to say that the Catholic relatives had asked that I not come, for the sick man might be frightened by the appearance of a priest and might worry before surgery that his condition was worse than it actually was. In short, rather than signifying healing, my appearance to that family signaled the approach of death. I could not but reflect that, while the sick hastened in crowds to see and touch Christ, here was a sick man who was afraid to see me, Christ's ambassador. This

---

6. First came Baptism with its anointings on the forehead, chest, and back; then Confirmation (anointing on the forehead), then Holy Orders (anointing on the palms), and finally, the Last Anointing (with anointing of all the senses).

family had been conditioned to expect the priest to prepare a patient for death—not to pray with him for life.

At the present time, as I noted earlier, the name "Extreme Unction" has been changed back to the original name, "Anointing of the Sick." Again authors are emphasizing the healing effect of the sacrament as today we return to a deeper sense of Christ's mission of healing the sick. (See Chapter 20: "Sacraments and Healing.")

The Religious Sense of Ordinary People

A remarkable thing, though, was that the people—especially the simple people—continued to pray with great faith for the sick through their various popular devotions. Since praying for healing was no longer performed by the living representatives of the Church, the priests, the people turned to the saints to pray for their ailments. Mary, the Mother of God, in particular was sought for healing at Lourdes and her other shrines, which were really centers of healing. My own province of Dominicans is, in large part, financially supported by the Chicago shrine of Saint Jude Thaddeus, Patron of the Impossible. Some 300,000 persons are on the shrine's mailing list because they believe St. Jude has helped them when they prayed for their needs. Devotees send countless letters to this shrine, so typical of many others around the world, to thank St. Jude that their prayers for healing have been heard. The popularity of shrines and devotions among Catholics in preference to the official liturgy was often ascribed to the fact that these offered a better emotional outlet than the simplicity and austerity of the Latin Mass. A deeper reason for their popularity was, I think, that these devotions met a basic human need of people who wanted to pray for their real material concerns. If God seemed distant, if it was his will to permit sickness, Mary, at least, seemed approachable.

Although the official representatives did not themselves ordinarily pray for healing among the people, the healing ministry in the Catholic Church was preserved through these shrines and devotions.

Similarly, among Protestant groups popular evangelists such as Oral Roberts and Kathryn Kuhlman have preserved the healing tradition when it was not promoted in the official church worship services (with the notable exception of Pentecostal Churches and certain ministers, particularly Anglicans, who instituted healing services in their churches).

These shrines and popular evangelistic services draw the same kind of crowds that Jesus attracted in his lifetime: wounded people who cry out along the roadside asking to be healed. They remind us of blind Bartimaeus, the woman with the issue of blood, the epileptic boy, the kind of people Jesus always attracted. Admittedly, these devotions are often sentimental, sometimes superstitious, and frequently embarrassingly commercialized. But, I believe, this all came about because the prayers for material and physical needs were moved from the center of the life of the Church and were shunted aside into the area of popular devotion. It was as if theologians moved off in one direction, while the simple people with their basic needs moved off in another.[7]

The crowds of people traveling to shrines and lighting candles at the side altars of the saints have been portrayed as having a religiosity that appeals to the heart and emotions; they need this kind of prop. But it goes deeper than that; these are people who are simply looking for help in their real human, material needs. If a woman finds she has inoperable cancer, where is she most likely to find prayer for healing?

---

7. Dr. Kelsey points out that in the most comprehensive survey of recent theology, John Macquarrie's *Twentieth Century Religious Thought,* not one of the 150 theologians surveyed discusses the effect of man's religious life on his mental or physical health. *Op. cit.,* p. 307.

From her pastor, or from St. Jude? From her minister or from Kathryn Kuhlman?

Now, of course, these great shrines seem to many to represent a pre-Vatican II spirituality. Nevertheless, to an older generation these devotions are still meaningful and crowds still throng such places as Lourdes. But to a younger generation of Catholics they represent an otherworldly Christianity, one they no longer feel comfortable with.

A Contemporary View of Man

Today, though, we find that psychology has effected a return to the Hebrew view of man: man as a person who is not separated into body and soul, but is a whole individual whose emotions and body very much affect his mind and spirit. Once again we see our souls not as imprisoned in the body but at home in the body—the resurrection of the body answers our deepest desires. This means that our view of man today is perhaps closer than ever before to the view of man that Jesus held. The Platonic, the Stoic, and the Manichaean views of man (in recent centuries we might add Cartesian and Jansenist influences—especially in the French and Irish Church) that have touched the post-apostolic Christian spirituality have all stressed a dualism in man, with spirit and mind being seen as noble while the body is, at best, a necessary evil. We are now returning to a glorious sense of celebrating God's creation with a realization that God does care for man—not just man's soul, but man, all of man.

The reason we have not prayed for healing in the past is not just because we have lacked the faith. It goes back to this "body as enemy" spirituality that has been with us for more than 1,500 years. But we are now recovering the full proclamation of the Good News, that salvation is for the whole person and that Jesus came to bring us the fullness of life in every possible dimension. The Gospel of St. Matthew explicitly reflects this; after describing how Jesus cured a leper, healed the centurion's servant, and restored Peter's mother-in-law to health, it states:

> That evening they brought him many who were possessed by devils. He cast out the spirits with a word and cured all who were sick. This was to fulfill the prophecy of Isaiah: "He took our sicknesses away and carried our diseases for us" (Mt 8:16-17).

Hopefully, we are now returning to the biblical view of man, to God's view of man: that holiness is wholeness. As a friend of mine once remarked when I was looking physically worn down, "Even God cannot play on a broken violin."

5

Let Him Carry His Cross Daily

ADMITTEDLY GOD CANNOT PLAY on a broken violin. Yet there are many people—good Christian people—who are broken. How can God use them? There is a kind of brokenness that all men suffer on their way to wholeness ("contrition" means literally a state of being broken); but unfortunately, too many Christians are broken in a destructive way —so badly broken that they cannot carry out the great commandment of loving God and neighbor. Their inner turmoil *prevents* them from carrying out God's will, and yet, paradoxically, they may still believe that such a sickness is God's will. Therefore, they feel no inclination to ask for release from what God evidently wants of them.

Take, for example, the person suffering from mental depression who finds it hard to believe in God's love for him. How can he in turn love God? Typically, such a one is too wrapped up in sadness to relate to others in a loving way or to become an active member of a functioning Christian community. He is too broken to fulfill even the very basics of a

Christian life. Moreover, his wounds probably stem from such deep childhood scars that he can do little to change himself, even with the help of a psychiatrist. Yet how many priests or ministers are ready to pray for a person like this, sure that God does not will such a state and will bring peace of soul if only it is sought? If God has come to save man, the total man, why are there so many Christians broken in body and spirit? One key reason is the remarkable shift from the days of the early Church when Christians looked at health and healing as the ordinary response of a loving Father to the attitude of today where suffering is often regarded as a sign of God's special benediction.

A Misunderstood Emphasis: "Carry Your Cross"

One familiar attitude toward suffering which has influenced many, myself included, is that those whom God loves most will have to suffer most, a view reinforced in a number of ways: "If you suffer the Cross nobly in this life, you will be rewarded by a glorious Crown in heaven," and the like. There is a picture at the beginning of the book, *The Ascent of Mount Carmel* by St. John of the Cross, which makes the same point by depicting a steep mountain with a narrow painful way leading to the top, while winding, pleasant side paths portray all the temptations that lead man astray from God. Older biographies of the saints (such as Blessed Henry Suso, quoted in the last chapter) usually emphasized the penances and sufferings these great spiritual heroes had to endure. The ordinary untaught reader of these books came away with the conviction that union with God was serious business and demanded great suffering if he wished to reach the heights of union to which God was calling him. The natural tendency of the less valiant was to shrink back and say, "I leave it to the saints."

Traditional popular spirituality has hammered the importance of suffering and penance—especially suffering that is *not self-chosen*—offering several benefits which follow:

1. For me as an individual: "It purged me of self-seeking and selfishness. If I can kill my excessive desire for pleasure by accepting suffering, I can then advance in detachment and purely unselfish love of God and neighbor."

2. For the *world*: "I can unite my sufferings with those of Jesus upon the cross and ask him to use them redemptively to help other people. Like St. Paul, I can ask Jesus to make up in my body what is still lacking in the sufferings of Christ for the salvation of the world."

In my desire for suffering, my chief aim would be to imitate Christ as perfectly as I might, to walk in his bloodstained footsteps so that I might become like him and share in his mission of redeeming mankind through suffering. Hasn't Christ explicitly stated that the person who does not take up his cross daily and follow him is not worthy to be his disciple?

Until rather recently spiritual directors would encourage those who were ill by telling them they were especially loved since God had singled them out to share more deeply in his crucified life. This ideal of living a crucified life was starkly heroic; it was reflected graphically in the handmade crucifixes brought from Spain that sometimes found their way into convents and monasteries. With glistening drops of blood and pain etched into the face of Christ, one felt guilty looking into that face, seeing how comfortable and unmortified one's own life was.

How could a person with a "cross"-centered spirituality like this ask for relief from pain? A healing would take away his opportunity to imitate Jesus and help redeem the world. Would he surrender to weakness rather than aspire to holiness? He might ask for spiritual blessings, but would hesitate to ask for material ones for fear they deprive him of the merits of suffering.

Unconsciously affected by this kind of doctrine, most Christians, certainly most Catholics, never thought of praying for a cure of their ailments, even though they knew that Christ and, after him, his apostles and the saints all helped people to become well. If I were to carry my cross, I had better hang onto the one that was given me rather than to ask for a lighter one: to ask for healing might be cowardice.

What Is the Correct View of Suffering?

The bible teaches an apparent contradiction: Jesus tells his followers to bear their cross; yet, whenever he meets people who are sick, he reaches out and cures them. Was he inconsistent, or have his words been misunderstood?

I think we can solve this problem by making an important distinction between two kinds of suffering:

1. The cross that Jesus carried was the cross of *persecution,* the kind of suffering that comes *from outside* a man because of the wickedness of other men who are evil. He suffered deeply within himself, too, but the source of his anguish was outside himself. Jesus wept over Jerusalem; he was reviled and mocked; he was nailed to the cross and died.

2. The suffering that Jesus did not himself endure, and which he took away from those who approached him in faith, was that of *sickness,* the suffering that tears man apart *from within,* whether it be physical, emotional, or moral.

The Life of Jesus

This twofold distinction seems clear in the life of Jesus. Precisely because he was good, he drew down upon himself the wrath of the authorities of this world; he endured calumnies, insults, and most painful torture and death at the hands of his enemies who were infuriated by his life and teachings.

But nowhere do the gospels recount that Jesus was ever physically ill. The long-Christian tradition has recognized that Jesus probably did not suffer from leprosy, epilepsy, schizophrenia, or any of the other diseases and emotional disturbances that plague mankind. We intuitively sense that these sicknesses result from a corruption of man's inner being and are not in accord with his nobility as a son of God. Sickness shows that, in one area at least, the sick man is being attacked from within his personality. Consequently, we instinctively feel that Jesus must have been an emotionally balanced and healthy man.

In his words and actions Jesus, too, distinguishes between sickness (attacking man's life and wholeness from within) and persecution (attacking from without). For instance, he tells his disciples that they will be persecuted, hauled before magistrates and judges, thrown out of the synagogues, that their enemies will be their own brothers and sisters, and that they are to rejoice when all manner of evil is spoken about them (Mt 10:17 ff.).

Contrast the rejoicing of Jesus at persecution to his reaction to sickness and demonic possession. The evangelists never show him counseling a sick man to rejoice, or to be patient because disease is helpful or redemptive;[1] instead, Jesus "cured them all" (e.g., Mt 12:16).[2] While we, by and

---

1. Quite the contrary, the earliest manuscripts of Mark say that when Jesus met the leper (Mk 1:41) he is described as "being angry," presumably because leprosy is an evil. In later manuscripts the verb is changed to "moved with pity."

A similar attitude toward sickness in which Jesus treats it rather like a demon to be exorcised is reflected in Luke's account of the healing of Simon's mother-in-law (4:38-39) in which Jesus "rebuked the fever and it left her."

2. Except, of course, in his own hometown of Nazareth: "He could work no miracle there, though he cured a few sick people by laying his hands on them. He was amazed at their lack of faith" (Mt 6:5-6).

large, have encouraged the sick to accept their illness as the
will of Christ, the Christ of the gospels seems to reveal a very
different attitude. Once when a leper came up to Jesus and
said, "If you want to, you can cure me," Jesus replied, *"Of
course I want to!* Be cured" (Mt 8:3).

As a friend of mine once said, "Every time you meet Jesus
in the gospels, he is either actually healing someone, or has
just come from healing someone, or is on his way to do it."

The Attitude of the Disciples and Apostles

It is clear that Jesus taught his disciples to take the same un-
compromising stand toward sickness. When he commis-
sioned the twelve to preach (e.g., in Lk 9), and when he sent
out the seventy-two (Lk 10), he also gave them the commission to heal the sick and drive out evil spirits. (The close association of the command to heal the sick and to drive out evil
spirits reiterates the attitude of the early Church that disease
is an evil—not a blessing sent by God.) Moreover, the man-
date to all believers to preach the gospel (at the end of Mark)
promises healing as a sign of belief: ". . . They will lay their
hands on the sick who will recover" (Mk 16:18).

St. Paul, who makes such a point of telling people to imitate him as he imitates Christ, and who adds that his desire
is to "share his sufferings by reproducing the pattern of his
death" (Phil 3:10), sees no contradiction in healing sickness:
"So remarkable were the miracles worked by God at Paul's
hands that handkerchiefs or aprons which had touched him
were taken to the sick, and they were cured of their illnesses,
and the evil spirits came out of them" (Acts 19:11-12). By
his actions, Paul, even with his emphasis on the cross, does
not encourage the sick to bear their illness as though it were
willed by God. Paul himself once fell sick ("You never
showed the least sign of being revolted or disgusted by my

disease that was such a trial to you") (Gal 4:14) but when it came time for him to boast of his sufferings for Christ, he did not mention his sickness, but rather the kind of suffering that comes from persecution and the labors inherent in his vocation:

> . . . I have worked harder, I have been sent to prison more often, and whipped so many times more, often almost to death. Five times I had the thirty-nine lashes from the Jews; three times I have been beaten with sticks; once I was stoned; three times I have been shipwrecked and once adrift in the open sea for a night and a day. Constantly traveling, I have been in danger from rivers and in danger from brigands, in danger from my own people and in danger from pagans; in danger in the towns, in danger in the open country, danger at sea and danger from so-called brothers. I have worked and labored, often without sleep; I have been hungry and thirsty and often starving; I have been in the cold without clothes. And, to leave out much more, there is my daily preoccupation: my anxiety for all the churches. When any man has scruples, I have had scruples with him; when any man is made to fall, I am tortured (II Cor 11:23-29).

To say, then, that God ordinarily desires men to be healed of their sickness does not connote a Christianity without a cross. I speak of the kind of Christianity preached by Christ himself and his apostles—where suffering is seen as an evil[3] —an evil to be overcome when it appears to overwhelm and destroy the inner life of a man; on the other hand, it is to be

---

3. It is significant, too, that the gospels usually connect healing with the casting out of demons; healing and exorcism are parallel ministries. They are both connected with evil; sickness is no more God's will than is being tormented by demons. ". . . They cast out many devils, and anointed many sick people with oil and cured them" (Mk 6:13).

endured and rejoiced in when it comes from the persecution of evil men or from the fatigue of apostolic labors. Although good can result from it, suffering is in itself the result of sin; it is only to be endured *for the sake of the kingdom,* not for its own sake.

In discussions about suffering, a problem nearly always comes up: What is the meaning of St. Paul's celebrated "thorn in the flesh," and of his inability to be rid of it even when he prayed? Paul says:

> . . . to stop me from getting too proud I was given a thorn in the flesh, an angel of Satan to beat me and stop me from getting too proud! About this thing, I have pleaded with the Lord three times for it to leave me, but he has said, "My grace is enough for you: my power is at its best in weakness" (II Cor 12:7-9).

The exact nature of this "thorn in the flesh" is obscure. Various commentators have suggested that it could have been sickness, persecution, or sexual temptation. Certainly, no one can use this text to bolster one point of view. What can be said is that St. Paul's initial response was to pray that the "thorn" leave him. He ceased praying when he learned that there was a purpose to it and that it was for the sake of the kingdom (lest his exalted revelations make him proud). Moreover, he calls it "an angel of Satan," and not a blessing sent by God.

On the other hand, the story of the epileptic demoniac (Mk 9:14-29; Mt 17:14-21; Lk 9:37-41) does seem to make it clear that: (1) *Jesus* expected his disciples to be able to cure the boy, and (2) the *disciples* themselves expected that they should have been able to cure the boy and were embarrassed at their failure. As Mark describes the incident, a crowd has gathered around to watch the disciples try to cast "a spirit of dumbness" out of the epileptic boy; but as the boy's father explains to Jesus when he rejoins his disciples, "I asked your disciples to cast it out and they were unable to." Instead of Jesus giving a calm reply (he might have said, "Now that I am here, just bring him to me") he replies, "You faithless generation: How much longer must I be with you? How much longer must I put up with you?" Apparently, he expected that the disciples should have been able to cure the boy themselves.

Then he talks to the boy's father to find out what is wrong. The latter concludes the pathetic story of his son's long-endured convulsions with a very human prayer, "If you can do anything, have pity on us and help us." Again Jesus reacts strongly. Mark says that Jesus *"retorts"*: "If you can? Everything is possible for anyone who has faith." Jesus is telling the father that he or *anyone* else should be able to do what he is being asked to do. The problem is not outside themselves— there is no "if" about it; the question is whether or not they have faith. Then Jesus proceeds to cure the boy.

After this the embarrassed disciples wait until they can speak to him privately; then they ask, "Why were we unable to cast it out?" "This is the kind," he answers, "that can only be driven out by prayer."[4]

Nothing in this episode gives the impression that Jesus is setting himself up as unique in the work of healing. Rather, it is as if he were training his disciples to cure people as part of their ordinary ministry; he is blaming them precisely because they are still not ready to do their work as by now they should.

The attitude of the early Church seems to have been that not only Jesus, but his followers as well, were to call upon God's power to cure sickness; they were guilty of shoddy work if they failed to cure the sick and drive out demons.

It seems that the New Testament record is solidly on the side of health as reflecting the mind of Jesus and his disciples.

4. Some of the early manuscripts have ". . . by prayer and fasting." But the earliest merely have ". . . by prayer."

As St. Irenaeus wrote: "The glory of God is man fully alive."
The reaction of the people to Jesus' cures was to glorify God
and praise him, as with the blind man who recovered his sight
and then followed Jesus, "praising God, and all the people
who saw it gave praise to God for what had happened" (Lk
18:43).

What Meaning, Then, Does Suffering Have?

Suffering is a mystery that all of us have had to wrestle with
in some form or other. If God can put a stop to suffering, why
doesn't he? I have talked to people who have suffered greatly,
who have seen the innocent suffer, and who said they were
now atheists because they could not believe in a God who
would want people to suffer. What is the answer? Certainly,
there is no simple one; but there are several key ideas that I
believe are biblical and represent a balanced point of view
that may help answer many of the questions we ask:

1. "The glory of God is man fully alive." God has revealed himself as being on the side of life (he *is* life), of
wholeness, of health in spirit, mind and body. *In general, it is
God's desire that we be healthy* rather than sick. And since he
has the power to do all things, he will respond to prayer for
healing unless there is some obstacle, or unless the sickness is
sent or permitted for some greater reason.

2. *Sickness is in itself an evil,* although good may result
from it. Sickness is ordinarily not directly willed by God, but
as the result of original sin, it is permitted. Through the power
of the resurrection, God's life is breaking into our wounded
world, and he gives us the power to cooperate with him by
healing and reconciling man and all of creation: "creation still
retains the hope of being freed, like us, from its slavery to
decadence, to enjoy the same freedom and glory as the
children of God" (Rom 8:20-21).

3. There comes *a time for a person to die*. This, of course, is obvious; but people do ask whether they should pray for elderly people who are ill with a terminal disease. The answer is that we should pray for light as to when to ask God to take away the sickness and when to pray for a happy death—which is a passing to a deeper life with God and not a tragedy at all. Agnes Sanford describes the need for guidance in praying for the elderly in her autobiography. Here she recounts the poignancy of making a decision about the sickness of her husband, Ted:

> But complete healing did not come. So I asked for guidance. There is a time for everyone to depart, that I know, and he was approaching seventy. I said, "Lord, how long does he have?" And the answer came, "Three years."
>
> His days were lengthened a little bit by continual prayer. He had three years and six months. But the last year and a half, after he was threescore years and ten, were truly, as Solomon said they would be, labor and sorrow. He had a massive stroke. . . . I did not pray for healing this time, for I knew that if Ted's life were prolonged it would be only labor and sorrow. I prayed only for whatever was best, trusting God to take him at the right time.
>
> However, others—all his people who loved him—did not consider these matters, but prayed definitely for healing. In all my books I counsel people to ask guidance before leaping into healing prayers, but few pay any attention. Ted did make a recovery, but indeed and truly he was not himself.[5]

It is normal for an apple to drop to the ground in the

_____
5. Agnes Sanford, *Sealed Orders* (Plainfield, N.J.: Logos International, 1972), p. 259.

autumn after it has spent the summer ripening to its full richness and growth. But if a green apple falls off the tree in July because a worm has gotten into it, something has gone wrong. Similarly, we can ordinarily assume that we should pray for desperately sick young people (for example, a young mother dying of leukemia) that they might live.

4. Some sickness may have *a higher purpose*. Sometimes it serves to chastise us or to bring us to our senses. At other times, it may turn us around and redirect our lives into a better course. A striking example was Paul, who was blinded on his way to Damascus and, consequently, found the Lord who completely changed Paul's life. His blindness lasted three days until he was healed by the prayer of Ananias. At a later time he fell sick in Galatia, but this provided the occasion upon which he was enabled to evangelize the Galatians.

Furthermore, there has been a long tradition of *redemptive* suffering among the saints who have asked Christ to share in his Cross as a special privilege. This tradition is too long to be lightly dismissed by those persons who like to see things in simple terms of black and white—of the devil and sickness completely on one side and God and health on the other side. Yet, at times, so much has been made of the redemptive value of suffering, that it has all but obscured the Good News of the gospel. All too often the hospital chaplain tells the patients indiscriminately, "God is offering you this cross to accept." By New Testament standards, it should be *normative* for the Christian to pray for the removal of sickness rather than its acceptance. Redemptive sickness is the exception, not the rule.

As an indication of the Catholic Church's early tradition of prayer directed toward healing rather than toward resignation, one of the *Roman Ritual*'s ancient prayers for visiting the sick reads as follows:

Let us pray. God of heavenly power, by your word you

drive away all weakness and sickness from the bodies of men. In your mercy, be with your servant now, so that his (her) infirmity may depart, his (her) full strength and health may return, and he (she) may bless your holy name. Through Christ our Lord. Amen.[6]

The Reverse Side of the Cross

The basic question, then, comes as to whether the healing effects of Christ's passion, as far as our bodies and broken emotions are concerned, are meant for this life or whether they are reserved for a time after death. Popular spirituality has suggested that our bodies are meant to suffer in this life, and that this is what it means to carry our cross in imitation of Jesus. But the renewed focus on healing coincides with today's realization that the resurrection is the central mystery of the redemption. The Spirit dwelling in Christ's body is leading men to claim the victory that Jesus has won, and not to confine this to their spiritual lives but to apply it as power and strength for the whole man—for the complete human person. This new awareness of the resurrected life available to us even now is beautifully exemplified in a vision described by Rufus Moseley (Rufus Moseley was an educator who had various mystical experiences and was known in certain Protestant circles in the 1930's and 1940's as a remarkable retreat master):

Suddenly and unexpectedly, a Presence, Power, and Glory, not of me, descended upon me and apparently had possession and full use of me. The whole body, as well as mind and soul, shared in the wonder. . . . My arms began to go out and my body began slowly to rise, and while I did

6. *Collectio Rituum* (New York: Catholic Book Publishing Co., 1964), p. 307.

not realize it at first my body was becoming or taking the form of a cross, a cross of life, of honor, of bliss, and of glory. The higher I arose the greater the bliss and glory. . . . When my body was apparently in the form of a perfect cross the glorified Jesus manifested Himself immediately in front of me . . . quickly He inbreathed or infused Himself within. I . . . said to myself, this is the fulfillment of John 14:20, "At that day (when He gives the other Comforter) you shall know that I am in the Father and you in me and I in you." . . . It was made known that the kind of union that Jesus has with the Father is precisely the kind of union that He is seeking for us to have with Him. . . .

I had asked for the truth about the Cross. . . . It was apparent that there was a glory side to the Cross that had been almost unseen in most of Christian history. In this experience in answer to my question, I was put upon a cross of life, while He went to a cross of shame. I had been put upon a cross of bliss, while He had been put upon a cross of agony. I had been put upon a cross of heavenly manifestation. . . . He was put upon a cross of desertion, where it appeared that even God Himself did not care, or had forsaken Him. . . .

The Cross is a way of life; the way of love meeting all hate with Love, all evil with good, all negatives with positives.[7]

7. Rufus Moseley. *Perfect Everything* (Macalester-Park, St. Paul: 1952). Revised edition, pp. 49-51.

6

Miracles--A Proof?

THE REAL PROBLEM for anyone who adopts an exclusively cross-centered spirituality, who embraces all suffering as God's will, is what to make of the gospels where over and over we read that Jesus "cured them all" (e.g., Mt 12:16). How account for the fact that everywhere in the gospel Jesus treated sickness as an enemy? Why, today, have the followers of Jesus encouraged the sick to accept their sickness as his will? Once when a leper came to Jesus and asked if he wanted to cure him, Jesus replied, "Of course I want to! Be cured!" (Mt 8:3). In contrast, we tend to say to the 20th-century leper, "Jesus probably doesn't want to cure you physically. Learn to accept your leprosy, for it is the cross he wants you to carry."

The previous chapters have mentioned some of the reasons for the radical shift of attitude from treating sickness as an enemy to welcoming it as a friend. But I believe the principal reason for this shift has been that we have tended to emphasize *doctrine* rather than experience, as if right knowledge coupled with willpower were enough to produce Christians. In many ways the Roman Catholic Church is discovering the inadequacy of such an approach; for example, its school system, financed with great sacrifice by the people, is in itself insufficient to create enthusiastic Christians. In some Catholic colleges no more than 20 percent of the students still participate in the Sunday liturgy; yet they have sat through years of courses in religion and theology. The general discouragement felt over the failure to discover a successful method of teaching catechetics is all part of the same sad situation: an intellectual approach is in itself not enough to Christianize a generation—or a nation. How often I meet young people who say, "I used to be a Catholic, but now I'm a Christian." What they seem to be saying is that their training merely made them conscious of rules and doctrines. They claim that it was only after they began to move outside Catholic circles that they found a personal relationship with Jesus and a new life. It is embarrassing to find a Catholic high school student who says he was not convinced of the reality of Christ's presence until he was "turned on" at a Jesus rally. This in spite of years of training by concerned parents and dedicated teachers. Admittedly, this "turning on" to Christ can sputter and die out; it is only a beginning, but it is a beginning—this personal experience of Christ's presence which is so needed for a living faith.

As a consequence of an overemphasis on doctrine, we also seem to have lost a lively sense of Christ's healing presence and power. In general Christ's cures have been presented as signs of the *truth* of his message. Since faith is beyond the direct argument of reason, the best way Jesus had of showing he was the Messiah was indirectly, by working miracles. ("Tell John the Baptist what you hear and see . . .") Jesus cured people to show that what he said was true—that he and the Father were one. Healing, therefore, came to be seen primarily as a sign of the truth of a doctrine, of a message, or as a proof of holiness. Seen from this viewpoint, healings came to have a threefold purpose:

1. They were worked *by Christ* to show that he was the Messiah and that he was divine.

2. They were worked *in the early Church* to show that the Church was carrying out the work of Christ and was truly the people of God. Once this fact was clearly established, the need for miracles subsided. After the first century, their occurrence was only intermittent—at Lourdes, for instance—to show a skeptical world that Christ was still with the Church. Textbooks (including those I studied in the seminary) taught that true miracles could not occur in the Protestant churches because God would not want to signify that these were true churches.

3. They were worked *by certain holy persons*—the saints—who could perform exceptional miracles to show precisely that they were Saints. The ordinary Christian, in this view, would never expect God to heal people in response to his own prayers, for he would be presumptuous to regard himself as a saint.

There is much to be said, of course, for seeing healing as a sign of proof. After all, Christ told his critics that if they didn't believe him because of his words, they should believe because of his works. What I see as harmful is the *overemphasis* on the proof aspect of healing, which tends to distort its true place in Christian living. Consider, for instance, each of the areas mentioned above—the life of Christ, of the Church, and of the saints. In each of these areas healing has deeper significance than being a mere proof of doctrine or of holiness.

The Miracles of Christ

Christ's motivation for healing was clearly something more than a desire to prove his messianic mission. In the first place, he frequently healed on the Sabbath, a practice that defied the teaching of the scribes and Pharisees. Far from convincing these men that he was the one sent from God, his cures convinced them that he was an imposter who should be done away with: "The scribes and the Pharisees were watching him to see if he would cure a man on the sabbath, hoping to find something to use against him" (Lk 6:7). Certainly, if Jesus had been primarily concerned about convincing people that he was the Messiah, he could easily have confined his healing ministry to the other six days of the week. His willingness to violate the tradition of his contemporaries shows the strength of his compassion for the sick; compassion was a stronger motivation for his actions than trying to prove his mission to the religious leaders.

Furthermore, after healing people Jesus often commanded them not to speak about their cures. He was not looking for publicity, but he was constrained by his own overwhelming love to help the sick even to the extent of jeopardizing his own life.

> The man went away, but then started talking about it freely and telling the story everywhere, so that Jesus could no longer go openly into any town, but had to stay outside in places where nobody lived. Even so, people from all around would come to him (Mk 1:45).

The picture one gets of Jesus—especially in Mark, the earliest gospel—is that of a man trying, if anything, to conceal his messianic identity; he is not trying to prove anything, and even seeks to escape the crowds who have come to be healed:

> And he asked his disciples to have a boat ready for him because of the crowd, to keep him from being crushed. For he had cured so many that all who were afflicted in

any way were crowding forward to touch him (Mk 3:9, 10).

Miracles as a Proof of the True Church and of Heroic Sanctity

The theory that healings take place in only one church to prove that it is the true church simply goes against the facts. Healings seem to be taking place in many of the churches— and even outside the established churches, for example, among the Jesus people. The main thing that God seems to want to show people by these healings is that he is real, that he loves ordinary people, and that he wants them to draw near to him. Christ appears more anxious to bring people to himself than he is to validate any one church. (This is a question of priorities and does not mean, of course, that it is unimportant for a person to belong to the church.)

Finally, we find no New Testament backing for the view that healings take place to show that a person is a saint. On the contrary, Jesus seems to assume that extraordinary actions will be performed by ordinary—or even evil—men.

When the day comes many will say to me, "Lord, Lord, did we not prophesy in your name, cast out demons in your name, work many miracles in your name?" Then I shall tell them to their faces: I have never known you; away from me, you evil men! (Mt 7:22, 23).

Moreover, he said that one of the signs that will follow those who *believe*—not necessarily those who are holy—will be that they will lay hands on the sick, and they will recover (Mk 16:17, 18). The rebuking of the disciples who failed to heal the epileptic demoniac indicates that Jesus wanted to bring his disciples to a point where they could cure even the most difficult cases.

Destructiveness of the Proof Emphasis

All these theoretical considerations are vital, for they affect our lives in important ways. The "proof" mentality seems to keep Christians from praying for healing. If I believe that healings are extraordinary events in the Christian life, proofs of holiness rather than ordinary Christian works, I certainly will be hesitant to pray for the sick for fear of elevating myself to a level of activity appropriate only to canonized saints.

Contributing to the lack of healing in the ordinary life of the churches is the attitude of many church leaders who hold that we don't need to pray for healing today because Christianity has sufficiently proved itself throughout history and in the lives of saints. Only the sensation seekers pant after the miraculous. In keeping with this attitude, church leaders, generally speaking, neither encourage healing services nor do they urge ministers and lay people to visit the hospital to pray for healing.[1]

Most important of all, if healing has meaning only as a sign and has no value in its own right, then healing must be extrinsic to the gospel message—an external proof pointing to the key thing: the gospel itself. But this viewpoint fails to see that healing is an integral part of the gospel message: if the Good News is that Christ came to save all men, then the *power* to save has to be there. If the power to save man extends to the whole person, part of the very message of salvation is that Christ came to heal us—spirit, mind, emotions, and body. To deny or minimize the healing ministry is to take away much of the power of the gospel and to leave in its stead a body of truths devoid of life. As St. Paul wrote:

. . . I still want to know, not what these self-important

---

1. Happily there are signs of change in communal services of anointing the sick now encouraged in the Roman Catholic Church and isolated congregations of various denominations where the ministers hold regular healing services.

people have to say, but what they can do, since the kingdom of God is not just words, it is power (I Cor 4:19b,
20).

Christianity is more than doctrine; it is power. It is power
to transform our lives, to destroy the evil that prevents us from
loving God and our neighbor. Jesus came to bring us a new
life, a share in God's own life. We have always believed these
things, but where is the reality of it? Where is the power
truly to change lives?

What we have done all too frequently has been to take the
Good News and to change it into Good Advice. The Good
News is that Christ has come to help us enter into the very
life of his Father and to transform us by his power into new
persons who can love and rejoice and help the poor in a way
far beyond our own capabilities. Good Advice is to hold up
a Christian ideal of life and service, and then to say in effect:
"Here's the ideal; now use your willpower to achieve it."

A good test of our Christian attitude would be the response to the question: What would you do if a drug addict
came to you and asked for help? Would you merely give the
addict all kinds of helpful advice and then try to encourage
him to use his willpower to stay off drugs? Would you then
call a local agency and help the addict enroll in a special drug
program like Synanon, or encourage him to commit himself
to a federal hospital? Any of these measures would be helpful,
but would you first of all as a Christian think of praying with
the addict, asking the Lord to free him from his addiction? If
you believe that prayer can accomplish his deliverance, then
you really have Good News to offer—of freedom for the
captive. Jesus not only holds up an ideal, but he gives us
the power to reach it. Christianity would be dreaming the
impossible dream if it were only words without the transforming power that frees us from bondage.

Rev. David Wilkerson, a minister of the Assembly of God, a church which emphasizes Christ's power to heal, has formed Teen Challenge centers all across the country, more than 40 of them at this writing. Wilkerson believes in Christ's power to cure the drug addict. More than that, he has evidence: more than 70 percent of the addicts who have submitted to his program of prayer have come off drugs and stayed off— compared to the less than five percent rate of cure in federal hospitals.[2]

Is the gospel just a talking game preparing for the here-after, or does Jesus aid a desperate person who needs help right now? For the drug addict or the alcoholic, healing is not simply a matter for academic discussion; it is a matter of life and death. It's not just physical life and death; it's spiritual life and death as well. What willpower cannot accomplish, Christ's healing power can and does.[3] Then, why weren't

---

2. The account of his work with drug addicts can be read in *The Cross and the Switchblade* (New York: Spire Paperbacks, 1964).

3. "The young man was gaunt-blond, trembling slightly, his strained face and close-cropped hair saying pretty clearly that he had recently been to war, and had picked up a communicable disease of that war— heroin addiction. Under his arm, he had a fatigue jacket and two Army blankets. He stood only in the back of Bethel Tabernacle—the squat, white Pentecostal church in Redondo Beach, California, where miracles are supposed to happen.

". . . Then one young man slowly rose from where he had been kneeling and picked his way through the sprawled congregation to the ex-serviceman in the back of the church.

" 'Welcome, brother.' A hand was extended, and tentatively, briefly accepted. 'You're welcome here.'

" 'Jesus can help you.' . . .

"It was all over in less than a minute. The young man's sobbing gently eased, almost as if mesmerized he began to join those surround-ing and supporting him in the simple prayers of thanksgiving. 'Oh man! Oh Jesus, thank you.' . . .

"Bethel Tabernacle's famous 30-second heroin cure had worked again. The guarantee of no withdrawal agonies, no sweats, no pain if you accept Jesus Christ had been fulfilled. One more thoroughly

more organizations like Teen Challenge and Alcoholics Anonymous, which are based on a belief in the power of prayer and the need for a community of love, formed within the institution of the Church? I think it is because we have stressed only that a sinner use his willpower, that he "take the pledge," as it were. But many of us never learned to pray with confidence that Jesus would free the addict from his habit; nor did we form that close community to support the alcoholic or addict and prevent his falling again.

Christians have always believed in the force of prayer and community; we have talked about them and written about them. But when it comes right down to the practical order, do we really believe that Jesus has come to free and transform men? Do we have only good advice to offer, or do we believe in the power of Jesus to change what we ourselves cannot?

With faith, we can begin to pray with the alcoholic that the Lord take away his inordinate craving for drink; we can begin to pray with the drug addict that the Lord help him kick his drug habit "cold turkey"; we can even dare pray for the lame man that he might walk again.

Then we will come to learn from our own experience what Jesus meant when he said: "I tell you most solemnly, whoever believes in me will perform the same works as I do myself; he will perform even greater works, because I am going to the Father" (Jn 14:12).

---

surprised but completely convinced member had been added to Bethel's rapidly growing, spreading, dispersing congregation."—

Brian Vachon, and Jack and Betty Cheetham, *A Time to Be Born* (Englewood Cliffs, N.J.: Prentice-Hall, 1972), pp. 1-2.

7

God Is Love

BECAUSE OF ALL the conditioning which makes Christians believe that suffering is sent by God, they are likely to feel guilty if they ask for healing; to feel cowardly if they ask for alleviation. As Christians, not only should they be able to endure their cross, they should run out and embrace it.

So people feel they must have an excuse, an unselfish reason for asking God for a cure. Typically, a mother will say something like: "I want to get well so I won't be a burden to my family." Or, a professional man will say, "I want to be cured, so I can do my work better."

In contrast, if either of these persons went to a doctor, they wouldn't feel they had to make such excuses. The man would go to an orthopedic surgeon simply because he had injured his spine and wanted to get well. He wouldn't need to justify his presence in the doctor's office by proving to the doctor that his getting better would help his family or enable him to do his work better. Reason enough that he is sick and wants to get well.

Why is it, then, that so many of us feel we have to justify our asking God to make us well? It's as if we can't believe that God loves us, but that he only values us for our work. How different we are from little children asking a loving father for a very natural favor.

As one British housewife, reflecting on the spirituality she learned, described her feelings:

Despite all the formal instruction we received on the Fatherhood of God, the lesson we really learnt was that our relation to God is as little like the normal relation of a child to its father as can be imagined. Picture your own child jumping nervously when it hears your voice; unwilling to play with others in case it gets dirty; always a little anxious because, even though you *say* nothing, you may be inwardly critical and disapproving; fearful of getting on your wrong side; uncertain of asking you for anything it wants because it thinks you will say it is too much trouble or too expensive or not good for it or too good for it—anything but a simple, affectionate "Yes"; obscurely convinced that the root of the trouble is that you don't like children, and its only chance of approval is to be as little like a child as possible. . . .

We *know* he loves us . . . ; we *feel* that his love is the dubious kind that used to result for us in spinach and the thwarting of natural impulse. We daren't formulate these feelings, because we know obscurely that if we did, we should have another set of concepts framed something like this: God is horrid . . . God is always trying to trip you up—and so on. These feelings are kept well out of sight and are only *consciously* present in the form of certain implicit expectations. . . .[1]

---

1. Pamela Carswell, *Offbeat Spirituality* (New York: Sheed & Ward, 1961), pp. 219-223 *passim*.

Part of the reason ordinary Christians have such a fearful relationship with God is that they have exchanged Christ's revelation of a Father who brings healing for their own more or less pagan conception of God as one who sends suffering as a punishment or a penance. Healing is essential to the gospel message and carries us all the way back to our very idea of God. *What kind of a being is God?* If we truly believe that God is love, then it should be easy to believe that healing is an ordinary, not an extraordinary sign of his compassion. Any other attitude toward healing robs the gospel of the reality of God's revelation of himself as a loving father: "If you, then, who are evil, know how to give your children what is good, how much more will your father in heaven give good things to those who ask him!" (Mt 7:11). What is at stake here is not something out on the periphery, but something right at the heart of Christianity: When I speak of God's love for me, do I speak of it in terms that I, a human being, can understand? Or am I talking about some unreal concept of "divine love" or "charity" that does not touch my real life?

I know what real human love is. I am certain that if I am in pain, if I am sick, my friends will do everything they can to get me well. They will take me to the doctor, buy me medicine, put me in a hospital, and may even help me pay thousands of dollars in hospital bills. Their actions show a love and concern that I can understand. But if, while I am lying in my hospital bed, the hospital chaplain, after trying to cheer me up with small talk, tells me that God does not ordinarily heal through prayer, I become confused. The chaplain is not portraying the love of God in any human way that I can grasp. Either Jesus meant something very definite when he said, "Ask and you shall receive," or the gospel has to be reinterpreted in such a way that ordinary people find it hard to understand in terms of their everyday lives.

C. S. Lewis, author of *The Problem of Pain,* set forth all

the understanding his brilliant mind could focus on the mystery and anguish of suffering. Some time after the writing of the book, his wife died. Faced with this terrible loss, Lewis' reasoned reflections were of no comfort; he began to rage against God for taking his wife. In his uncontrollable grief, he took a writer's way out of his pain: he wrote a journal describing his day-to-day battle with despair. When at last he regained his senses and emerged again into the light, he decided to publish his journal; but realizing that his treatment of pain endured was very different from his previous reasoning about it, he did not attach his real name to the work but chose a pseudonym, C. N. Clerk. (The book was later published under his real name.) Because of C. S. Lewis' reputation as an intellectual defender of Christianity, it is especially revealing to read his human reactions to personal suffering and temptations against faith:

> . . . But go to Him when your need is desperate, when all other help is vain, and what do you find? A door slammed in your face, and a sound of bolting and double bolting on the inside. After that, silence. You may as well turn away. The longer you wait, the more emphatic the silence will become. There are no lights in the windows.[2]

> Not that I am (I think) in much danger of ceasing to believe in God. The real danger is of coming to believe such dreadful things about Him. The conclusion I dread is not "So there's no God after all," but "So this is what God's really like. Deceive yourself no longer."[3]

> There is no answer. Only the locked door, the iron curtain, the vacuum, absolute zero. "Them as asks don't get." I was a fool to ask.[4]

---

2. C. S. Lewis, *A Grief Observed,* Copyright © 1961 by N. W. Clerk. (New York: Seabury Press), p. 9. Used by permission of publisher.
3. *Ibid.,* pp. 9-10.
4. *Ibid.,* p. 11.

No, my real fear is not of materialism. If it were true, we—or what we mistake for "we"—could get out, get from under the harrow. An overdose of sleeping pills would do it. I am more afraid that we are really rats in a trap. Or, worse still, rats in a laboratory. Someone said, I believe, "God always geometrizes." Supposing the truth were "God always vivisects?"

Sooner or later I must face the question in plain language. What reason have we, except our own desperate wishes, to believe that God is, by any standard we can conceive, "good"? Doesn't all the *prima facie* evidence suggest exactly the opposite?

We set Christ against it. But how if He were mistaken? Almost His last words may have a perfectly clear meaning. He had found that the Being He called Father was horribly and infinitely different from what He had supposed. The trap, so long and carefully prepared and so subtly baited, was at last sprung, on the cross. The vile practical joke had succeeded.[5]

I wrote that last night. It was a yell rather than a thought. Let me try it over again. Is it rational to believe in a bad God? Anyway, in a God so bad as all that? The Cosmic Sadist, the spiteful imbecile?[6]

The terrible thing is that a perfectly good God is in this matter hardly less formidable than a Cosmic Sadist. The more we believe that God hurts only to heal, the less we can believe that there is any use in begging for tenderness. A cruel man might be bribed—might grow tired of his vile sport—might have a temporary fit of mercy, as alcoholics have fits of sobriety. But suppose that what you are up against is a surgeon whose intentions are wholly

5. *Ibid.*, p. 26.
6. *Ibid.*, p. 27.

good. The kinder and more conscientious he is, the more inexorably he will go on cutting. If he yielded to your entreaties, if he stopped before the operation was complete, all the pain up to that point would have been useless. But is it credible that such extremities of torture should be necessary for us? Well, take your choice. The tortures occur. If they are unnecessary, then there is no God or a bad one.[7]

In these passages C. S. Lewis provides a striking example of what happens to the human heart when it is confronted with a tradition that God, rather than evil forces, brings suffering. He describes the human heart as crying out, unable to conceive how a loving God could be without compassion. Intuitively, he and all Christians know that God's love cannot be so different from human love as to be a complete mystery.

While in Peru, I was surprised to find that the most popular Christian feast of the year is that of *El Senor de los Milagros*—Our Lord of the Miracles. This feast, established by the people, is more popular than Easter or Christmas in spite of all official teaching, for the people look to God for help, for healing, for miracles. The month of October is spent much like Lent in other countries, preparing for the procession of the Lord of the Miracles. The Peruvian people in their simple faith look to God and their Church for help— not just for a doctrine of acceptance of suffering.

It is the devotion of simple people that has built most of the great Christian shrines. Expectant pilgrims continue to go to Lourdes in search of healing. They flock to Mary as a compassionate and loving mother, approachable and reaching out to heal. But if this is Mary's love, how much greater is the love of God who has said through the prophet Isaiah,

Can a mother forget her infant, be without tenderness for

7. *Ibid.*, pp. 35-36.

the child of her womb? Even should she forget, I will never forget you (Is 49:15).

In question here is our very notion of God. Against a God who wills men to suffer on earth, we may be tempted to rage as did Ivan in *Brothers Karamazov:*

> "Tell me yourself, I challenge you—answer. Imagine that you are creating a fabric of human destiny with the object of making men happy in the end, giving them peace and rest at last. Imagine that you are doing this but that it is essential and inevitable to torture to death only one tiny creature—that child beating its breast with its fist, for instance—in order to found that edifice on its unavenged tears. Would you consent to be the architect on those conditions? Tell me. Tell the truth.
>
> "No, I wouldn't consent," said Alyosha softly.[8]

But the revelation of God in Jesus Christ is that we have a merciful Lord who saves and heals. Jesus, as the visible manifestation of the invisible God, shows us that God is a loving Father. Repeatedly, Jesus asks for confidence: "Whatever you ask in my name will be granted." It is time to return to this childlike trust in prayer, to a confidence that God really loves us; for the most tangible sign that God loves is that he stoops, as Jesus did, to heal the wounded.

For if God has the *power* to help people, yet refuses to do so, the questions we naturally ask are:

1. Does God really *care?* If I have the power to help a friend when I see him hurt, I use all my powers to help him. If God has power to help but doesn't, I don't know what it means to say "God loves us." This is a very real question asked many times, especially by despairing people. "My condition," they say, "proves that God doesn't care. Maybe he

8. Fyodor Dostoyevsky, *The Brothers Karamazov* (New York: Signet, 1957), p. 226.

cares for you; but look at me, and you know why I'm convinced that God doesn't care about me."

2. If God cares, but lets people remain in their suffering, he seems to *lack the power* to help. He is irrelevant to my real life, to my real needs.

In either case, the very idea of God's goodness and love can be deeply shaken when we deny that he heals through prayer. Part of the present crisis of faith is, I think, related to a basic lack of confidence in prayer. Some preaching, emphasizing caution and stressing that God often says "No," has contributed to this lack of hope and faith. If God does not ordinarily answer prayer but only wants us to accept and endure suffering, what is the *Good* News? If someone says he is my friend, but then lets me suffer when he has the power to help, how can I help but question whether he really cares?[9]

---

9. This heartrending kind of question is asked in a letter I recently received:

My sister died last summer. She was a wonderful religious girl who went to Mass every day of her life until part of this year when her condition became worse. She was a very exceptional girl—never complained in her illness or pain. She had very severe treatments, lost her hair, could not eat or taste food at the end. But always a smile.

But my great concern now is my mother. My mother as long as I can remember was always a very religious person. Mass and Holy Communion every day of her life, down on her knees every night praying. My mother was our life and our strength.

My sister's death has completely shattered her. My mother truly believed a miracle would take place; when she became ill, we had Masses offered every week. She had hundreds of Masses offered up for her recovery.

My feeling now is, why? We believed, prayed and hoped. She had so much to live for and was so good.

But I know God's ways are not our ways. It is my mother whom I am greatly concerned about now. She has completely turned her back on God. No prayers, no Mass, no more belief in God. It is almost two months now and she screams and blames God for everything. This is not my mother, but no one in the family can seem to help or console her in any way.

A mother's love, a father's love, a friend's love, I understand. But what about God's love?

God has said in scripture that his love surpasses that of a mother (Is 49:15) or of a father (Mt 7:11). The marvelous revelation is that he is not an unapproachable God on the mountaintop of Sinai whom we dare not approach, but that he has become a man like us in everything but sin. The mission of Jesus was to share our suffering and then to transform it into new life, to heal us in body and mind.

Inspired by Christ, we have built hospitals with the assumption that it is God's will that men do everything humanly possible to care for the sick and help them get well. Only certain non-Christian religions would let people die on the streets, believing it to be God's will, fate, or Karma that brought them there where passersby should walk by and let them suffer it out.

The Red Cross, too, was founded through the compassion of St. Camillus, and Christian nurses and doctors are ready to give their entire lives to cure the sick. Why is it, then, that those who give spiritual advice usually counsel patients to accept their suffering as God's will for them, while everyone else in the hospital labors to restore the person to health? No wonder many people fear God when it comes time to die, for he does not seem to show love by healing as the patient's friends and relatives show their love by wanting to see him well.

Reflected in these attitudes is a kind of spiritual schizophrenia: Christian doctors and nurses work to make the patient well, obeying Christ's injunctions to help the sick and needy. On the contrary, preachers sometimes persuade the patient that acceptance of the cross is Christ's basic message. If the patient recovers through human ministration, fine; but God is somehow portrayed as mysteriously desiring man to suffer in a redemptive way. Little wonder, then, that in many parts of Latin America when disaster or sickness strikes, the people say, "It is God's will." To regain health they go, not to God, but to a *curandero,* a witch doctor, to pray for recovery. The roles have been reversed: the people treat God as if he were a pagan deity to be appeased by suffering. But for healing, they turn to the world of spirits and demons.[10]

There is a crucial need for a return to the vision of the God revealed in and by Jesus Christ, the tender, loving and compassionate God who raises men up and makes them whole wherever they have been cast down by the world of evil—whether they have sinned and need forgiveness, or are sick and need physical healing. Even now the kingdom of God is among us, saving and healing and destroying the kingdom of evil.

In short, the nature of God as manifested visibly in Jesus Christ is love. Jesus' compassion impelled him to reach out whenever he saw a sick man, even when it was against his own best interests. (When he cured on the Sabbath, far from proving anything, it showed many of his contemporaries that he was *not* the Messiah.) The healing works of Jesus were so important in Peter's mind that when he gave the household of Cornelius a thumbnail sketch of the life of Jesus, he said nothing about the content of his preaching, but only reported:

> I take it you know what has been reported all over Judea about Jesus of Nazareth, beginning in Galilee with the baptism John preached; of the way God anointed him *with the Holy Spirit and power.* He went about *doing good works and healing all who were in the grip of the*

---

10. The Maryknoll Fathers have recently put out a fine film, *The Healer,* which shows how a young priest, Father Innocente Salazar, discovers how the Aymara Indians in his parish in Peru are basically untouched by the Catholic Church. They see God as a vengeful God and go to the local witch doctor in search of cures for their misery and sickness.

devil, and God was with him. We are witnesses *to all that he did* in the land of the Jews and in Jerusalem (Acts 10:37-39, italics added).

After this, Peter speaks of Jesus' crucifixion, death, and resurrection; but he sums up the entire public ministry of Jesus in terms of what he did rather than of what he said, for Jesus established the kingdom of God through the power of healing as well as through preaching.

The healing of Jesus, then, is central to the doctrine of the gospel. To deny this is, in effect, to deny the gospel—to change it from Good News into Good Advice which lacks the power to transform man into a new creation.

In short, Jesus did not heal people to prove that he was God; he healed them *because he was God.*

Faith,

hope

and love

and the greatest

of these

is love.

1 COR. 13:13

PART TWO

Faith, Hope and Charity
as They Touch Upon
the Healing Ministry

8

The Faith to Be Healed

All the books on healing—including *the* book on healing, the New Testament—emphasize the role that faith plays in healing. "Go in peace, your faith has made you whole," is a constant saying of Jesus. Jesus asks of us the strongest kind of faith—a faith that admits of no doubt or hesitation:

> Jesus answered, "Have faith in God. I tell you solemnly, if anyone says to this mountain, 'Get up and throw yourself into the sea,' *with no hesitation in his heart* but believing that what he says will happen, it will be done for him. I tell you therefore: everything you ask and pray for, *believe that you have it already,* and it will be yours" (Mk 11:22-24; italics added).

This is an incredible, unbelievable statement! Nevertheless, we are asked to believe it; we are to have no hesitation in believing that we have already received whatever we ask for. (Later we will say more about how to pray "the prayer of faith" for healing, but for now, just notice the strong emphasis Jesus himself places upon faith.) Such strong statements are not rare in the gospels, as even the most cursory reading will show; on the contrary, faith in asking God for our needs is one of the common New Testament themes.

In consequence, most evangelists stress faith as a condition necessary for healing. "Have faith," they say, "and you will be healed. 'By his stripes you are healed.' Can you believe those words of scripture? If so, lay hold of that promise and you will be healed."

With absolute faith, Catholics accept another aspect of the healing ministry, the forgiveness of sins, provided the person meets the necessary condition: repentance. With a faith equally strong, many evangelists stress that physical healing will always take place, provided the person meets the necessary condition: faith. In both cases—the healing of sin and the healing of disease—preachers stress the same basic principle: Christ has already won these blessings for us through the cross; all we have to do is apply the fruits of the redemption to our own lives. "He took our sicknesses away and carried our diseases for us" (Mt 8:17).

But there is a problem; while we believe that forgiveness of sins always takes place, we can see that physical healing apparently does not always occur. Forgiveness is not a visible phenomenon; healing is. The blind man either sees, or he does not; the lame man either walks, or he remains in his wheelchair. Since not all the lame walk following prayer for healing, how can we have the same certainty of faith that we have when we pray for forgiveness of sin? What are we supposed to believe will happen? What kind of faith do we need?

What Kind of Faith Do We Need?

In order to talk about this entire matter of faith intelligently and avoid some of the oversimplification that has ended in harming people's faith instead of helping it, it may be well to describe four basic faith attitudes toward healing:

1) *Healing is simply man's responsibility.* There are many members of Christian churches who do not believe in the possibility of God's direct healing power, though they admit the use of natural means and secondary causes (including the power of suggestion).

Take for example the scorn for healing miracles evinced in the writings of the popular spiritual author, Louis Evely:

> . . . It seems that Jesus himself placed miracles beyond the pale of religion. Man left to himself would hope to better his condition through all sorts of wealth and power; but God has taught us to better it through love, by accepting it willingly, as he accepted his death on the cross. Nothing is more foreign to God than miraculous *tours de force,* phenomena which excite in man only fear or curiosity.

> With the acceptance of the theory of human evolution, with the development of scientific method and technical resources, it becomes more and more evident that the religion revealed by Christ is one that is fully human and fully divine—not an archaic religion of miracles and contradiction to human nature, but a religion of patient love and responsibility.

> If there are miracles to be worked, then it is we who must work them. Man, being man, has unlimited resources at his disposal.[1]

Certainly, such an attitude of self-sufficiency sees no need for a ministry of prayer for healing, which only prolongs an

1. Louis Evely, *The Gospel Without Myth* (New York: Doubleday & Co., Inc., 1971), p. 52.

illusion that prevents man from accepting responsibility for his own destiny.

2) *Healing is possible but extraordinary.* This attitude toward healing represents the belief of many Christians (Roman Catholics, in particular). Here is faith, certainly faith in God's *power* to perform miracles of healing; but there is doubt as to God's *desire* to perform such healing as a matter of course. Miracles are the exception—they prove something (e.g., the holiness of a saint), they are rare occurrences. In fact, if miracles should become common, they would lose their value as exceptional signs. The ordinary will of God, according to this view, is that sick persons should raise their sufferings to the level of the Cross; at that level they must learn to accept pain and not try to escape it. People should pray only for what will bring them spiritual advancement. Since suffering has redemptive value, men should not pray to be freed from pain but rather seek the royal road of the Cross.

The result is that the sick are not strongly encouraged to pray for healing, lest they lose the merits of the Cross. The situation is something like a football game; play as long as you can with an injury for the sake of the team, unless the pain becomes unbearable. A sick person asking for an end to pain may feel guilty, like the player—a quitter—asking to be taken out of the game. (Frequently, I meet people unwilling to pray for the cure of small sicknesses and hurts because they feel it is unworthy to ask for relief from such small ailments, for instance, an infected toe. Yet the same people will go to a doctor seeking a cure for the same ailment.) If persons with such an attitude do pray, they generally doubt whether God will condescend to answer their prayers, which they fear are contaminated by self-interest.

Experience leads them to believe in the truth of the self-fulfilling prophecy: Blessed are those who expect nothing, for they shall not be disappointed.

3) *Healing is ordinary and normative, but does not always take place.* It is this author's belief that the ordinary will of God is that man should be whole. Usually, a man glorifies God more mightily in every way when he is healthy than when he is sick. Therefore, man can and should pray to God with confidence for healing.

Yet, there are exceptions; sometimes sickness is directed toward a higher good, for the kingdom of God. (There are other reasons, too, enumerated in the chapter on "Eleven Reasons Why People Are Not Healed.") Consequently, healing does not always take place, even where there is faith.

4) *Healing always takes place if there is faith.* This kind of absolute belief is, I think, most strongly exemplified by persons who take the bible literally and present a very simple doctrine of healing. Such persons favor the writing of evangelists like Kenneth Hagin, who has written a number of booklets on faith as a precondition for healing. Typical of this teaching is the following:

> There are those who are especially anointed with the ministry of healing, but every believer ought to have a ministry of healing. I don't mean every believer ought to be anointed of the Spirit to minister in certain ways, but I mean every believer ought to be able to take the Word of God to a sick person and open that Word to them and give them what the scripture says on it.

> If those folks are receptive to the Word of God, then faith will come into their hearts. When you open the Word up to people, then they will see that the Word says, "By his stripes we are healed. . . ." Open the Word to the sick, and if their minds are open, that Word, through

their mind, will get down into their spirits. As they meditate upon it, they will come to see that by his stripes, according to the Word, I am healed.

If that person acts upon the Word of God, they will ignore what this outward man tells them. The body may tell them that the symptoms are still there, even the pain or the misery, or whatever it is. But instead of walking by natural, human faith, you walk by Bible faith. I have seen people with conditions that the doctors said could never be cured, but as I opened the Word to them, I have seen them with every symptom still present say, "I'm healed."

I asked them, "How do you know you are?" They said, "Because the Word says, 'Himself took my infirmities and bare my sicknesses.' " Those people are alive and well. Not just one of them, but many of them. They are alive and well today with no symptoms of the disease whatsoever. Yet, when they acted in faith and made their confession, they had every symptom they had ever had. As far as medical science was concerned, their condition was still incurable. What happened? They believed in their hearts.[2]

This is, no doubt, a powerful statement on faith, a real challenge. Yet there remain questions one might ask. For those who still exhibit the symptoms of sickness, is the *only* answer their need for more faith? One young couple, for instance, is trying to live up to this most stringent belief in healing, but they are having problems:

Pat and I have a few questions that we thought you might have the answers to:

---

2. *The Word of Faith,* January, 1972 (published by Kenneth Hagin Evangelistic Association. P.O. Box 50126, Tulsa, Okla., 74150).

We do not allow sickness in our new home because we know that faith and scriptures can drive it away, and Jesus bore our diseases for us. Why then do Spirit-filled Christians sometimes get really sick? X Y's singer,[3] the last I heard, was in a hospital, not allowed to move so that a blood clot could hopefully pass through without killing her. She does not believe in sickness. So why or how can this happen? We cannot teach healing positively and then end by saying, "If it is the Lord's will this time." That is not faith. I thought the bible had laws that were obeyed in faith, and that there were no "perhaps." Are there shades of gray in the bible?

Also, do we have dominion over animals? Our cat has coughing spells that really irritate us. We've prayed and laid hands on her, cast off bad spirits, etc. Veterinary bills are expensive and since we will not allow sickness in our lives, why allow it in our cat's life?

Of such small problems is life made up. Such real difficulties with the theory of the faith required for healing do lead to anxiety—or, in some cases, to a rejection of the whole idea of healing as incredible and contrary to the reality of a suffering mankind. It is necessary to make important distinctions in order to render credible the glorious ministry of healing to people who dare to ask questions. It's not just a matter of rendering this ministry credible to someone else; it's a question of the reality itself: How do we explain the sickness of Christians?

I do not pretend to have all the answers. Far from it, I bow down, like Job, before the mystery of healing in its con-

---

3. X Y stands for a noted evangelist who stresses a faith that disregards symptoms of sickness as a precondition for healing.

nection with suffering: "And now let us proclaim the *mystery* of our faith." But there are some distinctions we can make that will help us know the kind of faith, which is often—but not always—a precondition for healing.

1) *My faith is in God—not in my faith.*

My faith is not in my faith, but *in God*. This sounds obvious. Perhaps it is obvious. But if every person who prayed for healing really understood these words, we could clarify many problems that we now find in the healing ministry.

My faith is in God—in his faithfulness to his promises, in his wisdom, in his power, and in his goodness.

—In his *faithfulness* to his promises to hear and to answer my prayers. I have absolute confidence that God answers my prayers, whether I see the results or not.

—In his *wisdom*. Because of his wisdom, which so far surpasses mine, I trust that he understands, even when I don't, every motive, every circumstance involved in my praying for this healing of a particular person. Because of my ignorance I sometimes pray for a mistaken thing, or in a mistaken way, and so I do not see the results turn out as I think they should. But these will turn out as God in his wisdom sees best.

—In his *power*. I believe that everything is possible with God. Nothing then is impossible to the prayer of the Christian—even a resurrection from the dead.

—In his *goodness*. Because I believe in God's goodness I try to see everything as reflecting his love. Whatever is ultimately the most loving thing will happen in response to my prayer for healing.

But my faith is not *in my faith*. My faith opens up doubts

once I begin to look at its quality. When a blind person, one who has no eyes whatsoever in the sockets, comes forward to ask for prayer, I wonder if I have the faith required for such a healing. Most of us would have to admit our doubts. Once we begin to look at our faith, however, rather than at God, we begin to concentrate on our own inadequacy. (Those who claim to have no doubts sometimes seem more in need of healing than those they pray for; instead of examining their own ministry and asking realistic questions about why they are not always successful, they simply project the guilt for sickness onto those they pray for.)

In short, faith leaves me no doubts about God's power to heal, and about his desire to heal, contrary to those who feel God does not heal at all, or only in extraordinary circumstances. But I do doubt whether I know all the circumstances required to pray rightly for a given person. Is there something I don't understand in this situation? More often than not, I am at least partly in the dark. Consequently, I don't always know whether the person I pray for will get well. Unless the Lord reveals to me all the necessary details of the situation, I simply do not know whether healing will take place at this time. Does this mean I don't have faith? No, I don't think so; it simply means I am human. My faith is in God, not in my own powers—not even in my own faith.

Many people I have met, though, who do believe in healing feel guilty about their human doubts. They turn inward when they hear the challenge, "Do you have the faith to be healed?" Instead of confiding absolutely in God's power and goodness, they begin to probe within themselves to examine whether they are free entirely of doubt; and nine times out of ten, their answer is no. Then there ensues a painful conflict, in which the person begins to feel guilty; the more he examines his doubt, the bigger it grows. In the struggle to pass beyond the point of doubt, he ends by suppressing his real feelings.

The more he wrestles, the deeper his anguish. He may finally manage to surmount the doubt by a strong act of the will, moving beyond the doubt that still swirls around underneath. But faith is a gift that one cannot attain by his own efforts. As Dr. Bogart Van Dunne, a Methodist scripture scholar, once said in a seminar: "Protestants began by rejecting Catholicism for what they conceived was its reliance on works for salvation. But now, for some Protestants, *faith has become the works* they struggle to achieve."

This struggle to "achieve" faith reminds me of what often happens when I begin to lose a tennis game. I start overstraining; I hit the ball harder, trying to make winning shots in order to regain my confidence; I smash my serve harder to win a few quick, impressive aces. But all that really happens is that I hit the ball out of court more often, and I begin missing my first serve. My straining efforts worsen my game. So I try still harder. I begin talking to my partner, or myself, to generate a little more enthusiasm; I try running faster to refresh my drooping spirits. But I only end up beating myself. My efforts cannot cover up my lack of coordination.

Similarly, I see people in prayer groups, in the face of defeat (the person they are praying for doesn't seem to be changed), begin to pray louder and faster. They press the person with stronger and stronger exhortations to have faith. But they do not increase his faith. Instead, they only add to the tension. Their efforts cannot cover up the fact that the object of their faith is off center.

This anxious approach can do great harm. Persons who are not healed go away with the impression that they lack the faith they should have, or that God doesn't love them as he so obviously loves those who have been healed. They identify with the man born blind in John's Gospel who was being argued over by the disciples (not the Pharisees): "Who sinned, this man or his parents, for him to have been born blind?" (Jn 9:2).

I remember a woman at a large prayer meeting, who had been encouraged not to see a doctor, but to disregard her symptoms (seizures similar to epilepsy). During the meeting, she had an attack. The advice she had been receiving now only resulted in greater anxiety and sleepless nights, which, in turn, led to lower resistance and more frequent seizures. Far from increasing her faith, the advice she received only led her to condemn herself for lacking the faith to resist the attacks of Satan.

If we really believe that God makes himself responsible for the results of our prayer, we can do our part, which is to pray, and then leave the results to him. Glenn Clark, founder of the Camps Farthest Out, used to compare asking God for a favor with a hen hatching an egg. You put the egg under the hen and leave it for 21 days. If you keep taking the egg out to look at it, you inhibit the whole process; you may be helping your own anxiety, but you may also kill the egg. Why, he asked, can't we put as much trust in God as we do in an old hen? He used another simile:

> When you take a pair of shoes to the shoemaker to be half-soled you go off and leave them, don't you? How otherwise would the shoemaker be able to mend them? Likewise, how can God get at our problems if we continue to hug them to ourselves? Yes, the biggest problem in prayer is how to "let go and let God."[4]

When I try to suppress my doubts and to have faith in my

4. *Under the Shelter of His Wings,* p. 2. A pamphlet by Macalester-Park Publishing Co., St. Paul, Minnesota.

faith, I become man-centered rather than God-centered. I
begin to scrutinize my own doubts and my own fears, to feel
guilty about them; then I try to get rid of them by my own
willpower. I may *seem* to myself to be getting out of myself
and centering myself on God. In reality, I am doing the very
opposite: I am trying to create faith in myself, forgetting that
faith is a gift from God. So often, such an approach, far from
creating confidence and trust in God, ends in a sense of fear
and worthlessness:

> When I'm used as an instrument in a big physical healing
> I'm *scared to death*. There's no other way to describe it.
> Two examples have taken place in our community. I feel
> that a certain child remained in braces partly because of
> my lack of faith; then last Wednesday a blind man came
> in great faith to our meeting. We prayed over him and,
> though I believed that the Lord could heal him, at the
> same time I was afraid that he would. I can't help but
> feel that our lack of faith as a community could have pre-
> vented this man from seeing. I prayed about this and I
> felt led to I John 5, so I know the Lord wants my fear to
> go away. How do I strengthen my faith in this matter?
> It's not lack of faith in Jesus' power but in his using me as
> an instrument. I have no qualms about being used for
> prophecy, but this doesn't frighten me like healing. Why?
> (from a letter).

I would suggest that the teaching this writer has had on
healing has been faulty, she believes she should be able to
say, "This man will be healed at this time." Because she can't
do that—in all honesty she can't—she feels guilty. This leads
her to avoid prayer for healing.

If I can't force myself to believe that this blind man will
right now be healed, does that mean that I do not have faith

in God's promises? No, it simply means that I am willing to admit that I don't know all the factors involved in this situation unless God chooses to reveal them to me. To admit this does not mean that I lack faith.

No, faith is not in my faith, but my faith is in God—in his goodness and wisdom—in his unfailing listening and answering my prayers. To claim more than this, unless it has been specifically revealed that a given person is going to get well, is to make oneself into a counterfeit trying to play God.

The way, then, to pray in faith, is

—to turn *to God* in the complete trust that he knows what is best, that he loves us more than anyone else, and that he has the power to accomplish whatever we need;

—to accept *our doubts* about our own adequacy and our own prediction of results as normal;

—to see that the faith-*action* we need to take is to *pray for the sick* (when our guidance in prayer indicates this);

—to *leave the results up to God;* ordinarily we need not keep after the person we have prayed for to prove results.[5]

2) *"The gift of faith" is not the same as the virtue of faith.*

To every Christian faith is given—the *virtue* of faith which, in my opinion, implies the kind of confidence mentioned earlier: a belief in God's faithfulness, his wisdom, his

---

5. This is only to say we do not need to be anxious about results. In one sense we can pray for a person, then walk away, leaving the results up to God. On the other hand, we do need follow-up: we need to encourage the person to thank God for hearing and answering our prayers. Moreover, there may be a need for further prayer, and for that we need to know the results—or lack of results—for our initial prayer. Most important of all, many healings are progressive and require the continued support of a Christian community.

power and his love. It seems to me that this kind of faith
should include a belief in healing. This faith is a gift. But
though a gift, this is not the "gift of faith" enumerated by St.
Paul among those gifts given to some members of the community:

> One may have the gift of preaching with wisdom given
> him by the Spirit; another may have the gift of preaching
> instruction given him by the same Spirit; and *another the*
> *gift of faith* given by the same Spirit; *another the gift of*
> *healing,* through this one Spirit . . . (I Cor 12:8-9).

In the next chapter St. Paul again mentions many of these
gifts and adds, "If I have faith in all its fullness, to move
mountains, but without love, then I am nothing at all" (I Cor
13:2b). The faith to move mountains is an obvious reference
to Jesus' statement: "If anyone says to this mountain, 'Get
up and throw yourself into the sea,' *with no hesitation in his*
heart but believing that what he says will happen, it will be
done for him" (Mk 11:23).

This "gift of faith," or fullness of faith, is given to some,
but not to all, Christians. As I understand it, the "gift of
faith" is a ministry-gift which God imparts to help us pray
with confidence and "no hesitation in our hearts" for a given
intention. Since this confidence can come only by God's revealing his will at a given moment, the gift of "the word of
knowledge" is closely connected with the "gift of faith."
Through the word of knowledge, God intimates to the per-
son(s) praying that his will is to heal a particular person at
a particular time. Through this gift God may inspire us to
know:

a) that the one we are praying for or have prayed for
will be healed. The gift of faith then lies in accepting this
inspiration without hesitation and praying with absolute trust,

believing that this person will be healed;

b) sometimes the person may receive an inspiration to stop taking medication or to disregard symptoms. (The rules for testing the spirit certainly hold true here where the effects of false inspiration can be so harmful. If someone else tells a sick person to stop taking medication or to disregard symptoms, the one who is or has been sick should obey this suggestion only if he *himself* feels inspired to do so.)

The distinction between the faith in healing that all Christians should have and the special "gift of faith" is of particular practical importance. It explains why some Christians who believe in healing can always say: "I believe that God does heal, that he loves you and has the power to heal you. Let's pray for healing, but I can't predict exactly what will happen." Others can, upon occasion, pray with far more confidence: "God loves you and will heal you now if we just ask him to do so." It explains why evangelists like Kenneth Hagin can pray the prayer of command, "Be healed," with assurance. (God does not inspire him to pray for everyone; but he has, upon occasion, been interiorly prevented from praying for some of the sick who asked for healing.) Without the discernment, which is a gift from God to know when to pray and when not to pray, we are bound to have some doubts when we pray—not doubts about God, but about our own knowledge of God's will in a particular situation.

Praying in the Name of Jesus

Consequently, it is only when we pray "in the name of Jesus" that we can have absolute assurance and faith in prayer. For praying in the name of Jesus means much more than just using the formula of words (asking the Father in the name of Jesus Christ). In Hebrew thought, the name of a person stood for the entire person: to pray in the name of Jesus means to pray *in the person of Jesus*—as Jesus himself would pray. To pray in the name of Jesus means that we must put on "that mind which was in Christ Jesus," that we see people and situations as Jesus does, and then speak with the power and authority of Jesus. To see people and situations in this way is a gift. But it is only then that anyone can pray the prayer of command—commanding sickness to leave in the name of Jesus, commanding people to rise up and walk. The apostles prayed in this way, for they were inspired more directly by God than most Christians are today. They could say without hesitation, "In the name of Jesus Christ, the Nazarene, walk!" (Acts 3:6b). They spoke with the authority of Jesus because they had the mind of Jesus.

In brief, there are really two models of praying for healing. Each is perfectly valid but one is deeper and better than the other; yet it cannot be forced, for it is a gift.

a) For the ordinary Christian in ordinary circumstances: the prayer of healing is a *prayer of petition,* asking the Father to heal the person in the name of Jesus Christ (in the unity of the Holy Spirit). (This is the ordinary form of the prayers of the Roman Catholic liturgy.)

b) For the person with the gift of healing: at those times when he is truly inspired, the prayer of healing is more like a *prayer of command,* "Be healed." Or if his prayer is that of petition, it is far stronger than the ordinary prayer of petition, for it contains no element of doubt in it: "Amen. I see it being done. Thank you, Lord." It is a prayer in the name of Jesus, in the fullest sense of the word, where the person praying already knows in some mysterious way the mind of God, and so can speak in his person. It is as if the person praying were standing *with* God and speaking for him.

A diagram may be helpful in understanding these two styles of prayer:

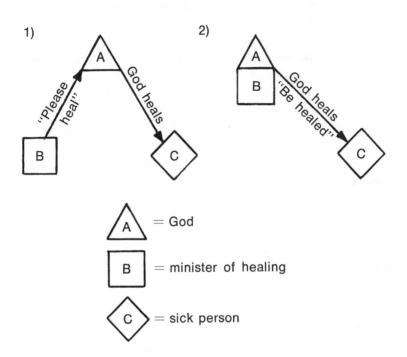

= God

= minister of healing

= sick person

The trouble with this diagram is, of course, that it makes God appear "out there," whereas God is immanent and heals from within. All the diagram is meant to illustrate is that in one case the person(s) praying is not altogether sure what God's will is in asking for the healing of this sick man at this time and is, as it were, speaking *to* God, asking him to heal the person. In the second instance, God in one way or another has revealed his will to heal at this time; therefore, the ministry of healing is not only praying to God but is addressing the sick person as God's spokesman and is speaking *for* God.

These two styles, both based on faith, are yet quite different. Many of the problems in the healing ministry are caused by persons who imitate the style of others who have gifts they themselves do not possess. The healer who does not really have the gifts of knowledge and faith may easily develop an empty and pretentious style of prayer. He can harm the sick by imposing guilt upon them, when, for instance, he tells people they have been healed, not because God has revealed this to him, but because he is imitating the prayers and actions of others who do have the gifts necessary to pray the prayer of command.

Each of us must search out where he really is, and learn to pray in a style that suits the reality of his own healing ministry. Each can learn from others, but he should not imitate others unless his own inner spiritual reality corresponds to the exterior form. Even if one has no exceptional gifts of knowledge, discernment, or faith, it should not stop him from praying for the sick, provided he is aware of his limitations. Do not pretend to be better than you are! Develop your own style, as the Spirit leads you.

Moreover, it is possible to *grow* in these gifts. Use what God gives you and you will see that God will use you more and more as his instrument. Agnes Sanford recommends that beginners pray for the cure of minor ailments, such as colds, that seem more amenable to healing than chronic and deep-seated ones like cancer, arthritis and blindness. (Even here I would not want to set up hard and fast rules, for I have seen people new in the healing ministry, whose prayers God has used in marvelous ways, beyond those who have been praying for the sick for many years.) As you exercise your faith and see God heal people through your prayers, you will find your own faith and courage growing. Use whatever gifts you have; learn to pray the prayer of faith which will be described in a later chapter, and, above all, love people, and you may yet see miracles.

3) *The faith needed for healing can be in anyone—or no one.*

It is comforting to know that God can work through man's weakness to accomplish the things he wants. ". . . my power is at its best in weakness."

Whose faith is needed?

a) The faith can be in the *person praying* for the healing, or

b) It can be in the *sick person* asking, even when the person asked to pray has little or no faith, or

c) Sometimes it just seems that God wants to manifest his goodness when *no one in particular* seems to have faith.

I remember, for instance, how a creative retreat master once told me about a sermon he thought had backfired on him. This priest used to work out clever introductions for his sermons to capture the audience's attention. On one retreat, he had what for him was a difficult audience: a college group. He wanted to speak to them about faith, about how important it is to hold on to the faith, in spite of appearances or emotions. To emphasize the fact that they should not look for emotional highs or for proofs, but should be willing to endure aridity and the cross, he decided to introduce his sermon on faith with a spiel on faith healing (in which he did not believe). So when the time came for him to give his sermon on faith, he told the students that he had the gift of healing; and he exhorted them to come forward to the altar railing and be healed. When he had finished giving his fake altar call, he was happy to see some 30 students come forward. His plan was to pray for them; then when they weren't healed, he could say, "You see! You were fooled. You are looking for miracles. Our faith is not like that; it is an assent to God's revealed truth simply because he has said it; you are not to be seeking signs and wonders."

As the priest went along the line, praying for the sick, he

copied what he had once seen Oral Roberts do on TV. With absolutely no thought that anything would happen, he prayed for the students by imposing his hands on their heads with great force proclaiming loudly, "In the name of Jesus, be healed!" "Then," he said to me, "You know what happened? They were all healed—or seemed to be. The headaches I can explain; they were cured by the power of suggestion in my sermon. But there was one boy with his arm in a sling who went back to his pew waving his arm and claiming he was cured; that bothered me. I was really glad next day when one student did come back to say she still had swelling in her sprained ankle which she had thought was cured. But all those other students acted as if they were healed. It spoiled the whole point of my sermon."

Who had the faith for healing in this case, if there was healing? Certainly it wasn't the retreat master who disbelieved the whole process. Was it the students? Perhaps. Or was it the power in the words of the prayer, "In the name of Jesus Christ, be healed"? Perhaps it was that, too.

Kathryn Kuhlman and other ministers of healing have seen sick persons who lacked faith be healed. We have also seen sick persons who didn't have faith in their own prayer healed through the prayers of another person such as a retreat master. Perhaps such healings are meant by God to help people receive the faith they do not yet have.

Faith is important for healing; but if we, in our weakness, do all we can, God will bless us far beyond our own merits. *Our faith lies in the obedience of praying for the sick,* despite our weakness, doing the best we can to show forth the mercy of Christ. We need to take ourselves less seriously—and God more seriously.

Though I am a nobody, there is not a thing these arch-apostles have that I do not have as well. You have seen done among you all the signs that mark the true apostle, unfailingly produced: the signs, the marvels, the miracles (II Cor 12:11b-12).

This is something that we must each discover: that, in spite of our weakness, when we step forward and pray the prayer of healing, doing the best we can according to the faith that God has given us, God blesses us in abundance, beyond our merits—even beyond the power of our faith.

9

The Mystery of Faith

AS I EXPERIENCE the paradoxes of the healing ministry, I become more and more aware of the mystery involved. Those who want simple answers and absolute clarity are bound to be disappointed. They will never have the beautiful experience that I have almost every day, of seeing a person touched and healed by God's merciful love:

> A thousand thanks for the spiritual healing. It was complete. Courage, joy and strength filled my heart at your prayer. God spoke through it to assure me of his love. It was the greatest consolation to know that you could understand my sorrow. After the prayer I went to chapel and there felt such a release! It seemed as if all the bitter memories were gone. From that moment I was filled with joy as the burden of years disappeared. (From a letter.)

True, there will always be a mystery, and anyone who tries to oversimplify will only end by causing confusion. St. Paul wrote, "The knowledge that I have now is imperfect" (I Cor 13:12b); surely we should not be ashamed to admit that our own knowledge is less than perfect.

Reliable authority has informed me that about 10 percent

of those who sought healing at meetings held by a famous healing evangelist were cured. The 10 percent is cause for rejoicing, but what happened to the other 90 percent who asked for health? (My own experience indicates that a much larger percentage of persons obtain healing in our retreats.) If the main factor the evangelist stresses is "Do you have the faith to be healed?" then people accept the converse, "If I am not healed it is because my faith is weak." Simplistic preaching causes guilt in those who are not healed and increases resistance in those who are skeptical about the very possibility of healing. Most people like simple solutions; they flee complexity which annoys them. As Dr. Paul Tournier wisely observed:

> It is the common experience of all, that humanity moves between these two poles of simplicity and complexity. People who have the sort of mind that sees only one side to every question tend toward vigorous action. They succeed in everything they do because they do not stop to split hairs and have abounding confidence in their own abilities. Your successful journalist, for instance, is inclined to simplify every problem and condense it into an arresting phrase. On the other hand, those with subtle and cultivated minds tend to get lost in a maze of fine distinctions. They always see how complicated things really are, so that their powers of persuasion are nil. That is why the world is led by those who are least suited to raising its cultural and moral standards. It is only very few who manage to combine both tendencies, and in my view a lively Christian faith is the best precondition for the accomplishment of this miracle, because it gives both profound understanding and simplicity of heart.[1]

1. Paul Tournier, *The Person Reborn,* pp. 20-21. Copyright © 1966 by Paul Tournier. Reprinted by permission of Harper & Row, Publishers, Inc.

As Tournier suggests, the popular preacher or evangelist
may simplify in order to make a point: "If you have faith, you
will be healed." Most of my educated friends are appalled by
such fundamentalist approaches. It is probably true that
many ministers of healing (those who launch into action without many doubts) are the least capable of explaining what
they do. On the other hand, those who might best understand
the complexity of this ministry are so immobilized by their
doubts, by their speculations, for instance, on the traditional
place given to the spirituality of redemptive suffering in the
Church, that they seldom launch out and pray for the sick
themselves. Prayer for healing is more associated with tents
than with theological seminaries.[2] That is why the world of
healing "is led by those who are least suited to raising its cul-
tural and moral standards."

----

2. The distance between the intellectual world and the experience of
healing is pointed out by Dr. Morton T. Kelsey:
    "Either there is a place for Christian healing in today's world or
there is not, and this can only be decided on facts. But Christian
theology does not seem to be looking at the facts—although, as we
have seen, these are certainly not lacking. Instead one has the distinct
impression of a foregone conclusion. The most comprehensive survey
of recent theology, John Macquarrie's *Twentieth Century Religious
Thought,* makes this quite clear. Healing is simply overlooked today.
Of the hundred and fifty theologians discussed in that book, *not one*
emphasizes the effect of man's religious life on his mental and physical
health, as do the more perceptive psychiatrists and students of psycho-
somatic medicine. Few of these religious thinkers, in fact, even bother
with the arguments against healing.
    "Of course there are some who, on the side, poke fun at theological
vagaries of Mary Baker Eddy and others, or decry the extravagances
of 'faith' healers. But the real reasons for ignoring the possibility of
healing are much deeper than this. Our culture has no place for such
experiences. Men feel helpless when confronting them, and theology
has no answer. Indeed, Christian thinkers cannot consider experiences
of healing today because of the tacit acceptance, philosophically and
theologically, of a world view which allows no place for a break-
through of 'divine' power into the space-time world." (Kelsey, *op.
cit.,* p. 307.)

To preserve the sense of mystery in a way that experience has convinced me is realistic and helpful, I suggest two basic principles:

1. Do not expand any one method or experience into a universal method;

2. Ask God to meet your needs with confidence; but do not tell him when or how to do it.

Let me explain these two principles more closely:

1. *Do not expand any one method or experience into a universal method.*

There is something in us that makes us want to find the right technique for every task, the right formula of prayer for every need. We still seek the alchemist's stone—a magic way of trying to control what God does. But God teaches us over and over again that he is beyond our limitations and will not be boxed into our neat compartments. To exemplify: There are those mentioned earlier who say that the only thing you need to do to obtain healing is "to lay claim to God's promises in faith"; there are others who feel comfortable with the concept of healing only in a sacramental context. Like the disciples, some men today, too, are always seeking the perfect answer: "Who sinned, this man or his parents, for him to have been born blind?" Jesus, as he does so often, takes the disciples completely out of the either/or of their thought patterns: "Neither he nor his parents sinned; he was born blind so that the works of God might be displayed in him" (Jn 9:2-3). So often we try to apply to all situations a technique we have found successful in one set of circumstances. (There will probably be enough successes, too, to encourage us to claim that our experience proves that we are right.) We selectively ignore our failures and find reasons to defend our way of proceeding.

I would like to cite in this chapter several examples to illustrate what I have just said. All apply to the healing ministry as practiced in the United States. One is the general tendency of some persons to treat all illnesses as cases of demonic obsession and to treat them by casting out the demons. In certain instances this may work; such successes encourage the exorcist to continue his work even though some of the people he prays for may be badly harmed by his approach, and intelligent onlookers may be so horrified by what they see that they are permanently prejudiced against any form of healing or deliverance ministry.

A second example is seen in the practice of "claiming your victory"—that is, accepting the fact that you have been healed once you have prayed for healing (see the quotation from Kenneth Hagin in the last chapter). From my own experience, this sometimes is the right thing to do, *if* it is what the Lord wants and if the sick person has been truly inspired to accept his healing as an accomplished fact, even though the symptoms sometimes still remain. I remember during a retreat one sister who was suffering from endometriosis. She asked the entire group of retreatants to pray for her. The next day she wrote about her experience:

> To tell you more about the second healing, the physical healing (she had earlier experienced a psychological healing), I've had no pain since the prayers for me, not one pain. Yet, for the last month and a half I have been intermittently plagued, especially after a meal. (But now I've had four meals and no pain.)
>
> This next part is funny. When I asked the group to pray, my thought was that I would continue taking the medication every two weeks until it was depleted in May (the retreat was held in February). Then I'd see if I was cured. The Lord had other plans. To give me a hint as

to what he wanted, he stopped the pains that had been present for three hours. Then—and this is the crucial point—he asked me quietly if I could prove my faith by not taking the shots anymore. I was struggling with this while everyone was praying, because after three and a half years of getting no relief these shots were a tremendous help in keeping me from becoming desperately ill. How could I stop taking them?

The Lord didn't make me think of not taking them until the plunge was made. Finally I said, "Yes, Lord; I'll go all the way. Now you will be put to the test to really heal me."

That I received the courage to respond in complete faith is in itself a healing, for there is no cure for endometriosis but surgery. Wow, that's faith!

To express how joyous I've been these days is impossible. For me a totally new life has begun.

It seems clear that the sister was really inspired to take the risk of faith and to trust that she had been healed—a healing that has now lasted for more than three years. This she did without the advice of others, moved solely by an interior urging. Just as a minister of healing may receive a "gift of faith" to trust in a private revelation and to pray the prayer of command, so a sick person may receive a genuine inspiration to believe that he, or she, has been healed—sometimes in spite of remaining symptoms. For them, obedience to their inner prompting seems to be the condition for their healing taking place.

The danger comes about when this special but rather common experience is elevated into a general principle—the claim of the healer that this is precisely what should happen in all cases, that everyone who lays claim upon the promise will be healed.

I was once present in a room where a man in a wheelchair who had suffered a severed spine in an accident was told by the leaders of the prayer group that they were confident he would be healed if he had faith. They had been praying and fasting for him and some had promised not to break the fast until he was healed.[3] As these good people gathered around him in all sincerity to pray for his healing, it was clear that the man was suffering from considerable pressure and anxiety. He was doing the best he could with his parents and friends around him, for they all knew that it would require a real miracle for the severed nerves to be reattached. As they prayed and encouraged him to get out of the wheelchair and walk, tension in the room mounted. As a matter of fact, he did not leave the wheelchair, and his last state of discouragement was worse than the first. This incident—and there are many similar ones—is painful to relate in a book designed to encourage healing. But such painful happenings do occur with harm both to the sick person and to the prayer group; and they do much to spoil the good image of the healing ministry in general. Through erroneously deducing universal laws from particular inspirations, grace becomes law all over again. In consequence, the ministry of healing, which should be one of the most glorious, most uplifting, and most consoling in the Church of Jesus Christ, our Savior, has been turned by some well-intentioned but unwise practitioners into a ministry of wounding and condemnation.

It is safe to say that for *some*, "claiming their healing" is what releases in them the current of God's healing power. But to say that this method is for *all* sick persons leads, I believe, to grave pastoral harm. To turn again to Dr. Paul Tournier:

---

3. In such instances it is possible that persons other than the sick person could know that he would be healed. But the sick person himself would ideally have this leading confirmed by his own interior inspiration. Certainly his freedom, his own view of the situation should not be coerced by outside pressure.

It is easy to build theories, to pursue one's adversaries with implacable logic, and to collect enthusiastic followers when one develops a corpus of doctrine that is coherent and intransigent. But when it comes to daily practice, how many impenetrable mysteries, how many paradoxes, how many failures and equally unexpected successes! I am always discovering more of the complexity, the subtlety, and the delicacy of the human mind. One makes a few experiments, but as soon as one tries to build a theory upon them, one finds that life refuses to be bound by them, and the same results cannot be obtained again. On the other hand, it is often just when one feels helpless, perplexed, and in despair when faced with the disaster of a person's life, that there takes place suddenly, one does not know how, a living "experiment."

. . . Thus each of us deduces from his personal experiences a system of thought, which he sets up as the truth against all other systems of thought.

Each of us calls to witness his personal experience in support of the system to which he considers it to be due. Each maintains the truths which the system he favors has revealed to him, and concludes that those who disagree with him are in error. . . .

Each of us hides his secret weaknesses, and the painful failures which still persist in his life, for fear that to admit them might call in question the system he holds to be true. And each points to the errors of others, and uses their inconsistencies and wrongdoing as a demonstration of the worthlessness of their teaching. . . .

In Leibnitz's celebrated words, all systems are right in what they affirm, and wrong in what they deny.[4]

---

4. Paul Tournier, *The Person Reborn,* pp. 93 and 98. Copyright © 1966 by Paul Tournier. Reprinted by permission of Harper & Row, Publishers, Inc.

2. *Ask God to meet your needs, but do not tell him when or how to do it.*

This is a helpful principle distilled from experience. God has certainly encouraged his children to ask for *what* they need—and to ask with insistence.

But, in his wisdom, God knows far better than we the time and place for healing to take place. Repeatedly I have seen an interval between the time of prayer and that of the actual healing. Once I was with a prayer group who prayed for a woman whose arm had been permanently immobilized through cancer and the consequent radiation treatment. According to her doctors, the impairment was permanent and would not improve with physical therapy. The group prayed with her on a Saturday night; several received a distinct impression that she had been healed, although she experienced no visible change. But on the following Monday morning, she found upon awaking that her arm had been restored to full mobility.

Oral Roberts in his book, *The Miracle of Seed Faith,*[5] describes how he made the same discovery—not in relation to healing, but to praying for financial needs. He suggested praying for *what* we need, but not trying to determine the *time* or *way* God would meet that need. Even though one may be tempted to pray, "Lord, inspire my wealthy cousin to help me in my need," he would do better by simply naming his need and leaving the rest to God. (Three times when I have had immediate financial needs, I have found this to be true. People I would never have expected to help me were prompted *in prayer* to put a check in the mail or to appear at the door and offer help.)

If a person seems not to be healed after we pray, we need not be anxious, provided we have done all that we could to seek God's guidance and wisdom. I have seen so many process

---

5. Oral Roberts Publications, Tulsa, Okla., 74102, 1970. Pp. 14-16.

healings (i.e., those that took place over a period of time), so many delayed healings, that now I just pray and entrust the results to God. "Maybe now is not the time. Maybe someone else's prayer will bring the final healing. Perhaps this prayer has begun a process which will, after a time, produce the long-desired effect."

The following is a beautiful example of how God meets his creatures' needs when they ask, but does so with a wisdom far beyond human planning in his choice of the time and the manner in which he will work. A woman had asked for an inner healing to repair the effects of a distant childhood relationship with her father which had badly affected her self-image as a lovable, worthwhile human being.

This letter comes to you so that you may know the beautiful way that the Lord worked on the retreat this past weekend to help me.

When I signed up to see you I wasn't really sure why. All the beautiful healings that I have received this past year flashed through my mind: I have been prayed over for a healing of what happened when I was only a few days old; another person prayed for childhood guilt feelings regarding sex; one of our sisters prayed for hurts of past years in religious life. All these healings were very real and powerful, so I questioned whether I had a right again. Yet, I knew I was still unsure of myself as a person.

Saturday after being prayed for by you and Sister Jeanne two things struck me. First, the beautiful gift of discernment that the Lord gave you regarding my need. I was amazed at how within a few minutes you could bring up two points of hurt of which I was unaware: my appearance and my father.

Secondly, I felt absolutely no release after you prayed for me. My past experiences with inner healing led me to believe firmly in its power, yet this time I felt absolutely nothing. Each time before there had always been a release accompanied by great peace, usually following a flow of tears. So I returned to my room and prayed prayers of trust in the healing, believing it had already begun, yet feeling like a pressure cooker ready for release.

. . . Gradually I experienced the first healing. I began to feel pretty, not unrealistically so. Yet, I could actually look in the mirror and smile at myself without feeling like someone to be shunned.

Then Monday afternoon at Mass I became convinced that the second healing would take place when I felt my father's arms around me. He loves me greatly and has always given generously to me of his wealth, but now I knew I needed him to express his love.

Wednesday evening when I returned to my home I knew I had to speak to my father and felt sick and teary. God is so good. I sat in front of my dad after mom had gone to bed and just began to cry and cry. He hugged me and asked what was the matter. I told him, so he embraced me while I cried and then we were both able to express our love for each other for the first time. It was beautiful and the Lord gave me the gift of tears for about a half hour, which gave me great peace and security in him. Praise God, our Father, for his love, which I know so clearly now. My return to my mission will be joyful, secure in his love—free finally to let Jesus flow through me to the people I love so dearly.

This is an example, too, of what I see so often: the Lord does not answer prayer on a superficial level; he wants people to work back to the source of the problem. How much more beautiful it was that a relationship between father and daughter was worked out and deepened in real life and not just in some imaginary way. The perfect, immediate outcome of prayer for this woman was an unsatisfied, "pressure-cooker" feeling, which proved to be the preparation for the final healing which took place four days later. Had I personally been overly concerned about the lack of immediate response to my prayer, I probably would have hindered its eventual success.

Mrs. Bob Cavnar of Dallas offers still another example of how one must be open to healing in whatever fashion God chooses. For many years Mrs. Cavnar had suffered from a painful back condition. On this particular occasion, she was present at a meeting at which a man was praying with people in a way which she felt was ridiculous—namely, the so-called "leg-lengthening" type of prayer (more about this in a later chapter). Nevertheless, something within her prompted her to join the praying group. She found that the prayer did not repel her in the way she had imagined it would. A gentle interior urging persuaded her to ask for prayer. She did so, and was immediately healed—by a method that she had earlier rejected as completely inappropriate.

Still another example of the unexpected ways that God works was the healing of Sister Avina Michels, O.S.F. (I have witnessed similar unanticipated cures a number of times. Apparently, the Lord wants to make sure that we have faith in him alone, and not in our own planned methods.) The group had prayed previously for Sister, who was confined to her wheelchair after she had been badly injured in an automobile crash in which two other sisters had been killed. In this earlier prayer her arm had been completely healed; consequently, with far greater confidence, several months later, Sister asked for a healing of her knees in order that she might leave her wheelchair and walk. The retreat team gathered around her wheelchair and, following the principle that it is good to be specific when making a petition in prayer, we asked for the healing of Sister's knees. Suddenly she put her hands to her face. As we watched the change of expression on her face, we saw her being healed of a facial paralysis and neuralgia that she had not even mentioned to us. In short, we prayed for her knees and the healing took place in her face. (Later, she received complete healing and is now able to walk without difficulty.)

These, and other experiences like them, have shown me that God has a sense of humor, and that he uses it to shake us out of our preconceived notions about how we think things ought to take place. Time and again we rediscover the complexity of the healing process; we are forced to seek God's wisdom on how to proceed. Then, without anxiety, we can leave the results to him.

Probably the most celebrated active minister of healing in the United States today is Kathryn Kuhlman, who has often had to ask herself why some people are healed in her services and others are not. In her long experience, she has come to the same conclusions set forth in this chapter. In an interview she shared what she has learned:

"I have decided that God doesn't have preferences in theology," she told me with a chuckle. "We are the ones who try to put a fence around God, to bring him down to our level. But it doesn't work. God is too big for us to confine.

"I've never written a book on the how and why of divine healing—even though I've been besieged with requests to do so—simply because I *don't know* the how and why. You see, just about the time the book was about to be published, the Holy Spirit would do something absolutely contrary to what I said. I'm still learning the mysterious ways in which God moves. I'll tell you one thing—I'm sure God has a sense of humor!"

Some of her own theological presuppositions have been shattered, the evangelist allows:

"There was a day, when I was very young and knew a great deal more than I do now, that I said, 'You must do thus and so, to be healed. There are certain conditions that have to be met.' I thought, for example, that faith on the part of the seeker was absolutely necessary.

"Then one day I got the shock of my life. A man said his deaf ear had just been opened in a service, but he had no faith at all. 'I don't believe in it,' he said. 'I never go to church.' Well, there went my theology out the window. . . .

"Take another example. Twenty years ago I believed that absolutely, come hell or high water, it was God's will for everybody, without exception, to be healed. But I've watched this thing very carefully. Now I see that we can't demand or command that God do anything. In general, I definitely believe that it is God's will to heal. But I can't say absolutely what is or is not his will in a particular case. There are some things I've learned just not to touch."[6]

It is because she has seen in her youth so many people hurt at evangelistic services when they were made to feel guilty because they were not healed, that Kathryn Kuhlman, in all the services in which I have heard her preach, makes an explicit announcement; that she does not know why some people are healed and some are not, why some who come to a service with complete faith go away not healed while others, who are quite skeptical, are healed at that particular service.

Healing is mysterious. The best that man can do is to bow down before the mystery that is God. When God chooses to reveal his mind, we can act with assurance. At other times,

---

6. Allen Spraggett, *Kathryn Kuhlman, The Woman Who Believes in Miracles*. Copyright © 1970 by Allen Spraggett. With permission of Thomas Y. Crowell Company, Inc.

when we are in doubt about a particular case, the most honest thing to do is to admit the doubt and bow before the mystery.

This was the answer Job gave to Yahweh:

I know that you are all-powerful:
    what you conceive, you can perform.
I am the man who obscured your designs
    with my empty-headed words.
I have been holding forth on matters I cannot understand,
    on marvels beyond me and my knowledge (Job
    42:1-3).

10

"But the Greatest of These Is Charity"

WHILE FAITH IS A REQUISITE for healing, both in the sick person and in the one praying for a healing, the primary disposition needed by the minister of healing is love. Yet seldom do I hear a sermon on the foremost place of love in the healing process. Glenn Clark once wrote about how important a loving climate is in a healing situation. It is this certain loving presence which he found characteristic of the ministry of Agnes Sanford:

> That "something besides" which Agnes Sanford possesses more than anyone I have met is hard to catch and put into words; it is something as evanescent and indefinable as the air we breathe. For want of a better word I shall call it the "climate" necessary for healing. . . .
>
> Anyone who steps into the presence of Agnes steps into the right kind of climate for healing. When I looked over the manuscript of this book I had only a secondary interest in seeing whether she had the "technique" of heal-

ing because I knew she had that. I knew that thousands
of people who had never healed anyone in their lives also
have the technique. My primary interest was in seeing
whether this book (prepared for a world where the spiritual temperature is so far below zero) could furnish a
"climate" that would make healing a living reality. To my
great joy I found that this is exactly what it does do. . . .

This book shows how this boy and scores of others
like him were healed through simple exposure to the
climate of faith and love. If to this faith and love there is
added the warm sunshine of enthusiasm, humor and good
cheer there is nothing more to be asked.[1]

Whatever else one does, it is absolutely essential that in
praying for healing, he establish an atmosphere of faith and
love. When love is present, I have never seen a person hurt in
any way by the healing ministry. What is true of Lourdes is
also true in these individual situations. Many people go to
Lourdes. Of these, some are healed and some are not; but all
leave with a sense of peace, convinced that God has touched
them, and loves them.

The minister of healing prayer in some way represents
God; he stands for the very person of Jesus. Therefore, the
sick person looking upon him should be able to sense in some
degree what God is like. This is, of course, embarrassing
because every man knows his weakness; it may even be a
frightening prospect to think that people actually hope to find
Jesus in the minister. But it is true; they do. If he shouts and
demands that the sick accept their healing, then the representation of God which people see in him may be very much like
an Old Testament image of a God angry with his people, at
times harsh and peremptory. But if the love of God shows

---

1. Glenn Clark, Introduction to *The Healing Light,* by Agnes Sanford
(St. Paul: Macalester Park Publishing Co., 1947).

through his face and in the tone of his voice, the sick person sees the compassion and tender love of Jesus incarnate in a fellowman. This goes back to what was said earlier about what kind of a God God is. Jesus cured not just to prove he was God, but because he was God abounding in love and compassion; sinners and sick came flocking to him because he reached out to touch every one of them. What one unconsciously *thinks God is like* affects not only his ideas about what to emphasize in the healing ministry, but also the way he prays with people.

1) *Emphasis on Power*

In healing, one can concentrate on either of two attributes: the power of God or the love of God. In every healing, there is a manifestation of both. But because of human limitation, there is the tendency to concentrate on one of these and to make the other subordinate.

Those who emphasize God's power in healing hold up the promises of God's mighty works and miracles to those who believe. They stress the faith that sick people need to receive these promises. To sum up: there is God's promise; then the sick person accepts and claims that promise in faith; and, finally, God honors that faith by acting in power and love, to heal.

The prayer of those who emphasize God's power is authoritative; it is usually uttered in a loud voice and accompanied by a forceful laying on of hands. This is a valid approach, in its reflection of God's authority and power, but as I mentioned earlier, it can place an undue accent on the faith of man and upon the legal elements of the bible. The preacher is much like a lawyer pleading his case. He holds up the book and says, "There are certain promises here. We have a written contract. God on his part is absolutely faithful to what he says. If you can accept these promises, then you will be healed. If you cannot accept these promises, cannot accept this contract, you will not be healed." I heard one evangelist say, "All you people out there—are you standing on the promises, or are you resting on the promises?" Now, while it is true that one should stand on promises, the very metaphor conjures up the picture of a little man standing on his bible, vehemently shaking his fist, as it were, and saying to God, "You must pay attention to me and honor your promise."

The fact is that one who knows that God is his loving Father, and that he is gifted with the Holy Spirit who enables him to cry, "Abba, Father," does not have to shout. No one in his own home has to claim the promises of his father. He can simply rest on the promises, certain that he has a loving father who will give him everything he asks for and needs. I think it is a greater proof of faith to think of oneself as "resting" on the promises rather than as "standing" on them. These are only figures of speech, of course, but they do reveal a person's conception of God. I cannot imagine, for instance, in my own home ever talking to my father the way some people talk to God. I cannot picture myself as a child sitting down at the dinner table and having to claim loudly to my father to send food down to my end of the table. Rather, I quietly ask him to pass the chicken. Serenity is a sign of trust and sureness; loud claiming indicates a deep insecurity. Some of the prayers I hear, proclaiming deep faith and trust in the promises, sound to me very anxious and uncertain—like the words of people who speak loudly to mask their own deep fears about being accepted.

2) *Emphasis on Love*

Another way of teaching about healing accentuates God's love, which, of course, includes his power. In proclaiming the mystery of God's love, one dwells on God's willingness to save and to heal all those who come to him with open and contrite hearts. Such preaching emphasizes man's receptiveness to God's love and the casting out of everything opposed to this love, especially hatred and lack of forgiveness of fellowmen. The answer to prayer is left to God. What matters is that God loves a person so much that he always hears and answers his prayers—sometimes in unexpected ways, sometimes by deferring an answer, but always by answering.

Personally I prefer to concentrate on the love of God made visible in Jesus, from which flows his healing power. The more one is centered on Jesus, the less desire there is for effect and the less anxious and more peaceful he is. It is easy, then, to be honest. Not everybody is healed: this is a mystery hidden from men. But we believe that God heals and that his ordinary will is that everyone be healed. People generally feel more comfortable with this approach than with one which tells people they have been healed, even though their symptoms do not reveal it, which tells people to claim their healing and which tells people to stop taking their pills.

Personally, I find it easier to be myself when I pray, thinking only of God's love. I find no need to raise my voice, no need to assume an authoritative posture. I can just be myself, knowing that anything good which results is accomplished through God's will, his power, and his love, and not through any efforts of my own to generate a faith that the sick person does not have. In short, it is important for men to take God seriously but not to take themselves too seriously. Healing is not so much a test of faith as it is the natural response to God's generous love.

HOW TO PRAY FOR HEALING

Clearly, then, a person's ideas about healing will influence the very way he prays for it. One who wants to show God's love as well as his power will speak gently. He will "put on the mind that was in Christ Jesus." His tone of voice will reflect his union with Jesus. His eyes will reveal Jesus' searching look of compassion. He will uncover whatever should be brought to light, but he will do this out of love and not out of condemnation.

It is necessary that the minister be free of the need to prove anything, that he be free of any personal desire for achieving results. To be cast down when his prayers have failed to effect a cure means it is time to examine his motives to see how much of his own fear of failure is mixed into his ministry. I may think I am defending the honor of God by demanding faith; but perhaps what I am really defending is my own self-image as a minister of healing. I must call to mind over and over again that the gift of healing is a manifestation of God's Spirit working *through* me. It is not "a thing" I have in my possession, which I can turn on or off at will, but a transient grace, a passing movement of God's Spirit working through me to help someone else. In most healings three persons are involved: God, the sick person, and the minister of healing. My part, as the minster of healing, is to pray the prayer of faith and then to move out of the way. In fact, the sick person is capable of asking for God's help himself without anyone else being with him at all. The key persons are God, who is Love, and the sick person, whose sickness elicits God's loving compassion. I am simply the human channel of God's love, and I should be humble about that. At times I am used; at times I am not used. I feel very uncomfortable when someone calls me a healer. The connotation is much like putting on a label of certification, a star on one's epaulets, a kind of rank—a something which one possesses permanently and over which he has control. But that is not true. Sometimes God uses my prayers and touch in order to heal; at other times, he does not. Why this is, I do not know. What I do know is that this inability to control keeps me humble; it helps me realize where the healing power comes from. So, the minister is simply to pray as best he can and, above all, to love all the sick who come to him.

I have seen extraordinary things happen when a climate of love was present. Sometimes there have been cures without explicit prayers for them. Within this past year, I remember twice being asked by married couples to pray for an increase of their love for each other. In one instance, as our retreat team prayed for Chuck and Alice, simply for an increase of their love, a cyst on Alice's shoulder that had bothered her for some time began to go down and then disappeared altogether with a sensation of heat. A similar instance happened in the summer of 1972. Several of us were praying for a Protestant missionary and his wife. Again, their prayer request was for an increase of the bond of love between them. After we had finished praying, the man was clearly surprised when he felt his abdomen; he kept saying, "It's gone, it's gone!" We were confused about what was happening until he told us that he had just been healed of a hernia that had afflicted him for several years. Time after time we find people healed, not only through direct prayer, but simply because of their love for each other. God seems pleased to work in a climate of love, to reach out and heal people who love him and each other so much.

The attitude on the part of the person praying for healing is in itself part of the healing process. As Paul Tournier says, it all depends on the spirit:

> You give a child advice. Your state of mind is far more important than the advice itself. You may be inspired by fear—the fear that he is "turning out badly." In this case you will suggest the fear to him, even without formulating it. And your advice, however proper it may be, by turning his thoughts toward evil, gives power to evil. If, however,

you are inspired by prudent and trusting wisdom, this same advice will be useful.[2]

Tournier's cautions have direct application to the healing ministry, for I have seen people who exercise a genuine gift of healing, who have prayed for many people with astonishing results, and yet who seem, at the same time, to engender a certain anxiety and fear. While they effect lasting healings, they also hurt many people by making them more anxious and more fearful. I believe that every healing should bring the person cured to a closer awareness of the presence of God, of his power and his love, and no one should be hurt.

This seems to be one reason for the success of Kathryn Kuhlman's celebrated healing services:

> In the miracle services a community of love and ac-
> ceptance is created. People feel secure enough to lay
> aside the barriers of fear, distrust, and egotism that have
> shut them off not only from fruitful contact with their
> fellowmen but from their own deeper selves. There is a
> yielding up of self-isolation. The individual loses himself
> in the group, the symbol of the loving family where one
> is accepted in spite of his faults and sins. He identifies
> with the needs of others. He sometimes forgets his own
> illness, his own needs, in praying for someone else whose
> need is greater. In this self-forgetfulness, as it happens,
> he is healed.[3]

In every prayer for healing, both God's power and his love should be invoked, but first place should be given to his love. The display of power, authority, and the claiming of promises

---

2. Paul Tournier, *op. cit.*, p. 58.
3. Allen Spraggett, *op. cit.*, p. 129.

may be fine for evangelists mature in the healing ministry. But for simple persons, who are servants not masters, the way of love has far less danger of self-deception. Furthermore, it brings peace, not anxiety, to the sick person asking for help. "If I have faith in all its fullness, to move mountains, but am without love, then I am nothing at all" (I Cor 13:23).

Lord,
you have
freed me
from my bonds
and I will
serve you
forever.

PS. 116:16

PART THREE

The Four Basic Kinds
of Healing
and How to Pray for Each

11

The Four Basic Kinds of Healing

To REPEAT: One of the real problems we see in the ministry of healing is a problem we find in every area of human activity: a tendency to oversimplify. We tend to take what we know from our limited experience and then apply it to every situation. For a long time, for example, most priests and ministers were trained to treat most problems as though they were moral problems that could be solved by *willpower,* through the help of grace. The alcoholic, for instance, was given sermons on repentance and on taking the pledge. Some were helped: Matt Talbot, for one, became a holy man. But it took Alcoholics Anonymous to show that there was a better way that would help more people—namely, that it took a community of support for most alcoholics to make a comeback. Now, beyond that, we find that even those persons whom AA has not been able to help can be cured instantaneously through prayer.

There are four different kinds of basic healing differentiated by the kinds of sickness that afflict us and the basic

causes of those sicknesses. Unless we know these differ-
ences, we will not be able to help most people. In fact, we may
harm them by insisting on one particular diagnosis and one
particular method of prayer when a different diagnosis and a
different type of treatment and prayer are needed. Someone,
for instance, who has had experience only with deliverance
and exorcism—who has no knowledge or experience of the
value of psychological healing ("healing of the memories")—
can do untold damage by insisting on casting out devils every
time he tries to help a person who has a psychological problem.
Some psychological problems seem to be caused by demonic
infestation but most problems in my experience can be explained by the natural causality of past hurts and rejections in
a person's life. Still other psychological problems are caused
by such physical causes as chemical and enzyme imbalances
in the bloodstream (e.g., postpartum depression).

So anyone who hopes to pray for the sick should realize
that there are three basic kinds of sickness, each requiring a
different kind of prayer:

1) Sickness of our spirit, caused by our own personal sin.

2) Emotional sickness and problems (e.g., anxiety) caused
   by the emotional hurts of our past.

3) Physical sickness in our bodies, caused by disease or
   accidents.

In addition, any of the above—sin, emotional problems
or physical sickness—can be caused by demonic oppression,
a different cause that requires a different prayer approach,
namely, prayer for exorcism.

Consequently, there are at least *four basic prayer methods*
we must understand in order to exercise a complete healing
ministry:

1) prayer for *repentance* (for personal sin),
2) prayer for *inner healing* ("healing of memories") (for emotional problems),
3) prayer for *physical healing* (for physical sickness),
4) prayer for *deliverance* (exorcism) (for demonic oppression).

Not all of us will have a deep ministry in each of these areas, but we should know our own limitations and be ready to refer a person to someone else who has more experience than we in one or the other area. I look forward to a time when Christians in every locality will be able to join their gifts to work as a team, much as doctors work together in any hospital or clinic. Most of us don't have the time or God-given gifts to work in all these areas of healing. But each of us needs to develop the discernment to judge what is wrong and the appropriate type of prayer to use.

This becomes even more important when we meet people who seem to need *all* these forms of prayer. For example, a middle-aged woman may ask for prayer to be cured of arthritis (physical healing); upon talking to her you find she was deeply hurt by her father when she was young (inner healing), and that she was never able to forgive him (repentance); nor has she been able as a woman to relate to her husband (inner healing probably); in her search for a way out of her predicament she has attended seances where she has supposedly met a "spirit-guide" from the dead who gives her guidance through automatic writing (a need for deliverance is here indicated).

THE SACRAMENTS

It is significant that the sacramental churches utilize sacraments or other rites (sacramentals) whose purpose includes these same four types of healing:

1) Repentance takes place sacramentally in the sacrament of *Penance* (reconciliation);

2) Inner healing can also take place in the sacrament of *Penance;*

3) Physical healing is meant to take place in the *Anointing of the Sick;*

4) Deliverance from demonic oppression or possession takes place in the *Rite of Exorcism.*

MEDICINE

Ordinarily, of course, God works through doctors, psychiatrists, counselors and nurses to facilitate nature's healing process. This may seem so obvious as to go without saying, except that there are some evangelists who set up an artificial opposition between prayer and medicine—as if God's way of healing is through prayer, while the medical profession is a secular means of healing, somehow unworthy of Christians who have real faith. Consequently, they encourage people to pray and not to see their doctor. But God works through the doctor to heal as well as through the prayer for healing—the doctor, the counselor and the nurse are all ministers of healing. All these different professions, with their different competencies, go to make up God's healing team. Any time we disparage any person who helps bring about the healing of the whole man we are destroying the kind of cooperative healing ministry that the Christian community might have and are setting up false divisions between divine and human healing methods.

As evidence of their harmful division we have already seen too many:

— faith healers who tell the sick they don't need to see a doctor,

— doctors who disparage the ministry of healing as a nonscientific appeal to the credulous;

— evangelists who disparage church sacraments as dead rites,

— ministers of the sacraments who have little concept of how much of God's healing power can flow through the Anointing of the Sick and Penance;

— persons who believe in healing but who prefer to ignore the ministry of exorcism,

— exorcists who disparage the ministry of inner healing ("healing of the memories").

These unhappy divisions and misunderstandings are sad, and totally unnecessary. The ones who suffer are the sick who may be dissuaded from the means of healing they most need because of the ignorance of the very ministers of healing who should be helping them.

We need to learn to work as a team, rather than as competitors, to bring God's healing power to the entire Christian body. Anyone who prays for healing should have a healthy respect for all four types of healing prayer as well as all the other methods of bringing the healing about. We must also be aware of our gifts and of our limitations. Where we are limited we should be ready to defer to the ministry of someone else, more gifted, wiser, or more experienced than we are.

I prefer now to give retreats with a team, for I experience a definite advantage when working with a team of persons who can pray effectively for inner healing as well as for physical healing, who can lead those who need it to personal repentance, who can counsel, and who can minister God's healing power through the sacraments (especially in the Eucharist have I seen healing take place).

Still, I look forward to a time when we will do even more of this teamwork, when all over the world there will be a collaboration between a) doctors, nurses and hospitals, b) with persons who have been given charisms for inner healing, physical healing and deliverance, c) working together with priests and ministers who experience the healing power of the sacraments.

When that time finally comes, I think we will be approaching a renewal of Christianity such as we have not seen since the early days of the Church.

These four types of healing, based on the four kinds of sickness we experience, with all the pertinent information we have given in this chapter can be summed up in the following diagram.

SICKNESS	CAUSE	PRAYER REMEDY	APPROPRIATE SACRAMENT OR SACRAMENTAL	ORDINARY HUMAN REMEDY
1. ... of the *spirit* - often contributing to emotional sickness - sometimes contributing to bodily sickness	*Personal sin*	*Repentance*	*Penance*	
2. ... of the *emotions* - often contributing to *spiritual* sickness - often contributing to *bodily* sickness	*Original Sin* (i.e., the person has been hurt by the sins of *others*)	Prayer for *Inner Healing*	*Penance*	Counseling (psychiatric and spiritual)
3. ... of the body - often contributing to *emotional* sickness - sometimes contributing to *spiritual* sickness	Disease, accidents, psychological stress	*Prayer of Faith* for physical healing	*Anointing of the Sick*	Medical care
4. ... any, or all of the above can, upon occasion, be	*Demonic* in its cause	Prayer of *Deliverance* (Exorcism)	*Exorcism*	

The following chapters will be based on these basic kinds of healing and their appropriate remedies (including medicine and the sacraments).

In summary we can say that the most basic questions we should ask before praying for healing are:

1) What is the *basic sickness,* the basic problem?

2) What is its *basic cause?*

3) What *kind of prayer,* or what kind of other remedy, should we use?

12

Forgiveness of Sin

THE FIRST AND DEEPEST kind of healing that Christ brings is the forgiveness of our sins. Our repentence and God's forgiveness—they are emphasized by every Christian denomination. No one doubts that Jesus died for our sins and took them away, provided we do our part and repent. This is salvation and healing at the deepest level.

What I have come to see, though, is how intimately the forgiveness of sins is connected with bodily and emotional healing. They are not separate. In fact, far from being a sign of God's blessing, much physical sickness is a direct sign that we are not right with God or our neighbor:

> . . . a person who eats and drinks without recognizing the Body is eating and drinking his own condemnation. In fact, that is why many of you are weak and ill and some of you have died. If only we recollected ourselves, we should not be punished like that. But when the Lord does punish us like that, it is to correct us and stop us from being condemned with the world (I Cor 11:29-32).

Here St. Paul ascribes some of the sickness and death affecting the early community at Corinth to the effects of sin; here, sickness is no blessing, but a punishment.

This connection of sin and sickness is now being brought to our attention again remarkably, not by the Church, but by psychologists and doctors who recognize that much, if not most, physical sickness has an emotional component:

> Even cancer has recently been linked to emotion. Researchers are finding that cancer victims are often people who have long felt hopeless, who have believed that their lives are doomed to despair. The onset of the disease in many cases is associated with a series of overwhelming losses that make the person finally give up entirely.[1]

Although there is a danger of our playing amateur psychologist and reading too much into a person's physical sickness, these findings do show how appropriate was the angry reaction of Jesus to sickness ("He rebuked the fever")— much more appropriate than the reaction of some later Christian writers who saw most sickness as redemptive. Far from being redemptive it is often a sign precisely that we are not redeemed—that we are falling apart at a deeper level:

> Ulcerative colitis is thought to develop when a predisposed person fails to express chronic resentment and anger. On an unconscious level, the mucous membrane of his colon *does* respond to these repressed emotions. The ensuing engorgement and hyperactivity produces bleeding. . . .
> Ulcerative colitis is often accompanied by severe de-

---

1. Howard R. and Martha E. Lewis, *Psychosomatics: How Your Emotions Can Damage Your Health* (New York: The Viking Press, 1972), p. 7. This whole book, giving a popularized version of medical research that connects many diseases with an emotional and moral component, is well worth reading.

pression and feelings of hopelessness and despair. The typical victim is immature and dependent, particularly on his mother. He often is perfectionistic and rigid and tends to be wary of other people.[2]

There is good evidence, then, that there is a very natural connection between much of our sickness and our spiritual and emotional health. For very human reasons we can see why physical sickness can symbolize a deeper sickness of the human person. (This profound realization caused Dr. Paul Tournier, as a physician, to abandon the merely physical treatment of his patients and to deepen his prayer life and to study psychology so that he could help to heal the entire human person who was sick at all levels of his being.)

Because of these relationships between all types of healing I have found it often helpful—sometimes essential—to consider a prayer for repentance or a prayer for inner healing first before praying for physical healing.

The story of the paralytic who was let through the roof by his friends and then forgiven his sins by Jesus before Jesus told him to pick up his cot and walk is often used to show that the physical cure was a sign to the unbelieving Pharisees of Jesus' real power to forgive sins. That it was. But I also believe that Jesus was proceeding to heal the paralytic by stages in both areas of his life where he needed healing. Perhaps the sin and the paralysis were interconnected.

In my own ministry I have seen this connection borne out in striking ways. Once while giving a retreat at the Carmelite Retreat House in Aylesford, Illinois, we (Mrs. Barbara Shlemon, Sister Jeanne Hill, O.P., and I) conducted a communal penance service in which I stressed the need to forgive enemies and then gave the people (some 200 were making the retreat) the time to forgive anyone who had ever hurt

2. *Ibid.*, p. 160.

them. The communal penance was followed by a prayer for inner healing. Nowhere in this service did I mention physical healing. Yet, two persons testified immediately afterwards that they had received physical cures. One was a man who had suffered constant chest pain since undergoing open-heart surgery. During the communal penance when he was asked to think of someone who had hurt him, he thought of his boss, a man he regarded as unjust. At first, he wasn't going to forgive him, but then with all the time allowed, he entered into a prayer of forgiveness. At that moment all the painful effects of the open-heart surgery left him. A similar thing happened in July, 1973, when I conducted a repentance service at the West Virginia Camp Farthest Out. Afterwards a young woman came up to me and said that a pylonidal cyst had been instantly healed at the moment she was able to repent of a long-standing grudge.

Forgiveness: The Most Important Form of Repentance

These examples indicate that the key form of repentance we need is to forgive our enemies. I have found that many sins do not block God's healing power to the same extent as does a lack of forgiveness. I understand better than I used to why Jesus laid such a heavy stress on forgiving enemies when he talked about prayer. He doesn't talk nearly as much about drunkenness and lust as he does about being unforgiving. Furthermore, he often seems to connect forgiving enemies with the Father's answering our prayers:

> I tell you therefore: everything you ask and pray for, believe that you have it already, and it will be yours. And when you stand in prayer, forgive whatever you have against anybody, so that your Father in heaven may forgive your failings too (Mk 11:24-25).

I used to consider such passages as a kind of jumping from one subject to another: in one sentence Jesus enjoins faith in prayer; in the next he enjoins us to forgive. But now I see that the two ideas are intimately connected. It's as if God's saving, healing, forgiving love cannot flow into us unless we are ready to let it flow out to others. If we deny forgiveness and healing to others, God's love cannot flow into us. It's all part of the great commandment in which loving our neighbor is part of the same commandment as loving God. "I love God only as much as I love my worst enemy." There is a direct relationship between our willingness to love others and the healing ministry:

Be compassionate as your Father is compassionate. Do not judge, and you will not be judged yourselves; do not condemn, and you will not be condemned yourselves; grant pardon and you will be pardoned. Give and there will be gifts for you: a full measure, pressed down, shaken together, and running over, will be poured into your lap; because the amount you measure out is the amount you will be given back (Lk 6:36-38).

To paraphrase: if you forgive, you will be forgiven; if you are willing to heal all others, including your enemies, you will be healed. The first condition if we seek healing is to cast out sin, especially the roots of bitterness.

Yet, for some reason, we seem to be insensitive to our worst sins: those of bitterness and resentment. Sins of drunkenness we detect with the same sensitivity with which the non-smoker sniffs cigarette fumes lingering from last night's party, but we are not nearly so sensitive to our bitterness and anger.

Illustrative of the bitterness that often wracks Christian churches that are very sensitive on such issues as smoking and drinking is a section of history I was just reading today:

All went well with the "Tomlinson Church of God" until the death of its founder in 1943 when a power struggle developed between his two sons, Milton and Homer, for control of the church. In a bewildering set of moves and countermoves, the younger brother Milton, who was not a minister but a printer, was elected as "General Overseer." After Milton's accession to power, Homer was inexplicably expelled from the church. Following this development, Homer went to New York City where he founded a third denomination which he christened "The Church of God, World Headquarters." In March 1953, the former "Tomlinson" Church of God with Milton as Bishop and General Overseer changed its name to "The Church of God of Prophecy," which it is claimed, designates it as the one, true "Church of God."[3]

We feel we have a right not to forgive; in justice let there be an eye for an eye, a tooth for a tooth. We have a good reason for exacting vengeance we feel (witness the attitude of some Christians toward amnesty for true conscientious objectors who fled the U.S. to avoid serving in the Vietnam War).

Yet we have the Lord's words, "You have learned how it was said: 'eye for eye and tooth for tooth.' But I say to you: offer the wicked man no resistance" (Mt 5:38-39). Upon this John L. McKenzie, S.J., comments:

The law of revenge was an ancient custom of the Near East that protected individuals by obliging the next of kin to avenge injury or murder. . . . The laws of the Pentateuch are actually restrictions that limit the injury inflicted by the avenger to injury proportionate to the damage done by the aggressor. The customary principle of self-defense

3. Vinson Synan, *The Holiness-Pentecostal Movement in the United States* (Grand Rapids, Mich.: Eerdmans, 1971), pp. 195-196.

is rejected by this saying of Jesus; and the customary principle is not replaced by another principle of self-defense. This saying is probably the most paradoxical of all the sayings of the passage and has certainly been the object of more rationalization than any other. . . . It is difficult to see how the principle of non-resistance and yielding could be more clearly stated. The rationalizations of the words of Jesus do not show that his words are impractical or exaggerated, but simply that the Christian world has never been ready and is not ready now to live according to this ethic.[4]

In praying for healing the most common phenomenon we experience is the sensation of heat, which we ordinarily associate with human love, with the warmth of friendship. On the contrary, cold is associated with the presence of evil.

One sensation recurs frequently, both in accounts of demoniacal possession and in those of metaphysical experiences. The subjects and the assistants experience a sudden feeling of glacial cold, which often seems to emanate from the walls. At a Sabbath, the devil's arrival is signalized by an icy chill and a sensation of freezing physical contact. Cold hands close about the neck of the possessed; a cold wind blows suddenly. Fear, making the flesh creep, and the chill of the extremities, partly explain this sensation of cold; but sometimes it seems inexplicable. It is generally accompanied by sexual frigidity.[5]

Heat and cold, symbolizing love and hate are not, I believe, accidental concomitants of God's total healing and its opposite,

---

4. "The Gospel According to Matthew," *The Jerome Biblical Commentary* (Englewood Cliffs, N.J.: Prentice-Hall, 1968), pp. 72-73.
5. Jean Vinchon, "Diabolic Possession" in *Soundings in Satanism,* ed. Frank Sheed (New York: Sheed and Ward, 1972), p. 4.

the death wish of the devil. Life and death are here in conflict. Too often, though, we ourselves block physical healing through our own coldness, our own resentment and lack of forgiveness. I can see more clearly now why St. James in his passage on praying for the sick with anointing, also encourages confession of sins: "So confess your sins to one another, and pray for one another, and this will cure you" (Jas 5:16).

I remember being asked by a woman to pray for an inner healing. When we talked about her childhood, she indicated that her deepest problem, an unreasoning hatred of men, including her husband, went back to harsh treatment and derision that her brothers had heaped upon her as a little girl. Before praying for that healing, I asked her to forgive her brothers. This she refused to do. I told her that this would block any healing. She still refused. When I asked her why she hung on to her resentment, even if she was being destroyed by it, she thought for a while and then replied that, if she forgave her brothers, it would take away her last excuse for being the kind of person she was (she could no longer blame them). After praying a short time more she realized how contrary this was to her Christian commitment and to her professed desire to be whole. With tears she forgave her brothers as best she could. She then received the deep healing she was seeking.

To sum it all up: the more I pray with people for healing the more I discover the close interrelation between all forms of healing. The churches have long known the power of Christ to forgive sins, but what I realize with increased intensity is that:

1) Our physical sickness, far from being a redemptive blessing, is often a sign that we are not redeemed, not whole at a spiritual level.

2) Physical healing often *requires first a forgiveness of sin* or an inner healing.

3) The most important repentance is of *bitterness or resentment,* sins which Christians often do not recognize as sins in themselves.

4) Again, *love* is the best remedy to break through the coldness, the hurt and bitterness that block God's healing power from flowing into us.

With all these considerations I understand better than before what Jesus was getting at when he pointed to the woman who had poured ointment all over his feet at Simon's banquet:

> "Simon," he said, "you see this woman? I came into your house, and you poured no water over my feet, but she has poured out her tears over my feet and wiped them away with her hair. You gave me no kiss, but she has been covering my feet with kisses ever since I came in. You did not anoint my head with oil, but she has anointed my head with ointment. For this reason I tell you that her sins, her many sins, must have been forgiven her, or she would not have shown such great love. It is the man who is forgiven little who shows little love." Then he said to her, "Your sins are forgiven." Those who were with him at table began to say to themselves, "Who is this man, that he even forgives sins?" But he said to the woman, "Your faith saved you; go in peace" (Lk 7:44-50).

Somehow, the woman's love has been unblocked, her warmth makes it clear that forgiveness, the healing of her spirit, has taken place. To Jesus, the flow of her love is the sign that she is receiving the forgiving, healing love of his Father.

13

The Inner Healing of Our Emotional Problems

SOMEWHERE BETWEEN OUR SINS and our physical ailments lies that part of our lives where we find many of our real failings as human beings—our emotional weaknesses and problems. For many of us who went every week to the sacrament of Penance there came a point when we found that we kept on repeating pretty much the same thing. The cure of some of our failings did not depend altogether upon our willpower. Over and over we tried; again and again we failed: "Three times last week I was impatient." "Was it your fault?" "I just don't know."

Later, when I myself heard confessions and tried to counsel these persons who came for advice to the visiting parlor of the seminary where I taught, I came to realize that I seemed to have very little to offer the people who were hurting the most. If the person was well balanced I could offer some helpful suggestions, but if he had a really deep emotional wound, then he usually could not merely use his intelligence and willpower to solve his problem. Unfortunately, the only help I was trained to give was to encourage him to use will-power (under the influence of God's grace), coupled with the frequent reception of the sacraments and to recommend some practical advice. What troubled me was that this advice usually was not sufficient. The mentally depressed sister, who had been enduring, rather than enjoying, life for as long as she could remember, remained depressed. The best I could do was to encourage her to keep going. Also, I could recommend that she see a psychiatrist.

I found, of course, that my concern and caring were in themselves a healing force. But I didn't have time to listen to all the disturbed people asking for appointments. The psychiatrists, too, were overbooked and unless a person had done something desperate, they had to wait a month for a first appointment. What could I tell the mentally depressed woman who could not believe that God loved her and whose whole experience of life simply demonstrated to her that no one really cared about her—especially if her husband had deserted her? The only one who would listen to her was a psychiatrist at $50 an hour. What could I say to the homosexual who simply was not attracted to women and whose tendency went all the way back as far as he could remember? What hope did he have for a change; what did the Church offer him as a real help?

In the 60's, as the priests I knew studied the findings of psychology they gradually came to realize that *repentance* was insufficient advice for many of these problems that went deep into man's subconscious—and hence, were largely involuntary. They finally learned the wisdom of recommending that such suffering persons see a psychiatrist, after a time of resistance in the 1940's and early 50's. In time, it seemed that I, like many other priests and ministers, was serving mainly as a referral service for other, more professional services, which could better handle the needs of suffering humanity.

At the same time, however, psychiatrists were referring their patients to me for spiritual direction; through this experience I could see both the help that some patients were given by the psychiatrist's direction as well as observe the number of patients who progressed only minimally. (I recently talked to a mother and father who spent $70,000 on psychiatric help for their daughter. This professional help kept her alive and gave her a vocabulary to describe her problem but did not cure her. She has since been healed by prayer.)

This caused me to reflect seriously: why, if Christ came to bring salvation and freedom, wasn't there any realistic hope for some people who were badly wounded psychologically? Especially, it didn't seem fair to persons who had given their lives to Christ as best they could—sisters, for instance. They would tell me, "I don't think God loves me." Physical sickness I could see as potentially redemptive. But if persons are mentally depressed they are prevented from experiencing many basic aspects of the Christian life:

1) The Christian is supposed to experience inner *peace and joy,* but the depressed person cannot.

2) We are to believe that *God loves us,* but the depressed person cannot.

3) We are supposed to relate to others in *community,* but the depressed person is often so saddened that he withdraws from community, nor does he have the energy to *work* as a normal person does.

4) Jesus had said that we should not be anxious, yet the depressed person is often in a continual *state of anxiety.*

In the traditional terminology of the Church, such a person is, objectively speaking, living in a sinful state of depression, of lack of hope, but is not subjectively guilty for it. Yet, guilty or not, there seems no way out for the suffering person. What does the message of the freedom and salvation brought by Christ mean to such a person? Medicine and psychiatry do not always help, nor does repentance, the traditional remedy of the Church. Something clearly is missing. It is not right that such sufferers *should be overcome by evil,* when their willpower cannot touch it. When we come to this area of emotional sickness, it is hard to see how the person's suffering can be spiritually helpful: the mental depressive finds it almost impossible to trust his fellowman; the scrupulous person feels that God is the enemy, not his friend. Consequently I was never able to accept the fact that psychological sickness was God's will for a suffering individual; it was destructive, not redemptive.

So, when I first heard about inner healing, through Mrs. Agnes Sanford, her message filled me with hope. "Healing of the Memories," as she termed it, made so much sense. It was as if the whole wall of an unfinished building suddenly went into place. It made sense not only because Christ came to free us from the evil that burdens us, but also because it was in accord with what psychologists have discovered about the nature of man: that we are deeply affected not only by what we do, but by what happens to us through the sins of others and the evil in the world (original sin). Our deepest need is for love, and if we are denied love as infants or as children, or anywhere else along the line, it may affect our lives at a later date and rob us of our peace, of our ability to love, and of our ability to trust man—or God.

The basic idea of inner healing is simply this: that Jesus, who is the same yesterday, today, and forever, can take the memories of our past and

1) *Heal* them from the wounds that still remain and affect our present lives;

2) *Fill with his love* all these places in us that have been empty for so long, once they have been healed and drained of the poison of past hurts and resentment.

I have found by experience that this kind of prayer is

usually perceptibly answered. At times the healing is progressive and takes several sessions, but I believe that it is
always God's desire to heal us of those psychological hurts
that are unredemptive and that prevent us from living with
the inner freedom that belongs to the children of God.[1] When
this kind of prayer is seemingly not answered I assume that we
simply haven't gotten to the bottom of the matter, either
because

1) There is a need for *repentance,* usually a need for
the person to forgive someone who has hurt him.

2) There is a deeper, *more basic hurt* we have not yet discovered or reached.

3) There is also a need for *deliverance* (see chapter 15).

When to Pray for Inner Healing

Inner healing is indicated whenever we become aware that we
are held down in any way by the hurts of the past. We all
suffer from this kind of bondage to one degree or another, some
severely, some minimally. Any unreasonable fear, anxiety, or
compulsion caused by patterns built up in the past can be
broken by prayer, provided the person is also doing his best to
discipline his life in a Christian way. So many Christians are
hindered in their lives by such things as a haunting sense of
worthlessness, erratic fits of anger or depression, anxiety and
unreasoning fears, compulsive sexual drives, and other problems which they would like to change, but find they cannot
cope with on the basis of repentance and a decision to change.
More and more books are being written, such as *I'm OK—
You're OK,*[2] which show the influence of the past upon our

1. For a book on praying for inner healing I would recommend Agnes
Sanford's *The Healing Gifts of the Spirit* (New York: Lippincott,
1966).
2. By Thomas A. Harris (New York: Avon Books, 1973).

present, and the need for breaking free of the patterns of im-
maturity. Some of these patterns we can change through adult
decisions, but often we find that the powerful memories of the
past rise to fill us with fear and anxiety, whether we wish these
fears or not. We cannot wish them away by an act of will.

What Is Inner Healing?

The idea behind inner healing is simply that we can ask
Jesus Christ to walk back to the time we were hurt and to free
us from the effects of that wound in the present. This involves
two things then:

1) *Bringing to light* the things that have hurt us. Usually
this is best done with another person; even the talking out of
the problem is in itself a healing process.

2) *Praying* the Lord to heal the binding effects of the
hurtful incidents of the past.

Some of these hurts go way back into the past; others are
quite recent. Our experience coincides with the findings of
psychologists: that many of the deepest hurts go way back to
the time when we were most vulnerable and least able to
defend ourselves. There is a good deal of evidence that some
hurts go back even before birth while the child was still being
carried in the mother's womb. Just as John the Baptist leapt
in Elizabeth's womb when she heard Mary's greeting, so every
child seems sensitive to its mother's moods. If the mother does
not really want the child or is suffering from anxiety or fear,
the infant seems somehow to pick up the feelings of the mother
and to respond to them. (In praying for inner healing I have
seen an adult woman reexperience in an amazing way the time
before birth and verbalize it during the prayer. "I'm not going
to come out; I'm not going to be born!") These earliest
memories up to the time we are two or three years old seem
to be the most important in setting the patterns of our future

behavior—long before we are free to make our own personal decisions.

If a person has always felt unlovable or has always been restless or fearful, the need for inner healing probably goes all the way back to the very earliest years of life.[3]

The Setting for Prayer

Since the need to talk about these deepest, earliest memories is painful—often involving feelings of guilt or shame—the prayer for inner healing is ordinarily something to be done privately with only one or two persons present. Here, I think, the Catholic tradition of respecting the privacy of an individual in confession is of real value. In fact, the sacrament of Penance can well be extended to include the use of prayer for inner healing to help the penitent with the fullness of Christ's healing power.[4] There should always be freedom for a person to ask for prayer without being forced to pray in a large group or to have to pray with a particular person for whom he or she feels no special affinity. This kind of prayer is so sensitive, so delicate, that the person asking for prayer should have the freedom to select the person or persons he would like to confide in and pray with. (Often, too, these traumatic childhood experiences have to do with sexual matters that the person finds it most painful to talk about.)

The ideal, then, is that people qualified, by a gift of the Spirit, coupled with a knowledge of psychology, or with great

---

3. E.g., "Although there may be exceptions, the general rule is that we do not learn to be loving if we have never been loved. If the first five years of life consist totally of a critical struggle for physical and psychological survival, this struggle is likely to persist throughout life." Harris, op. cit., p. 129.

4. This approach is expertly set forth in Father Michael Scanlan's booklet, The Power in Penance (Notre Dame: Ave Maria Press, 1972).

sensitivity, be available for persons who wish to pray for inner healing. Those who do the praying should never force themselves upon others. A sign that you may be called to pray for inner healing is when the person has first come to you and unburdened himself of the things that are hurting within and that are beyond his conscious control. (This can happen, of course, in such a natural setting as morning coffee when the neighbor comes over to share confidences.) You can ask the person then if he or she would like you to pray for inner healing. (If the person has never heard of inner healing you can explain very simply what it is.)

If the person is deeply suffering, chances are he will not feel that he has much faith. This is especially true for mental depressives; do not ask the person to claim any more faith than he has; one of the symptoms of depression is his previous experience that no one has been able to help—that even God does not care. In fact, you can expect him to say, "I've prayed about this many times before, and nothing's ever happened." In praying for physical healing we do well to ask the sufferer to make an act of faith, but in praying for psychological healing sometimes we only add to the sufferer's feeling of hopelessness if we ask for more faith than he can elicit. Assume that any faith required must come from you. The atmosphere should be of great peace and gentleness. The time you give to the person should be generous and unhurried. (If I don't have at least 20 minutes I usually don't feel I can pray adequately for inner healing. An hour is a good amount of time: 45 minutes to talk and 15 to pray. Sometimes it takes longer still, and there should be provision for a follow-up.)

Getting to the Root

In preparing to pray there are questions that usually reveal the basic wounds to pray for:

1) *"When* did this all begin?" Mrs. Sanford gets at this by asking if the person had a happy childhood; if not, the person will say, "No," and then naturally tell about what happened. If the person says, "Yes, I had a wonderful childhood," you can then ask when things first went wrong. I find that most deep emotional problems go back into our distant childhood, although many people have later been badly hurt in school, or through unhappy sexual experiences, or still later through broken marriage relationships or through prolonged strained relationships in religious communities.

2) "Do you have any idea *why*—what caused it?" Often the answer to the first question reveals the reasons for the ancient wounds—most of which go back to rejection and to broken relationships. Our relationships with our parents are especially important—whether or not we truly experienced the felt love of our parents is truly crucial. If there is a lack of love between the child and one or the other parent, chances are the person will carry that hurt on into adult life. If the mother did not hold the child enough, if the father came home from work tired and seldom talked to the child or punished it harshly, if there were too many children for a sickly mother and she had no time to show them affection, or if one of the parents died while the child was little—all these painful events leave their wounds which deeply affect the person's basic feelings about himself, about others and about life. Sometimes the person does not really know what happened; then we ask for God's revelation or wait until such time as the deep need comes to the surface. If the person can remember how it all began and why, we then ask Jesus to walk back with us into the past while we picture, in as an imaginative a way as possible, his healing each of the principal emotional hurts the person sustained. Since it is the inner child of the past who is being healed we need to pray in as childlike, imaginative a way as we can.

Jesus, as Lord of time, is able to do what we cannot: he can heal those wounds of the past that still cause us suffering. The most I was ever able to do as a counselor was to help the person bring to the foreground of consciousness the things that were buried in the past, so that he could consciously cope with them in the present. Now I am discovering that the Lord can heal these wounds—sometimes immediately—and can bring the counseling process to its completion in a deep healing.

At times, these hurts may seem slight to an adult mind, but we must be sensitive to see things as a child would. I remember once praying for a woman whose complaint was that her inner life was always bleak and boring, even though her professional life was in itself full and exciting. When we finally found what had caused her to shut off the flow of life it was an incident that happened when she was 10 years old.

"Our Hearts Are Restless Until . . ."

After the prayer for the healing of the hurt (the negative part, as it were) we can pray for Jesus to fill up in a positive way whatever was missing in the person's life. Since we have such a basic need for love, the conclusion of a prayer for inner healing usually involves a filling with God's love of all the empty places in our heart.

If the person does not feel loved by God I ask Jesus to speak to the person within his own heart and spirit—at a depth where no human voice can reach—to call the person by name and to say that he loves the person, even in the midst of weakness and failure. If the person lacked a father's love I ask Jesus to fill the person with the love of his own Father in fulfillment of his priestly prayer to his Father: "So that the love with which you loved me may be in them" (Jn 17:26b). Then I ask the Father to make it as if the person had a father who sat the child on his lap in the evenings to talk over the day and

to tell stories, who took the child by the hand and went walking down the street, sharing his vision of life and ideals, who
carried the child on his shoulders and threw him up in the air
and caught him. If the person missed out on a mother's love in
any way I ask Jesus (if the person is a Catholic) to send his
mother Mary to hold and to warm the child, and to do all
those other things that mothers do to give their children love
and security.

These prayers may sound very simple, very childish—and
they are. On paper they may seem sentimental. But when
we actually say such prayers they are very moving. Through
them God heals the brokenhearted.

There is much more to say about this and sometime perhaps I will try to write a book on inner healing and all the
insights we have learned about this beautiful ministry.[5] Inner
healing brings so much peace and joy to people it is a pity so
few understand and pray this kind of prayer. Nor is everybody
equipped with the gifts needed to pray for inner healing;
moreover, it takes time to pray; it is exhausting. But it is
worth all the time and effort to see the transformation from
sorrow into peace or joy that almost always follows. Typical
of God's transforming love is the following testimony of a
young sister who had prayed to be released from a long-standing inner problem:

> Peace and all good things to you. It's 10:15 "the morning
> after." I thought I should share with you somehow some
> of what has happened since we prayed together yesterday.
>   You may recall that during our visit I kept asking,
> "Where is the fire? I thought I would be on fire," etc.
> Then we prayed and I felt—not a burning—but a quiet
> cooling of my whole spirit.

5. Both Father Michael Scanlan and Mrs. Ruth Stapleton have recently finished books on inner healing which will shortly be published.

We parted then and as soon as I was able to be alone I became conscious of a strange sensation. I was being washed and/or cleansed. Closing my eyes I could "see" waterfalls and rushing rivers. I *was* that river, that running water!

Throughout those first few hours and during the Mass, each time I was quiet and reflected and not distracted, I would become conscious of it again. Coming home, I sat for a while in the quiet darkness and just rested in the Spirit—in the whole experience. I thought that after a few hours it would go away, but it is still with me.

I opened the bible once today, to John 4. The first words on the page were an introduction to the text: "This passage introduces us to the symbolism of living water. . . . Just as Moses made water spring from the rock, Jesus will give living waters springing up to life everlasting. Christ, when glorified, will give the Holy Spirit, living life in abundance for all who believe. . . ."

The passage itself is about Jesus and the Samaritan woman. The verse that touched my depths, naturally, was: "Anyone who drinks the water I shall give will never be thirsty again; the water I shall give will turn into a spring inside him, welling up to eternal life." Praise Jesus! (If I go on I will begin to "babble like a brook"—or is that what the Spirit is already effecting?)

One thing more: I was alone here this morning except for one other sister who I thought was a bit tired of testimonies. So I began to write this letter; then sister came in and I said, "Look, I've got to share this with someone," and then we read the passage together. At verse 14 ("but anyone who drinks the water that I shall give will never be thirsty again . . ."), I broke down and cried like a baby. That probably is not important except that I almost *never* cry, and perhaps this is part of the whole healing process, the healing of the emotions.

Praise Jesus—my heart is very full.

At times some people question whether inner healing is "scriptural"; it is simply the application of Christ's healing power to what we now know of the emotional nature of man. In no way does it deny the gospel, but builds upon it and applies it to what psychology has to say about the nature of man.

A remarkable incident that seemed to confirm the confluence of revelation with science occurred just three months ago. I was praying together with a husband for his wife who was suffering from a feeling of inferiority and anticipated rejection; she was always afraid of making a wrong decision for fear of what others—and especially God—might think of her. These fears went back to the deep hurt of her own mother abandoning her at birth. After a beautiful, moving prayer, we left her to pray alone while her husband drove me back home. In the silence of prayer the thought came to her, "Read the *Song of Songs,* chapter 3, verses 1-4." She didn't know the bible that well to have any idea of what was contained there, so she opened up her bible and to her profound consolation read:

> On my bed, at night, I sought him
> whom my heart loves.
> I sought but did not find him.
> So I will rise and go through the City;
> in the streets and the squares
> I will seek him whom my heart loves.
> . . . I sought but did not find him.
>
> The watchman came upon me
> on the rounds in the City:
> "Have you seen him whom my heart loves?"

Scarcely had I passed them
than I found him whom my heart loves.
I held him fast, nor would I let him go
till I had brought him
into my mother's house,
into the room of her who conceived me.

This was a beautiful confirmation of exactly the healing for which she had prayed—an extended application of scripture as it applied to her situation.

Man's most basic need is to know that he is loved—not for anything he can achieve or do, but simply because he is. If anyone does not know God's love in this way, Jesus eagerly desires to show us how much he cares for us by healing us of those ancient hurts that have withered or broken our hearts and spirits.

He will not break the crushed reed,
nor put out the smouldering wick
till he has led the truth to victory:
in his name the nations will put their hope
(Mt 12:20-21).

14

Praying for Physical Healing

OF ALL THE KINDS of healing physical healing is perhaps the hardest for us to really believe in; it is far easier to believe that prayer can lead to repentance or can change a person psychologically. Yet real physical healings take place regularly in the prayer groups I know. Often a dozen or more occur on retreats when we take the time to pray for the sick. So if you have the faith that the Lord still heals people as he did 2000 years ago, launch out and learn to pray for the sick. For, although physical healing may stretch your faith (have you ever prayed for a blind person?), it is also the simplest kind of prayer. It is much simpler and shorter, say, than a prayer for inner healing.

The Confidence to Launch Out

To pray for the first time requires courage. I used to feel very foolish, as if I were pretending to be someone special when I knew I was just an ordinary person. Who was I to pretend to be the great healer, to act like Christ? All this was, of course, merely false humility since, as we know, Christ himself instructed his followers to pray for the sick. Mrs. Barbara Shlemon believes that healing requires more courage than faith.

What a joy when we find that God really answers our prayers and heals the people we love! The praise of God spontaneously rises from our hearts. The following excerpts from three letters show the kind of healing that often takes place as we learn to share in the healing love of God:

March 16, 1973

Dear Father,

I am the diabetic over whom you prayed at the retreat March 2 and it is with great joy I want to tell you that the Lord has healed me. Praise the Lord with me, for since March 4 I have taken no medicine, and I feel great. Never in a million years did I think that this would happen to me. . . .

On October 22, 1973, she wrote:

. . . I have the doctor's verification, for I went to see him last week and he can't find anything wrong with me. I shared with him last April when I returned from the retreat, and he was amazed, but this last week he was convinced that strange things do happen. (He is a Catholic, but even Catholics are slow to believe in miracles.) I thank the Lord every day for healing, as now I am able to do my housework, which last year I could not do. My heart has been healed, too; I do not feel the pressure I felt before, when it was enlarged and was beating irregularly. I could not walk up the stairs, and now stairs do not bother me at all. I feel ten years younger, praise the Lord.

In answer to my letter she wrote again on Feburary 5, 1974:

> . . . As you know, I had been a diabetic for ten years; my eyesight was failing, my heart was very bad, I could not walk up the stairs without resting every few steps, my feet were swollen all the time, I had to be on a special diet, I lost a lot of weight, and had to take seven pills a day just to live. It is almost a year now since my miraculous healing, and I feel as strong and healthy as in my youth. I can walk up the stairs, and run if I want to. My eyesight is improving, and my heart is peaceful and strong. Praise be to God, and thanks to you, for you did intercede for me.
>
> There will be a Mass of thanksgiving said in my parish on March 4 on the anniversary of my being healed. As to the doctor's confirmation, I was taken care of by a Jewish doctor who has since retired. . . . I went to another doctor on my return from Florida, and then again two months later to see what he would say. He could not find anything wrong with me, but as to putting it in writing, he was not sure he knew my case well enough. Well, I am sure, for I know how I feel. A year ago my husband had to do all the housework for me, now I can do it all, and be on my feet ten hours without any trouble.[1]

If you have confidence that Jesus might use your prayers to heal the sick then there are just a few simple steps to learn. They are easy enough to remember; we do not need a graduate degree to learn to pray for physical healing. My friends, Father Ralph Rogawski, O.P., and Sister Helen Raycraft,

---

1. Letters from Mrs. Sophie Zientarski, New Buffalo, Michigan.

O.P., are teaching the poor people of the barrios of Santa Cruz, Bolivia, to pray for the sick in their neighborhood, and they report that about 80 percent of these unlettered people are healed or notably improved as they pray for one another. There is no one method or technique that always produces results; God wants us to depend on him—not upon a technique. But there are some simple steps that flow out of the very nature of prayer for healing, and these I want to share with you.[2]

1. LISTENING

The first step is always to listen in order to find out what to pray for. Just as the first step for a doctor when he meets a patient is to find out what to treat, so we need to find out what we are meant to pray for.

A doctor is looking for the right diagnosis. In prayer for healing we are looking for the right discernment—which is the same thing as right diagnosis in the realm of prayer.

We are really listening to *two* things:

a) To the person who asks for healing and tells us what seems to be wrong; and

b) to God, who from time to time shares with us (through the gift of knowledge) the true diagnosis whenever the person isn't sure what is wrong.

My friend Rev. Tommy Tyson, who is one of the best listeners I know, says that he gives only one ear to the sick person. The other ear he gives to God. In this way the Spirit comes to enlighten us when we seem to be in the dark about

---

2. The book I have found most helpful in describing how to pray for the sick is Mrs. Agnes Sanford's, *The Healing Light* (Plainfield, N.J.: Logos, 1972—in paperback).

what to pray for. To some people this special knowing seems to come in a very special way in the form of definite mental images or verbal impressions: to many of us, however, the knowledge of what to pray for comes in a very natural way, like a simple intuition. We may not be sure whether we are inspired by God or not; we learn by experience to sift out our intuitions and to find out what works out in practice. "By their fruits you will know them. . . ." Often, after I have followed what seemed to me a simple intuition about what to pray for, the person I was praying for has told me that I touched on those very things he had not directly mentioned but had hoped that I would pray for. When these intuitions work out time after time, you learn to trust that God is working through them.

Among those things we learn to listen for are the following:

a) *Whether or not to pray*

There are multitudes of sick people. Some of them are not ready to be healed, even when they ask for prayer; for others who will be healed I am simply not the right person to pray for them. I cannot presuppose that I am supposed to pray for every sick person I meet.

My friend Rev. Rudy Evenson, who now runs a prayer home for alcoholics, tells the story of how he was set on fire with enthusiasm when he first heard about healing. A former prizefighter, Rudy attacks every problem directly with courage and zest. Armed with his newfound faith, Rudy decided to try it out in the local hospital. Upon entering the first ward, he proceeded to go from bed to bed, laying on hands and praying for healing. When the hospital authorities found out about what was happening they threw Rudy out. This didn't bother Rudy too much. After all, we must expect persecution.

What did bother him was that none of the patients got out of bed; none were healed. In his room that night, Rudy prayed in anguish: "Lord, I believed in you. Why did you let me down? What went wrong?"

Then it seemed to Rudy that he heard a voice, "Rudy, who told you to pray for the people in that hospital? Did you ask me?"

"No, Lord," replied Rudy. And he got the point.

The first discernment we need is whether or not we are meant to pray for this person at this time. Some people know this very clearly; they are the ones with the special gift of faith.

Others know that they are supposed to pray for someone by reason of a sensation of warmth, or something like a gentle flow of electricity that courses through their hands, as a sign to them that God's healing power is present.

For others the knowing is almost natural: a feeling of peace or joy when they should pray; a feeling of darkness or heaviness when they are not meant to pray. (This has to be carefully sorted out from the feeling of heaviness that may oppress one when a deliverance commences.)

> It is not the duty of every Christian to pray for everyone. Our prayers will help some and will not help others, for reasons beyond our understanding or control. Only the Holy Spirit can safely direct our healing power. And if we will listen to the voice of God within, we will be shown for whom to pray. God directs us most joyfully through our own desires. The impulse of love that leads us to the doorway of a friend is the voice of God within and we need not be afraid to follow it.[3]

When I first began the healing ministry I met a man who

---

3. Agnes Sanford, *The Healing Light,* p. 86.

was introduced as a true worker of miracles. Yet, at the time, he was suffering from mental depression and exhaustion, because people had found out about the wonderful way God used him, so they would call him at all hours of the day or night to visit the sick. If someone had been in a car wreck friends would call him to the hospital in the middle of the night. Because he was compassionate he would get out of bed, dress and drive over to the hospital where he would stay all night in prayer with the mangled accident victim. Several years of this and he himself had a breakdown and needed rest and prayer. God really does want us to pray about whether or not we are to pray for someone—even when their needs are crying out to our own humanity. One of the hardest things I have had to learn to say is "No" when someone in obvious need asks for prayer.

God often uses our natural intuitions and desires as a channel to lead us, if we will give him the chance. Those experienced in following these intimations sometimes receive a strong impression that they are *not* to pray for healing for a given person. (You can still pray for the person or give him a blessing.) After talking to many people experienced in the healing ministry, I have been impressed by the variety of ways in which God guides people as to how and when they are to pray.[4] In all this, our main desire must be to sort out genuine spiritual guidance from the inclinations rising from our own human subconscious which may be colored by our own human limitations and prejudices.

Even those of us who seem to receive no clear guidance one way or another can still pray for healing. In the absence

---

4. For some, the first intimation they have they are called to a healing ministry is this current of energy vibrating in the hands (often during a prayer meeting) which seems to be God's way of alerting some people and encouraging them to pray for the sick.

of other guidance we are safe, provided we make no presumptuous demands on people (to claim their healing, for example) if

(1) we pray for persons who come forward and ask for prayer. I assume, barring any counterindication, that God has inspired them to ask for help. In these poor and suffering ones Christ is present;

(2) we pray when our compassion inclines us to want to visit or pray for someone who is sick.

Extraordinary manifestations of knowledge and of sensations of healing power are all helpful, but they are not necessary. Many of the extraordinary healings I have seen have taken place without any unusual side manifestations at all. All that happened was that a person came forward and asked for a prayer for healing; the group prayed for what the person asked; and the person was healed.

b) *What to pray for*

The person, of course, is the one who usually tells us what we need to know about what to pray for. As we listen, we are trying to pick out the basic things, the root system of the problem that we need to emphasize in our prayer for healing. As we listen we must decide which of the four kinds of healing the person needs. Even when the person has a physical ailment, we should be alert to the possibility that some deeper healing may be needed.

If we are just dealing with physical healing, we don't need to spend a long time discussing symptoms. On the other hand, inner healing requires a fair amount of time for counsel (20 minutes to an hour at least) with the possibility of follow-up.

If there is also a need for repentance, the person may want an opportunity to receive the sacrament of Penance. If the person also needs deliverance, we will ordinarily need the help of several experienced people who have plenty of time to follow through and help the delivered person afterwards. Since these types of prayer are so different, it is for us to listen well and make a wise decision about what to pray for.

In addition to listening to the person, we should also be alert to the promptings of the Spirit who may enlighten us, especially when we don't know what to pray for. It is not healthy to be unduly problem-oriented and symptom-centered. If we are truly united to Jesus Christ and his Spirit, the sources of the life which is to heal, we can rely upon their positive inspirations about what to pray for. In the abundance of their health and life, sickness will be overcome, in the brilliance of their light, darkness, and ignorance will be dispersed. (Examples of the kind of inspiration often given by the Spirit are given in the chapters on "Inner Healing" and the "Eleven Reasons People Are Not Healed.")

2. LAYING ON OF HANDS

In actual praying for the sick, the laying on of hands is a traditional Christian practice: ". . . They will lay their hands on the sick, who will recover" (Mk 16:18). Certainly it is not essential; if you feel that the person you are praying for would be embarrassed or would feel more comfortable if you stay at a distance, then by all means be sensitive to his feelings. But if it seems right, there are several advantages that give support to the New Testament example of laying on of hands.

In the first place, there does seem to be a current of healing power that often seems to flow from the minister of healing to the sick person. Precisely what this is we are not sure, but it seems like a transfer of life-giving power.

Jesus himself seems to have experienced this flow of power in such a way that he could sense it:

Now there was a woman suffering from a hemorrhage for twelve years, whom no one had been able to cure. She came up behind him and touched the fringe of his cloak; and the hemorrhage stopped at that instant. Jesus said, "Who touched me?" When they all denied that they had, Peter and his companions said, "Master, it is the crowds round you, pushing." But Jesus said, "Somebody touched me. I felt that power had gone out from me" (Lk 8:43-46).

Some people experience this same transfer of power, sometimes like a gentle electric current, sometimes like a flow of warmth. Whatever it is, it is often connected with healing. It almost seems like a transfer of life. I have a theory that some persons with long-standing ailments could be prayed for maybe 15 minutes a day with the laying on of hands, almost like cobalt-radiation treatment.

Rev. Tommy Tyson talks about "soaking prayer" in which you just soak the person in a prayer of God's love.

This brings us to the other benefit of laying on of hands and that is the human one: concern and love are communicated far more by touch than by words alone. After a group has gathered round and prayed for a person, that person is usually sorry to see the prayer end. There is a sense of community and love experienced in a very deep way. I remember once praying with a 60-year-old sister who was to have an operation the next day. We gathered her whole community around her with the laying on of hands. When it was over tears were streaming down her cheeks and she said, "I have never felt the love of my community as deeply as I have tonight."

3. THE ACTUAL PRAYER

In praying for the sick person—with or without the laying on of hands—we can be spontaneous in making up the prayer for healing (which some people call the prayer of faith, because it summons up our faith to believe that God will truly heal the sick person). We can assume any posture that is most comfortable for us—sitting, kneeling, or standing—where we can best forget ourselves and relax and concentrate on the presence of God.

Ordinarily the prayer for healing involves:

a) *The presence of God*

We turn our hearts and minds to the Father, or to Jesus; we know that it is only through their love that anything will happen. The traditional form of the liturgy is to pray *to* the Father, *through* the Son, *in* the Spirit. But some people feel more comfortable simply addressing the prayer to Jesus. After welcoming their presence and praising God, we then turn to

b) *The actual petition*

Most ministers of healing suggest that we be specific in our prayer, that we visualize as clearly as possible what we are asking God to heal.[5] For instance, if we are praying for the healing of a bone we can ask the Father (or Jesus) to take away every infection, to stimulate the growth of the cells needed to restore the bone and to fill in any breaks. Such a

---

5. I do know one couple, though, who pray for healing and simply relax, empty their minds of all thought and effort, and simply let the love of God flow through them. And people are healed. It's just another reminder that we shouldn't absolutize any method.

specific request seems to enliven our own faith, as we see in
our imagination what we are praying for. It also stimulates
the faith of the sick person as he listens and pictures in his
own mind what we are asking God to accomplish in reality.
This helps him become more actively involved in the prayer,
even if he says nothing. (If the sick person is up to saying a
prayer himself, so much the better.)

Such an imaginative prayer should be *positive,* emphasizing not the present state of sickness but the hope of the body
as we would like to see it—whole. Agnes Sanford for a long
time had no success in praying for the sick at a distance when
she was asked to do so. Contrasting this with the positive
results achieved through a prayer group she knew, she won-
dered why she failed and they succeeded until she realized
that, while praying, she imagined the persons in bed, sick;
the prayer group, on the other hand, thought of the distant
patients they prayed for as whole and well. After changing to
a more positive way of praying she, too, found that the persons she prayed for at a distance became well. In this kind of
prayer mental suggestion can, of course, have some influence;
but this is much more than that: we are not playing psychological games but are trying to share in the way God sees this
person in his perfect imaging of how the person should be—
whole and alive and well.[6] Certainly this positive visualization
helps our faith. Imagine, for instance, someone coming to
you asking you to pray for the filling of a tooth. If you should
decide to pray for such a request, visualizing the tooth being
filled would be a real test of faith—much harder than just
praying for the subsiding of the pain or for healing in general
for the person. Many things we don't understand; but we
know by experience that they seem to help. For that reason

6. Jo Kimmel in *Steps to Prayer Power* (Nashville: Abingdon Press,
1972), has a fine chapter on "Visualization Prayer."

Agnes Sanford and others recommend that we visualize in a concrete way the desired effect of the prayer.

> Every time that we meditate upon God's life and light instead of meditating upon a headache, we are building into our inner consciousness a new thought-habit of health. Someday that new thought-habit will be stronger than the old one, and headaches will be no more.
>
> If the thought, "Oh dear, I'm afraid I'm getting the flu," crosses our minds, let us correct that idea right away.
>
> My nose and throat and chest are filling with God's light and if there are any germs there, they are being destroyed immediately. I rejoice and give thanks, Oh Lord, for thy life within me, recreating all my inner passages in perfect health.[7]

4. WITH CONFIDENCE

Jesus answered, "Have faith in God. I tell you solemnly, if anyone says to this mountain, 'Get up and throw yourself into the sea,' *with no hesitation in his heart* but believing that what he says will happen, it will be done for him" (Mk 11:22-23).

As mentioned in Chapter 8 this kind of faith is a gift— to know that *this person* we pray for *will be healed at this time*. But we can all have the faith that God in some way will hear and answer this prayer—always. For a long time there has been a kind of tradition which led most of us to end all our prayers with the phrase, "if it be your will." The idea behind it, of course, is that we don't know God's will, so we don't have the confidence that everything we ask for will be given us, but only those things that are really good for us.

---

7. Agnes Sanford, *The Healing Light*, N.J.: Logos, pp. 28-29.

This is true. Yet, this seems to weaken our confidence in prayer. It returns to "I don't really believe anything is going to happen." This is a far cry from the words of Jesus, "Everything you ask and pray for, believe that you have it already, and it will be yours" (Mk 11:24). The answer is that we should pray for the discernment to enter into God's mind when we pray; having entered fully into God's mind we can then pray with confidence for what we know he already desires for us. When we pray, we do not pray to change God's mind, but rather we are entering into his mind to restore the wholeness that he has long desired for us.

By experience we find that the phrase "if it be your will" seems to weaken the effect of prayer because our inclusion of that phrase usually indicates that we don't believe that *ordinarily it is God's will to heal persons who ask.* For most people that phrase puts an element of doubt where doubt does not belong: we attach the "if" to God's basic will to heal us of our diseases. "If it be your will" is a convenient escape hatch, so that if a person is not healed through our prayers, we can say, "Well, it doesn't seem that God wants to heal you." With the doubt centered on God no wonder such prayers are seldom answered. "If you can do anything, have pity on us and help us," said the father of the epileptic demoniac. In the response to this "if," Jesus retorted, "If you can? Everything is possible to anyone who has faith" (Mk 9:32). Yet, there is a healthy doubt: a doubt as to whether I know all the factors in the case—whether I know the root cause of the disease in order to pray for causes and not just symptoms, or whether there may not be some hidden purpose in the sickness, or whether I am the person whose prayer God will use to bring about the healing.[8] All these are open questions unless God should reveal to me that he intends to heal this per-

8. *Cf.* Chapter 18 of this book, "Eleven Reasons People Are Not Healed."

son at this time through my prayer. If he does reveal this, I can pray with utter certainty—even a prayer of command: "Stand up and walk."

But if I am praying without such a revelation it seems best, as Agnes Sanford suggests, to say, "Let this be done *according to your will.*" This may seem only slightly different from "if it be your will," but there is considerable difference in that the doubt in this case does not center upon God's basic will to heal, but it places the doubt upon whether we *know* all the factors needed to bring about a healing. Yet, we do believe God is answering the prayer "according to his will," as he sees best.

I do know, however, of at least one prayer group that prays, "if it be your will," and through their prayers healings have taken place, because they do believe in God's basic will to heal. Their understanding of "if it be your will" does not place the "if" upon God's will to heal, and they do pray with confidence, "with no hesitation in their hearts."

For most of us, though, it helps to leave out "if it be your will" because of the phrase's ambiguity. If we feel inclined to add anything, let it be "according to your will."

5. WITH THANKSGIVING

St. John writes:

> We are quite confident that if we ask him for anything, and it is in accordance with his will, he will hear us; and knowing that whatever we may ask, he hears us, we know that *we have already been granted what we asked* of him (I Jn 5:14-15).

If we believe that God answers our prayers always (not always as we think he will, but always, nevertheless) we naturally will have a heartfelt desire to thank him. We can thank him even during the prayer: "I thank you Lord that even now you are sending your healing love and power into Bill and are answering our prayer. . . ." Our attitude should be that of St. Paul: "There is no need to worry but if there is anything you need, pray for it, asking God for it *with prayer and thanksgiving. . .*" (Phil 4:6).

6. PRAY IN THE SPIRIT

Those who pray in tongues, when they are not sure precisely what to pray for, turn the prayer over to the Spirit, believing that:

> The Spirit too comes to help us in our weakness. For when we cannot choose words in order to pray properly, the Spirit himself expresses our plea in a way that could never be put into words, and God who knows everything in our hearts knows perfectly well what he means, and that the pleas of the saints expressed by the Spirit are according to the mind of God (Rom 8:26-27).

Often when I have been pressed for time, with a crowd waiting for prayer and no chance to speak to each one, I have simply gone from one person to another, laying my hands on their heads or shoulders, praying in tongues about 30 seconds for each person. I do the same thing in foreign countries when I do not know the language. In this way many have been healed; several remarkable outpourings of God's grace have occurred at such times as this, when I simply turned the prayer over to God's Spirit, not even knowing what the needs were of each Peruvian, Colombian, or Bolivian.

15

Deliverance and Exorcism

ONE MIGHT WONDER what a chapter on praying for deliverance from evil spirits is doing in a study on healing. To tell the truth, I did think of leaving it out—especially since it is such a controversial subject. Nevertheless, it is a part of healing in the broader sense of freeing man from all the evil that burdens him and prevents him from being fully alive and free. Anyone who exercises a ministry of healing must at least understand the four basic kinds of healing, including the last among them—deliverance.

Here I would like to make a distinction between

1) *exorcism,* which I understand to be a *formal* ecclesiastical prayer to free a person *possessed* by evil spirits, and

2) *deliverance,* which I understand to be a process, mainly through prayer, of freeing a person who is *oppressed* by evil spirits. Formal exorcism in the Roman Catholic Church requires the permission of the bishop and is rarely exercised. Deliverance, on the other hand, is a relatively common occurrence—at least in some Christian communities.

I tried to avoid the ministry of deliverance as long as possible, since I was already worn out praying with all the people who desired prayer for inner and physical healing. Why get involved in the unpleasant business of praying for deliverance?[1] Healing is such a beautiful and positive kind of prayer that I had no desire to get involved in something I felt was ugly. The little I had seen of this ministry in prayer groups seemed to me unbalanced and exhibitionistic. As a psychiatrist friend had observed, "Who will exorcise the exorcists?" I still have enough intellectual pride not to want to be associated with the stigma of fundamentalism coupled with fanaticism. My fellow Dominican and friend, Father Richard Woods, in writing about diabolism reflects the common disdain of the intellectual world for the image of the exorcist when he writes, "Catholic priests and Protestant pastors (so far, no rabbis) have told me contentedly of the informal exorcisms they regularly perform, clucking their tongues at the sad number of young people still, however, in the grip of Satan."[2]

Nevertheless, in spite of my fear of losing a somewhat respectable image, the past three years have made me realize that there were some people I simply could not help merely by praying for inner healing. Prayer for deliverance sometimes was clearly called for. Some people who came to me knew this and were quite calm and rational in describing truly extraordinary manifestations of apparently demonic attacks. Just this past week, for instance, I received a letter from a

---

1. Don Basham in his book, *Deliver Us From Evil* (Washington Depot, Conn.: Chosen Books, 1973) describes a similar reluctance to get involved in the deliverance ministry. Of the books I have read on the subject I would recommend Basham's as offering the most practical advice. In addition I would recommend *Exorcism*, The Report of a Commission Convened by the Bishop of Exeter, edited by Dom Robert Petitpierre, O.S.B. (London: S.P.C.K., 1972).
2. *The Devil* (Chicago: Thomas More Press, 1973), p. 14.

sister who asks about a pastoral problem common to anyone who has experience in the healing ministry:

Do you know where I can get some information on deliverance and healing? What's the difference between praying for deliverance and exorcism? How does one know when a person needs either? There's a 12-year-old boy on our block who exhibits strange "symptoms." I visited the parents the other day and without saying what I think (and I don't have any background on these things) the child might be suffering from, I talked and prayed with them.

The boy, they say, has an unidentifiable disease; he keeps twitching, except for a few intervals, gets real bad at night, sometimes says words they don't understand or vulgar words and doesn't communicate. His eyes are like far away and his mother says that at night he moves his head, with his eyes open, back and forth. His hands look paralyzed and he just keeps twitching.

One night I asked him to say, "Jesus Christ help me." He could say, "Help me," but he couldn't—or wouldn't—say "Jesus Christ." We prayed for a while and he fell asleep before I left. He stopped twitching, his hands went limp and were no longer stiff and twisted. I feel there is much more to do.

Meeting such strange cases myself, as well as having these questions addressed to me, I realized I would either have to learn something about deliverance or not help such tormented persons (beyond referring them to the psychiatrist). I would willingly have referred these cases to someone with a proven expertise in deliverance, but there simply weren't that many experts in deliverance that I knew about. Some of the people I heard about who were performing exorcisms didn't seem to have balance or to use common sense; some were claiming every sickness was demonic and were thereby splitting prayer groups apart. People who needed deliverance were phoning in from the East and West coasts to ask for appointments; I wanted to refer them to someone in their own cities for help. But I didn't know of anyone to refer them to. One person called a local chancery to ask for prayer for exorcism and was told abruptly to see a psychiatrist. In view of all this, I realized I would have to learn something about deliverance in order to complement what we had already learned about repentance, inner healing and physical healing.

Is There Such a Thing as Demonic Possession or Oppression?

As I have said, my initial avoidance of the deliverance ministry came from a fear of moving into an area that savors of superstition and primitive religion. Some of my closest friends find it easy to accept healing as a beautiful ministry of God's love, but to them any emphasis on the demonic seems like a retreat from reason into the realm of superstition. The evil that is in man, they say, is enough to explain what is wrong with the world; when Jesus is reported to have driven out demons, he was just speaking according to the mentality of his age which attributed mental illness to evil spirits. Talk of demons seems like a throwback to the Middle Ages or to the witch-hunts of Salem.

Consequently, I assume that some intelligent readers will question the very existence of demons and wonder if the resurgence of exorcism isn't more of an unhealthy regression than a move toward health. To propose adequately the need for such a ministry is clearly beyond the scope of this chapter, but I would simply like to indicate that, beyond the evidence of the gospels, I personally have been convinced by

1) A constant tradition in the Roman Catholic Church

of the reality of this ministry, most recently emphasized by Pope Paul VI in the following statement (which was, incidentally, much criticized):

What are the greatest needs of the Church today?

Do not let our answer surprise you as being oversimple or even superstitious and unreal: one of the greatest needs is defense from that evil which is called the Devil. . . .

Evil is not merely a lack of something, but an effective agent, a living, spiritual being, perverted and perverting. A terrible reality. . . .

It is contrary to the teaching of the bible and the Church to refuse to recognize the existence of such a reality . . . or to explain it as a pseudoreality, a conceptual and fanciful personification of the unknown causes of our misfortunes. . . .

That it is not a question of one devil, but of many, is indicated by various passages in the gospel (Lk 11:21; Mk 5:9). But the principal one is Satan, which means the adversary, the enemy; and with him many, all creatures of God, but fallen, because of their rebellion and damnation; a whole mysterious world, upset by an unhappy drama, of which we know very little. . . .

This question of the Devil and the influence he can exert on individual persons as well as on communities, whole societies or events, is a very important chapter of Catholic doctrine which is given little attention today, though it should be studied again. Some people think a sufficient compensation can be found in psychoanalytical and psychiatric studies or in spiritualistic experiences. . . . People are afraid of falling into old Manichean theories again, or into frightening divagations of fancy and superstition. Today people prefer to appear strong and unprejudiced. . . .

Our doctrine becomes uncertain, obscured as it is by the darkness surrounding the Devil. But our curiosity, excited by the certainty of his multiple existence, justifies two questions: Are there signs, and what are they, of the presence of diabolical action? And what are the means of defense against such an insidious danger?[3]

2) In addition to this long tradition in the Church, reflected in the rite of exorcism in the Roman Ritual, my own *experience* has convinced me more than anything else.

a) *Before* prayer for deliverance many of the phenomena, such as the behavior of the boy described in the letter, impress me as most easily explained as demonic in origin. Admittedly, this kind of criterion needs to be used cautiously, but the gift of discerning spirits finds its purpose in this kind of judgment. To call a person a schizophrenic or a mental case still does not explain how and why those particular symptoms were caused. *If* the cause is demonic, then the proper cure would be exorcism. At one time I thought that if a person was psychotic the only remedy was to refer the person to a psychiatrist or mental hospital. I now have come to believe that many of these same patients can be helped through prayer for deliverance *if* the cause of the psychosis is demonic. This kind of prayer should be done ideally working in conjunction with the psychiatrist.

I have, for instance, before me two letters from a woman who was in a mental hospital for 12 years being treated for schizophrenia. In February, 1973, I and another priest said a prayer of deliverance for her and an immediate change took place. On June 9 she was released from the hospital and on October 5 she wrote:

---

3. "Deliver Us From Evil": General Audience of Pope Paul VI, Nov. 15, 1972. Reported in *L'Osservatore Romano*, Nov. 23, 1972.

I went to see my psychiatrist today. He said I was well.
I told him I wanted to visit the hospital because I miss
the dances there. He said that he didn't agree; the hospital
is for people who are sick and I am well.

In short we have tended to diagnose various personality
problems as neurotic or psychotic; but such labels do not
necessarily get at the root causes of the problems. We believe
that a view which holds that some of these problems could be
demonic in origin is primitive and superstitious. Yet to call
a person "schizophrenic" only describes symptoms and may
not help the person recover at all.

In dealing with someone who is psychotic it would be
unwise to jump to the conclusion that such a person needs
deliverance. On the other hand, those who are not open to
the possibility that such problems as schizophrenia can be
caused by demonic intervention I believe are blocking the
way for the cure of that patient, *if* the cause of sickness of
that particular patient is demonic in whole or in part.

b) *During* prayer for deliverance I have seen unusual
phenomena take place which I think can best be explained by
demonic activity. Such phenomena would include what pur-
port to be demons speaking through the person (e.g., "You
will never drive us out; we are too many and too strong for
you")—often much to the person's surprise. I know that these
phenomena can be explained in other ways, but to me now
the best explanation is the more direct one: that these voices
are demonic in origin. I know some of the people who have
prayed for deliverance from one or another problem, and
they are as rational and sophisticated in their understanding
of these matters as anyone. Yet during the exorcism they
were surprised by what they found taking place (e.g., sometimes the person is thrown to the ground).

c) *After* prayer for deliverance there is often a transforming change that takes place in persons who have not been helped by any other means. This change is sensed immediately by the person ("I just felt something leave; I feel a tremendous weight lifted off me") and is recognized by others in the new freedom and joy the person experiences.

As one person wrote after praying for deliverance:

I feel so privileged and special to God that he led me to this weekend, so that I might be healed and transformed into a new person.

You might have some idea how very, very important this is to me—a matter of life and death. My gratitude will take the form of total surrender to God. At last I have the ability to open to him completely without the old obstacles keeping me from him.

These past few years' experience has convinced me of a vital need to understand the deliverance ministry.

Problems with Terms

When people talked about exorcism I used to think about people being "possessed." Clearly this was a rare phenomenon; there were a few famous cases like the celebrated exorcism at Earling, Iowa, back in the 20's. But these rare, dramatic instances were hardly worth reading about unless we were influenced by morbid curiosity.

The problem is in the term "possession." Real possession when an individual's personality is submerged by an alien, evil force is certainly rare. It is nothing most of us need to be concerned about. But the word in the New Testament which is often translated as "possessed" actually means, in the original Greek, something like "demonized"—which is a much broader term. I find that possession is rare but people who are "demonized," who are attacked or *oppressed* by demonic forces, are a relatively common occurrence.

If a person is oppressed by evil spirits, then an informal exorcism, a prayer for deliverance, is in order. Derek Prince has compared this kind of oppression to the invasion of a city in which the person has control over the main part of the city, but where *certain areas* of the city are under enemy control. When a person has a problem of compulsive behavior in a particular part of his life—drug addiction, for instance—it *may* be an indication that prayer for deliverance will free the person.

Indications That Deliverance Is Needed

The following are signs that may indicate a need for prayer for deliverance:

1) There is that element of compulsion that was just mentioned. When a person tries over a period of time to change but is unable to, even after doing everything possible to achieve self-discipline, then either prayer for inner healing or prayer for deliverance (or both) may be the answer. Common problems that often involve inner compulsion include drug addiction, alcoholism, self-destruction, compulsive masturbation. Discernment is always needed to decide the proper approach to each of these problems: repentance and self-discipline, or healing, or inner healing for the wounds of the past, or deliverance. But compulsion is one indication that demonic forces may be an influence.

2) The person asking for prayer often himself knows that the problem is demonic and will tell you. Of course, the person may have too lively an imagination and after reading vivid accounts of demonic activity may have decided that his problems must be demonic, much as suggestible people who

read medical books imagine that they have contracted the diseases they have read about. So, if a person comes asking for exorcism, we are right to question them closely. Most of us, however, have been trained to be suspicious of any such tale of demonic horrors and to ascribe it to hallucination or other psychic aberrations. Some of the people who describe these wild stories are psychotic, too—which does not help in the sorting out. My own impression is that priests and ministers who have an adequate intellectual background tend to disbelieve any story of diabolic activity, while unofficial exorcists with little or no training tend to believe everything is exactly as told and create all kinds of havoc by seeing demons when there are none. In this way those who should be performing whatever exorcism or deliverance that needs to be done abandon the field to those least qualified—and then criticize the results.

My own experience leads me to believe that many people have had experiences of evil they would like to talk about and be freed from, but the skeptical response they have so often met from their priest or minister has led them to keep quiet about their deepest suspicion about the real source of their problems.

3) If prayer for inner healing seems to accomplish nothing, then it may be an indication that deliverance is needed. I have come to expect that prayer for inner healing will ordinarily have a perceptible effect. If, after prayer, a person says, "I still have a feeling of being tied up inside," it may indicate a need for further counseling, or support in community, or more prayer for inner healing—or, possibly, for deliverance.

From what I have seen of the activity of demons they ordinarily try to convince the afflicted person that he is unworthy, unlovable, doomed to failure, headed toward death and disaster, hated by God and filled with irredeemable guilt.

All these problems of a "loser's script" can also be caused by the psychological wounds of an unhappy past. It is clear then that any deep personal problem can have a number of possible causes; one person who is mentally depressed needs to repent of a secret sin that weights him down; another has a problem of hormonal imbalance and needs medical attention, or prayer for healing (e.g., postpartum depression); still another never experienced the love of a mother and father and needs psychiatric help and/or inner healing; still another, oppressed by demonic powers leading to thoughts of depression and despair, needs prayer for deliverance.

In all this it is clear that the gift of *discernment* is necessary to know what is wrong and how to proceed. Because of the delicate nature of this ministry, the one who prays with someone for deliverance, more than any other minister, needs this gift. When you pray for healing and it does not take place, then, providing the ministry has been in an atmosphere of love, the patient is still blessed. But if you pray for deliverance and nothing happens, then the person may fall under a pall of condemnation believing that you have seen demonic activity in him which has not been driven out and which still remains.

Deliverance should be ministered, then, with great caution, and only if in prayer you judge that demonic activity really is present, and that the Lord wants you to pray *for this person at this time*.

Prayer for deliverance is radically different from prayer for healing in two ways:

1) Whereas prayer for healing is addressed to God, a prayer of deliverance or exorcism is directed to the oppressing *demons*.

2) Whereas prayer for healing is ordinarily a petition, prayer for deliverance is a *command*. For a person who has the gift of faith, prayer for healing can be a command—"In

the name of Jesus Christ the Nazarene, walk!" (Acts 3:6b)—
but prayer for deliverance is always a command to the demonic forces, ordering them to depart in the name of Jesus
Christ, as did Paul to the spirit influencing the soothsaying
slave girl: "I order you in the name of Jesus Christ to depart
that woman" (Acts 16:18b).

The exorcist, then, is one who, invested with the authority of Jesus Christ, commands the evil forces to leave. This
commanding need not be done with shouting, as I have seen
it done in some prayer groups, but it does need to be done with
firmness and authority.

For a variety of reasons this ministry should be reserved
to those who have been called to it:

—Because it is a prayer of authority, those who feel
strained in situations of authority—who are timid or insecure
—are not suited to this ministry. They will either be so frightened that nothing will happen through their prayer, or they
will mask their insecurity by false posturing that will only
make their ministry appear ridiculous.

—On the other hand, just because it is a prayer of command, involving confrontation, persons with aggressive tendencies may feel called to this work, when, in reality, they are
working out their own aggressions. Since their motivation is
mixed, the results of their ministry are likely to be mixed. The
sensitivities of the person being prayed for may be deeply hurt
by what one observer once described as "spiritual rape."

—Because of the need for sorting out the complexities of
good and evil and knowing when to pray, what to pray for,
and how, the exorcist must be experienced, wise and discerning. Simplistic people who tend to see everything in terms of
black or white often seem drawn to a deliverance ministry
where they help some people while they harm many others.
This, in turn, gives deliverance a bad image, frightening away
the very persons who might be best able to exercise a discern-

ing ministry of deliverance. (For these reasons formal exorcism in the Roman Catholic Church has been reserved to
priests who have received permission from the bishop to exorcise a given person.)

Just Before the Prayer for Deliverance

The following points represent the consensus of those persons
I know who have the most experience (and prudence) in the
deliverance ministry:

1) Prayer for deliverance should not be entered into without real prayer and discernment beforehand. Like major
surgery it should not be lightly suggested. Many people have
a need for prayer of deliverance, I believe, but the time cannot
be hurried and there is a great need for follow-up. If follow-up
cannot be provided, if there is no Christian community to help
the person grow, we should hesitate before embarking on a
prayer that cannot be finished; the last state of the person may
end up worse than the first.

Bob Cavnar, of Dallas, at one time was engaged in praying for a number of people for deliverance. They were all in
great need, calling upon him at all hours of the day and night.
But when he stopped to pray about the situation, his guidance
was that he should pray for only one man who was in the most
severe need. This Bob did, and over a period of months the
man was freed from the oppression that had held him paralyzed in his bed. During those months of prayer Bob learned
a great deal by this experience, almost as if he were being
given a course on deliverance.

2) Ideally the prayer should be in private, so as not to
appeal to the curious (the crowds packing in to see the movie
The Exorcist show how deep this curiosity is) and only mature
persons should be allowed to participate.

3) Ideally, prayer for deliverance should be done with a

team, rather than alone. At times, I have had to pray for deliverance alone, but a team is preferable for a variety of reasons—the most evident being that the diversity of gifts belonging to the Christian community can be brought to bear. One person, for instance, may be more suited to say the actual prayer of deliverance (ideally a priest or minister) because of his spiritual authority. Another may have a gift of discernment to know what to pray for at any given moment, while still others can offer prayer support to the person prayed for, as well as the one praying the prayer of deliverance. Sometimes the prayer is short, but at other times the prayer can go on for several hours—in which case simple fatigue and the need to concentrate make a team approach the most suitable.

The Actual Prayer for Deliverance

1) As the prayer begins it is wise to pray for *protection*. I pray that the power of the blood of Christ surround and protect every person in the room. Then I pray that Mary, the Mother of God, St. Michael the Archangel, all the angels and saints, and all the court of heaven intercede with us for the person we are praying for. I pray that no evil force be able to harm anyone in the room—or anywhere else—as a result of demons being cast out through our prayer for deliverance. The way each person prays will, of course, be different, but it is wise always to pray that no harm befall anyone as a result of the fallout from the prayer. Often we find that spirits, once cast out or stirred up, redouble their attacks upon the afflicted person—or upon others:

> The evil spirit replied, "Jesus I recognize, and I know who Paul is, but who are you?" and the man with the evil spirit hurled himself at them and overpowered first one and then another, and handled them so violently that they fled from

that house naked and badly mauled (Acts 19:15-16).

In this instance the exorcists (the sons of Sceva) apparently did not have the spiritual authority needed to perform the exorcism. Similarly, problems can arise for us if we do not pray for God's help and are not called to this ministry which deals with powerful spiritual forces.

2) I always pray then that the force and power of any demons *be bound* and lose their force to resist. I do this by a prayer of command in the name of Jesus Christ. This prayer seems to help the deliverance take place more quickly and more effortlessly.

For example—and for those who have not witnessed these things I simply ask you to suspend judgment until you have had a chance to investigate them for yourselves—during prayer for deliverance some persons feel as if they are being choked by some invisible hand, or they may be thrown to the ground, or they suddenly go blank. All these manifestations temporarily interfere with the prayer until they are dealt with. Consequently, I pray that the powers of evil be bound and in this way avoid as many unpleasant side effects as possible.

3) Ordinarily we need to find out the identity of the demon we are driving out. Usually these demons are identified by their predominant activity: e.g., a spirit of self-destruction or a spirit of fear.

Again, I know this must sound strange to someone who has not been involved in this type of prayer, as it once did to me. Nevertheless, the demons do seem to have identities and names[4] which they reveal to us in several ways:

---

4. In July, 1972, I prayed for a woman who had been consecrated to Satan in Brazil at the age of 11. The particular demon she had been consecrated to serve she knew was mentioned in Job 18:14. In the *Jerusalem Bible* this demon is personified: "He is torn from the shelter of his tent, and dragged before the King of Terrors." In the *New American Bible* the capital letters are removed and it is changed

a) *The person asking for prayer knows* what the demon is or what its characteristic activity is. For instance, *if* homosexuality in a given instance should happen to be demonic in causation, then the prayer can be directed against a spirit of homosexuality. (This is not to say that all homosexual problems are demonic; only that *if* this is the case, then . . .)

b) Through the *gift of discernment* the persons doing the praying know what should be prayed for. This is the most direct way, the quickest, of knowing what to pray for. But the genuine gift—which is not guesswork—is relatively rare in my experience. (There are three people that I know and trust whom God inspires with discernment in the kind of situation we are describing.)

c) Through *commanding the demons to identify themselves*. They answer this command, either by speaking through the oppressed person (often to his great surprise) or through suggesting very strong mental pictures or ideas to the person's mind. These thoughts are ambiguous signs in that they can be simply the subconscious of the person, so here again real prudence and discernment are needed on the part of those praying to be able to sort out precisely what is happening.

4) If an area of demonic interference is recognized, then the person should *renounce any sin* connected with it. If, for instance, a spirit of hatred identifies itself, then the person should forgive any persons who have ever wronged him, and thus cut away the sin or wound that has given the demonic force a hold upon him.

In addition, he can *renounce the spirit* of hatred, or whatever else it is, himself. If the evil spirits do not have a deep hold upon a person, self-deliverance is a real possibility.

---

into a nonpersonified "king of terrors." It is important to realize that these powers are not impersonal forces of evil, but we are dealing with real entities that have a name.

(Chapter 17 in Don Basham's *Deliver Us From Evil* describes how this can be done.)

Furthermore, if the person has been involved in spiritualism or other forms of occult activity, he should renounce by name each one of these activities.

5) Next I ask the tormented *person himself to cast out* the demon by a prayer of command. Sometimes this is enough to cause the demonic force to depart.

6) If the demon (or demons) has not yet departed, then I myself pray for deliverance. This deliverance prayer has several definite components:

i) "In the name of Jesus Christ . . ."
   (for a priest . . . "and of his Church")

> It is not by our authority that we cast these demons out, but we name the power to which these demons must bow " 'Lord,' they said, 'even the devils submit to us when we use your name' " (Lk 10:17).

ii) ". . . I command you . . ."

> This is a prayer of authority, not of entreaty. This kind of prayer is like a parent telling a child to do something; if there is doubt or hesitation, the child picks it up immediately and will not obey. The person commanding can speak quietly but must really believe that the authority of Christ will rout the forces of evil.
>
> In praying for deliverance I find it helps to look directly into the eyes of the person being prayed for.

iii) ". . . the spirit of . . ."

> Identify the spirit, if possible, by name: "spirit of hate," "spirit of despair," or whatever else it is.

iv) ". . . to depart . . ."

v) ". . . without harming ———— (the person being freed) or anyone in this house, or anyone anywhere else, and without creating any noise or disturbance. . . ."

> There have been instances where other people have been attacked by the demons leaving or the person being prayed for has been needlessly tormented. These problems can all be precluded by praying for God's protection. Since deliverance tends to be a spectacular or ugly performance, if the demons are unchecked, it is advisable to command the demons to be quiet and not to create any disturbance.

vi) ". . . and I send you straight to Jesus Christ that he might dispose of you as he will."

> Some persons prefer to command demons to "return to the abyss" or something of that sort, but personally I prefer to leave what happens to the wisdom of Christ. As David DuPlessis once told me, there is an occupational hazard of exorcists becoming infected by what they combat; they may become harsh and judgmental over the years. As St. Jude remarked:

"Not even the archangel Michael, when he was engaged in argument with the devil about the corpse of Moses, dared to denounce him in the language of abuse; all he said was, 'Let the Lord correct you' " (Jude 1:9).

7) The person being delivered seems to know when a given demon has departed. Sometimes there is no discernible change to an onlooker; the person just looks up and says, "It's gone! I feel so much better now."

If there are many demons, the person, too, seems to know when they have all gone. There is a sense of freedom, of joy; at times, it's like the lifting of a weight or some other very physical relief such as the removal of some gripping pain.

Often, too, the demons come out with a struggle: sometimes they cry out or throw the person to the floor (phenomena mentioned in the gospels) or they come out in a fit of coughing or retching. All these symptoms are, of course, unpleasant and make the work of deliverance an unsavory task. If these phenomena become too exhibitionistic I command the demons to keep quiet or to stop tormenting the person or to cease whatever else they are doing. The coughing or retching (why it happens is a mystery) does seem to have a part in expelling the demon; when it is over the person usually has a definite impression that a particular demon has departed.

All these phenomena are bizarre and distressing. Much as we may dislike them, we must be prepared to face them if we are going to help those persons who need deliverance.

Other Considerations

In dealing with demons it seems that there is ordinarily a principal one, something like the taproot of a tree around which the rest of the root system clusters. Getting rid of them is something like digging out a tree stump. Sometimes it is best to drive out lesser spirits that have less of a hold upon the person; it's something like chopping off feeder roots, so you can get more easily at the main root. Other times, the lesser ones won't move until you identify and drive out the principal spirit. I say "lesser" because some of these demons seem stronger than others. I have found here that sections of the old spiritual theology that deals with "capital sins" and "daughter sins" have been especially helpful in all this. These demons, like vices, seem to go in clusters. When you find "anger," for instance, you may also find "resentment," "jealousy," "depression," "sadism" or such specialized forms of anger as "hatred of women."

Demons usually identify themselves by the title of a particular vice:

"In the name of Jesus Christ, I command you, evil spirit, to identify yourself. Who are you?"

"Lust."

"In the name of Jesus Christ, I command you, spirit of Lust, to depart. . . ."

Several of the spirits that tend to surface early and block the prayer for deliverance are:

—mockery (The person may start to laugh derisively and may say something like: "You can't drive us out. You don't have enough experience.")

—dumbness (The person can't move his mouth or talk.)

—confusion (The person becomes very confused and can no longer think.)

(Here again the persons praying must have the discernment, knowledge and experience to be able to know the difference between the very natural human distress that the person may be experiencing and not misidentify this as demonic activity.)

After praying the prayer of deliverance it is helpful for the leader and others to praise God or to sing (and for those who pray in tongues to do this). This kind of prayer goes on until the demon releases whatever hold it has upon the person and leaves. If there is no change then the person leading the prayer needs the discernment to know how to proceed from there.

If the person being freed has had any dealing with spiritualism or with the occult (such as the Ouija board), the person should ask God's forgiveness for this. If there are demons (such as a demon of divination) that entered through this kind of influence, they should be the first to be driven out; otherwise they will block anything else from happening.

Following the Deliverance

There are three important factors following upon any deliverance. If there is no follow-up, chances are the condition of oppression will return:

1) There should be a *prayer immediately after* the deliverance to *fill* the person with God's love and grace. Anything left empty by the departure of the demons should be filled by the presence of Jesus.

2) The person should be taught *to break the habitual behavior patterns* that originally led to the demonic infestation. If the problem was in the area of despair, for instance, some kind of spiritual discipline, mutually agreed upon, is needed to combat the area of human weakness that caused the problem in the first place.

In addition, the person should be taught how to rebuke any forces of evil and keep them away, once they have been driven out. "Give in to God then; resist the devil, and he will run away from you" (Jas 4:7). I once spent two hours praying for a person to be delivered from a number of evil spirits, a principal one being resentment. The person was delivered but within an hour an incident occurred which aroused resentment in the person. Unresisted it led immediately to a return to her previous state (although the subsequent prayer for deliverance was much easier and only took about 40 minutes).

3) The person should also adopt a regular schedule of prayer, of reading scripture and (if he belongs to a sacramental church) of receiving the sacraments of the Eucharist and of Penance.

4) Ideally, the person should then become part of a Christian *community*. Just as alcoholics have found that they cannot, for the most part, remain dry without the help of people who understand and care (such as members of Alcoholics Anonymous), so people who have been delivered need the prayer and loving support of community. A real tragedy in today's churches is that there are not enough such communities. I simply don't know where to send people who can't make it without the help of community. The few strong communities we know about that have households that take in people who need support are already overburdened with more people than they can adequately handle.

Final Considerations

I might mention here that whenever I have prayed for deliverance I have almost always also found prayer for repentance or for inner healing was necessary. Usually there is a very human weakness, such as an experience of rejection in early life, that opened the way for the demonic. Unless this deep weakness is shut off, there may be more problems later. The person is something like a tree where there has been a deep gash in the bark; if this is not covered over, the tree is always in danger of succumbing to the attack of insects or fungus which will then get within the tree and rot it out.

On the other hand, most emotional problems, such as depression, are caused by very natural, human factors and the appropriate response is not deliverance but prayer for inner healing and/or psychological counseling and/or spiritual discipline and growth.

Of all the areas of healing, deliverance is the most susceptible of abuse and creates the most problems. Yet, I see it as most necessary that more of it be done by the right people. Nowhere are discernment and prudence more necessary than in this ministry. But nowhere are there more ignorance and lack of experience—especially on the part of the clergy, who are the natural candidates to perform this ministry.

For those who have had no experience in any kind of deliverance ministry, some of what I have written in this chapter may seem problematic if not downright medieval. I would only ask that you put it all on the back burner, as it were, until such time as you have a chance to see for yourself. In this area you will find books and articles voicing very strong opinions pro and con. Here I would simply like to share the beautiful aftereffects of deliverance from a priest who has personally experienced it:

> So many wonderful things have happened since the Lord delivered me that I feel I must write and let you know.
>
> First and above all, my faith in the powerful love of Jesus has grown tremendously. The positive assurance I have that he is with me in prayer alone, with others, and in the Eucharist astounds me. When I pray with people for healing or deliverance, I couldn't be more sure of his presence and desire to serve this person with me. Indeed, I feel that my already growing ministry of deliverance is just what I've needed to build my faith. Somehow, with each one (there have been eight in the last two weeks)

my faith and love of Jesus grow immeasurably.

My own ministry of deliverance has somewhat surprised me. And yet something seems to tell me that I've known all along that I was ordained for this. . . .

I have not delivered anyone whose reaction was as violent as mine, although some have approached it. And I have already helped a young man in a two-hour session that included all four types of healing. . . .

The most striking effect in my personal life has been the permanency of my cure. As I look over a list of demons cast out I am grateful that none of them has a hold on me anymore. My outlook on life is different now: I no longer feel like an outcast because of my problems. I am no longer beleaguered by doubts, fears, inadequacies or lust.

Of course, I am tempted in all the areas in which I was delivered. But it is so wonderful to have human and not demonic temptations! They are infinitely easier to resist. . . . I never realized that a free Christian could give his life to the Lord so completely. . . . My life is filled with joy such as I have never felt before. It at once quiets me and moves me to serve in love.

16

A Case History: Flor's Story

IN NOVEMBER, 1972, and February, 1973, our team gave retreats in Bogota and Cali, Colombia. On these retreats Senora Flor de Maria Ospina de Molina received a remarkable series of healings that illustrate the four kinds of healings I have just described.

Her story also illustrates the complexity of these different healings and how they intertwine. Notice how Flor's daughter was not healed until her mother was inwardly healed, some months after we had first prayed for the daughter. Moreover, Flor apparently received a deliverance when she received an inner healing; whatever grip any evil spirits (such as resentment) had upon her was loosened and broken when she forgave (repentance) and received an inner healing. Furthermore, this case history illustrates how healing often takes time and happens in a series of steps as one log after another in the logjam that impedes the flow of life is taken out of the stream, until finally the key log is removed which sets a person free.

This beautiful story of how God sets one of his people

free is a translation from the Spanish (by Dorothy Curran) of the testimony given by Flor on February 18, 1973, in San Juan Battista Catholic Church, Cali, Colombia.

In October, 1972, I was invited to take part in a study of the charismatic renewal by Padre Guillermo; I attended every one of the conferences and this produced good results. Afterwards we went to Bogota to attend a retreat given by Father Francis MacNutt, Sister Jeanne Hill and Mrs. Ruth Stapleton. While there, we experienced a great and tremendous thing which initiated us into the movement: I felt a deeper life in the Spirit. It was there for the first time that I spoke in tongues. On the second day of the retreat following the prayer for inner healing by Mrs. Ruth, I found Father Francis in the hall and I asked him to pray for me and my children. He put his hands on my head and told me to pray. This day I first learned to pray in tongues.[1] I felt happiness and I began to cry. A young man was standing there when this happened; having witnessed this experience, he kissed and hugged me and said: "The Lord was with you."

Four months later I heard that Father Francis was coming to Cali, Colombia. I remembered my experience in Bogota and all that I learned from him. I asked God not to let me miss one conference at my parish church and at the Presbyterian church. So I attended every morning conference, Monday through Friday. I brought my sick daughter, Maria Fernanda, with me the first day and I asked Father Francis to pray for her sickness. I was also accompanied by my two half-sisters.

On Thursday, the day before the conferences finished,

---

1. This was not what I was praying for; I was praying for her children as she had asked—another instance of the mysterious and beautiful way in which God answers our prayers.

Father Francis prayed for the inner healing. In the prayer he included all those persons who might not have been wanted by their parents or who never received the love they needed. At this time Father asked us to reflect back on our lives—to think back to our infancy and childhood. It was then, too, that Father asked us to pray for our parents if, by chance, they had not brought us into this world through love. At this moment, I felt a tremendous convulsion and a great desire to cry, because I was one of these unwanted children. I asked God to give me the tranquillity which I needed at this moment because I was in the presence of my two half-sisters, children of my mother's second marriage, who probably would not understand what was happening to me. The only thing I felt at that moment was a desire to scream out and say that I was one of those unwanted children! I had been full of hate and revenge since my infancy and childhood; it seemed that I could hear my mother's first words when I had reached the age of reason, when I first was able to comprehend and understand. She said to me: "You and your brother are children of my first marriage. I don't know why destiny brought me to that marriage. You are the shadows of that cross; you always make me remember that part of my life."

Since I was a small child I didn't understand what it was all about. My brother never lived with me or our mother; he always lived with my father's mother. I felt ashamed of my brother who suffered from asthma from the time he was a year and a half old.

I remembered how my mother married my father when she was very young. My mother had told me about my father in a great rage. She told me that my father had many bad habits and that he was irresponsible. They married very young, perhaps without love. My mother was an orphan, and perhaps she married as a last hope, thinking that through this marriage, she could change her life.

The first child, my oldest brother, died in 40 days. Afterwards my brother was born, but he was never reared with me. When I was born, my parents were already separated due to lack of understanding in the home. I asked my mother if my father saw me after I was born. She said yes. He came because she called him and he loved me a lot. After that my mother never permitted him to visit and see me, because she did not want to live with him anymore.

Then, when I was one year old, my father was murdered—a terrible and horrible death during the time of the Violence [the civil war in Colombia]. This happened in La Cumbre, Valle, Colombia. He died at 28 years (almost the age that I am now) from bullet wounds in the stomach, causing all his intestines to pour out on the sidewalk of this small town. My mother told me that the death of my father gave her great happiness; she said it was better for a husband of this kind to be dead. From this moment, a legal battle started to decide on whom his children belonged to. The law decided to leave my brother with my paternal grandmother while my mother claimed me.

Thursday morning, I was reliving my infancy and childhood: I grew up without a father. The only thing I knew of him was the worst. I had a distorted and horrible image of him—an image of sin and irresponsibility; even his death was horrible. I remembered, too, what my mother had said when I was about 13 years old when I had a terrible argument with her in which I told her she should respect him in his death. I reminded her that I never ordered her to marry him—she had freely chosen to marry him. My mother replied that the marriage was a disgrace and an inexplicable destiny. It was something she never desired. Whenever I asked my mother for anything, she would say, "Your father never left you an inheritance so why should you be asking for things?"

At this time, too, my calvary began with my stepfather. I was still a child when he told me he desired me (my mother was out of the house), and that if I did not accept him, I would have to leave the house, or he would leave it. I had always been close to God and God was close to me. When my mother returned home that day, I told her what my stepfather had said. From that time on, hate was poured on me from both my mother and my stepfather; I was face to face with humiliation as my stepfather continued to insist on his love for me.

When I was 16 years old, I escaped from home. I realized that I could no longer find security there. My mother couldn't help me since she had five small children from her second marriage. I told her that I could no longer live in this house filled with hatred and maliciousness. So I went to work for another family as a servant. After two months, I met my future husband and in four months we were married, another marriage of circumstances! Although I never really desired this marriage with a man ten years older than I, since I was like a child compared to him, I promised myself to be a good wife and a good homemaker. I have kept this promise. I am married ten years and I have three children. With God's help, I am giving good example.

On Thursday morning, I reviewed all these memories. I recalled my past sufferings of my childhood and young adult life, which was never a happy one. I felt a desire to cry. I felt torment, a tremendous interior congestion within me. I asked God to help me because I was sitting between my two half-sisters who probably never knew the terrible suffering that their father had caused me.

I stayed on in church while my half-sisters went to get a cup of coffee. I felt a great need to talk to someone. Fortunately, Padre Guillermo of my parish was there praying. I told him all that I was experiencing and suffering that morning. I felt I was also suffering for my brother. I reflected that what I felt inside of me, my brother probably felt too. Just recently, my brother came to visit me and he asked about "that woman" whom he hates so much. I told Padre Guillermo that my brother hates our mother. I felt that perhaps the largest wound I have is that of my brother's hate for our mother, because he does not know God as I have had the opportunity to know him.

Then I asked Padre Guillermo to pray for my brother. But I felt a great need for an interior healing. I felt I needed to be cleansed. I wanted it because I felt a tremendous torment and confusion. The main thing I felt was remorse that I had never prayed for my own father whom I never knew, and also for my mother. For the first time in my life, I knelt down and prayed to God for my father and my mother. I asked God to erase the horrible image within me that I saw! I was not clean inside of me. I also realized that I was not free. Something inside me prevented me from being completely free; something prevented me from gaining the complete freedom to live for God. I came to realize, from the talks Father Francis had given, that I needed still more; so I began to analyze my life further.

On Friday morning, Father Francis divided the group. I went to the basement of the church to pray for interior healing. There we formed a circle where others outside the circle would pray with us. At that moment I truly felt God's presence in me when Father put his hands on my head and prayed for my interior healing. Perhaps others can give a better testimony than I of what happened to me at that moment, for it was said that *something went out of me*. From that moment, I felt completely electrified. I began to tremble. The person (Marlene Bundy) next to me began to tremble also. It seemed as if an electric current went through me—as if it were the grace of God, as if it were a cleansing. We felt that our Lord himself had descended upon us. God acted forcefully; I rested interiorly. I felt peace for the first time, because I forgave while I, in turn, was forgiven for what I had done, for what I had kept hidden within me for such a long time. When I returned to myself (I suppose I can say this) I felt wonderful!

There before me was Pastor Jose Fajardo of the Presbyterian church and Father Francis. Pastor Fajardo was crying really hard. He said: "Flor, it could be that you have been chosen for something great. Let's give thanks to God for you. You will with your testimony help many more people."

After this, we sat down to rest and I recalled my three children, especially Maria Fernanda who has been suffering with eczema for five of her six years. I remembered that I had tried everything—doctors, specialists, pilgrimages—although I never tried spiritualists or any other form of witchcraft.

Thinking of my sick child, I asked Father how to pray for my child. "I brought her to you Monday and you prayed for her," and I repeated my request: "Teach me how to pray for my child! She does not get better." Father replied: "Flor, many times the sicknesses of children are not all the child's fault, but are connected with their parents. You were suffering with something that has now been healed by God. I believe that now that you have forgiven and have been healed by God, your child too will be healed." This was on Friday. On Saturday, the child was a little better. On Sunday, the day I give this testimony at the Church of San Juan Battista, Maria Fernanda's hands are dry. They no longer have pus or any other infection. Praise the Lord!

Hold up your limp arms,

steady
your
trembling knees,

the injured limb
will not
be wrenched,
but grow
strong again.

HEB. 12:13

PART FOUR
Special Considerations

17

Discernment of the Root Sickness

IN TALKING ABOUT HEALING we have seen clearly how discernment is needed in this area. Our spiritual and physical sicknesses are so interrelated that we need God's light often to untangle the complexity of human existence so that we will know how best to pray.

God is a mystery—and so is the human person.

Rev. Tommy Tyson shared the following incident[1] which illustrates a combination of several things we have talked about: discernment through listening to God, the need for repentance—especially in relation to forgiveness—and the need for the healing of man's spirit before certain physical healings can take place:

As I understand it the gift of discerning spirits is essentially this: as spiritual beings it is utterly impossible for us

1. Tommy spoke about this in a talk he gave for the Christian Preaching Conference Convention in Toronto in 1968. This incident has been transcribed from the tape recording of his talk.

to live alone. We are always identified with other spiritual realities—bad or good or neutral. That is my premise, my understanding which governs my own approach.

Now, the gift of discernment of spirits is the gift whereby you are able to see that spiritual reality to which another person is most closely identified. Sometimes this comes as a visual representation—sometimes it is given as a word of knowledge. That sort of thing began to happen to me one evening when I was holding a preaching mission down South. The pastor drove me out in the country until we had come upon a beautiful little mountain ridge overlooking a farm. The pastor said, "Tommy, I guess this is the reason we came on this drive, not just to see the view, but there is a home down there; I had forgotten about those people, but we should visit them."

We went down to this lovely farm home. There on the porch sat a man and his wife in their mid-60's. Mae and Nelson were their names. Mae was sitting in a wheelchair with her right arm folded against her paralyzed right side. Nelson was sitting in the porch swing. The pastor and I pulled up a chair in front of them. I began to turn inwardly, being bathed in God's love. (I never give a person both ears anymore. I just give you one ear, but not my best one. While I'm listening to you from one ear, I'm really seeking to get heaven's interpretation from the other ear.)

The Lord began just to bathe my heart with love. People are aware of the power of love, aren't they? So I said to Mae, "Mae, something is happening—the Lord is giving me great love for you and I know he wants to minister to you." She said something through clenched teeth—she was paralyzed you know. As I sat there some pictures began to come to my mind. I said, "Mae, if this is of the Lord you'll know it, and if it isn't, I need to know it."

I have discovered in this kind of discernment you can afford to be very cautious; you don't have to tell people that the Lord is showing you something. That might frighten them. A lot of people might be afraid if you say that God is showing you something. But you can say, "This idea has come to me," or "This idea seems to be of the Lord," or "May I share this with you?" I have found this to be much more helpful than just telling people everything you know. Just because you know something is not in itself a license to tell it, is it?

But as I say—this picture was coming to me: I saw a lovely home in a little village—I even saw a weeping willow tree in the yard. When I described the home Mae said, "That was the home I was raised in." I saw her as a young girl riding off in a horse and buggy with a young man, and I could tell they were running—it was just a mental picture. Then the whole thing dawned on me. I said, "Mae, I take it that Nelson came into town, and your folks didn't want you to have anything to do with him, so you ran off and eloped with him."

She said, "Yes, that's right." Then, as the picture developed, I saw her sitting at an organ—just losing herself as she played. Then, from that picture this interpretation came. I said, "Mae, you were disappointed in your marriage, weren't you? You discovered that your folks were right and rather than leave him, you lost yourself in your music. You have compensated for a disappointing marriage through music."

She was crying now as she replied, "Yes, that's right." Then, I only could see a big block, so I said, "Maybe the Lord wants you to tell me what this is, or maybe we should just sit and wait for a while." Then she nodded at Nelson and said, "You tell him." Nelson said, "I suppose what you see now in this block is what happened down at the church. . . . Everything you have said has been true. What happened at the church was that a woman there who has a large family had a falling-out with Mae; they had a big argument. This woman said, 'Mae, either you or I with my whole family will have to leave this church!' Since there were only the two of us, we thought it best for Mae and me to leave."

I said, "Mae, how soon after that did you become paralyzed?" She guessed it was about three months. So I said, "Mae, where is your hand of fellowship? Where is your forgiveness?"

There it was; that was the problem.

In this case I don't mean to imply that all paralysis comes from lack of forgiveness. I think it is dangerous to imply that certain diseases have a definite spiritual cause, unless you are sure about it. Unless you are cautious you can bring people under grave indictment and guilt. I don't believe in doing that, but in this case her body was the sacrament of her soul: what her soul went through her body also underwent, and this had been going on for three or four years. I told her what I thought.

Nelson looked at me and said, "There is one thing God hasn't shown you that maybe you ought to know. In the three years Mae has been paralyzed I've tried to make up with her and we've become sweethearts again." (God uses suffering, doesn't he?) Then I said to Mae, "Will you accept forgiveness and cleansing from all this?" She said, "Of course I will."

She had confessed her sin and I had heard that confession, so I laid hands on her and said, "Mae, in the light of God's word, you are cleansed from your sin and you are washed clean in the blood of Jesus." When I pronounced her forgiveness she became radiant, and we had a great time rejoicing. As I started to walk off the porch, I turned impulsively and said, "Mae, in your new life, let me be the first one to offer you the right hand of fellowship."

I reached out my hand and hers—that had been paralyzed—came out to meet mine. For the next hour we helped her to learn to walk all over again.

18

Eleven Reasons Why People Are Not Healed

FOR THE MOST PART we need encouragement to believe that God *does* heal people. But after we do summon up the courage to launch out and start praying we may get discouraged when we realize that people are not always healed through our prayers. This is especially puzzling to those who have been exposed to a very simplistic approach to healing: "All you have to do is to claim your healing."

I remember in the early days of our prayer meetings in St. Louis one priest who had an agonizing interior struggle moving from his position of suffering-sent-by-God to one of a suffering-as-part-of-the-evil-Christ-freed-us-from, would often get up in the prayer meeting and give a short teaching on the redemptive value of suffering. Finally, he read a book on the authority of the believer which persuaded him that he ought to start praying for healing instead of for the acceptance of sickness. The person he chose to pray for was a most difficult beginning: a patient dying of cancer. He gathered a group of friends and with his newfound expectancy that she would be healed, he took his group to the hospital and prayed the prayer of faith. A short time later she died.

Crushed by this experience, he didn't pray again for anyone for another year.

We need to understand then why people are not healed, so that we can understand the kind of faith we need to pray for healing. The best point of view, I think, is to see that *God's normative will is that people will be healed, unless there is some countervailing reason.* He gives some individuals the "gift of faith" to know that particular persons they pray for will be healed. The rest of us need to believe in God's healing power and pray for healing, while at the same time realizing that there is a mystery involved and that the person may not be healed. To avoid simplistic approaches to healing we should be aware of the reasons people are not healed. In my ministry I have discovered at least 11 of these reasons and I imagine that there are several more that we will discover:

1) *Lack of faith*

When the disciples could not cure the epileptic demoniac Jesus upbraided them for their lack of faith (Mt 17:14-20). I believe that this is still the reason we do not have more healings taking place in our churches today; there is a general skepticism about healing as anything more than a natural psychological process.

But even for those of us who believe, we need to grow in faith. I find I have more faith than I did a few years ago. This is true even of someone of the fame of Kathryn Kuhlman; many more are healed in her services today than there were in the early days of her ministry. We need to grow in faith— even those of us who have seen miracles of healing—in order that God may use us still more.

2) *Redemptive suffering*

Physical healing is not in itself the highest value in the world. At times God uses sickness for a higher purpose. There has been a long history of saints whom God called to suffer redemptively in union with the suffering of Jesus on the Cross. If a person is called to suffer for the sake of the kingdom, or to learn a lesson, or as a punishment, or for some other reason, then clearly he should not pray for healing.

I remember in 1969 when Agnes Sanford was visiting the Trappist Monastery in Dubuque, Iowa, to give some lectures on healing to the Trappists. It was just then that an epidemic of Hong Kong flu struck the monks down. On the second day of the seminar Agnes herself, the renowned expert on healing, came down with flu and had to be taken to the Franciscan Sisters' hospital. But a higher purpose seemed to be served by this as it gave Agnes a chance to talk to many sisters and nurses and, as a result, she was asked to give a workshop to the Franciscan Sisters and in this way, influence a congregation prominent in nursing. St. Paul recognizes the higher purpose that sickness sometimes serves when he says, ". . . Even at the beginning, when that illness *gave me the opportunity to preach the Good News to you,* you never showed the least sign of being revolted or disgusted by my disease that was such a trial to you" (Gal 4:13-14. Italics added).

3) *A false value attached to suffering*

Having said that some suffering is redemptive and is for a higher purpose, we must balance that statement by saying that most sickness does not appear to be redemptive (*cf.* Chapter 5). I have been asked to pray for persons who didn't really want to be free of their suffering; it seemed to me that their sickness was destructive and was not a blessing sent by God, but they had been so conditioned by their training that they felt guilty about asking God to take away their suffering. When you see a person depressed and unhappy under the weight of disease you can be fairly sure that he is not being blessed by God. But if he believes that God has sent the sickness, then he often feels guilty about asking for healing. Nor should we pray for a person contrary to his wishes. Even if someone talks him into praying, there will be a strong subconscious resistance that will block the healing.

4) *Sin*

If there is sin connected with the physical ailment (as was mentioned in Chapter 12)—especially resentment, no healing is likely to take place unless the sin is dealt with first. Once on retreat we prayed for the healing of a sister suffering a truly destructive illness, but nothing happened. The whole group remained in prayer filled with an expectancy that something should happen. Then someone sensed that the disease was hooked up with a real resentment of authority and a number of angry relationships. When this was brought up, the sister concurred that she felt this was truly the case; she asked forgiveness for her rancor. Immediately the healing began to take effect.

5) *Not praying specifically*

Especially in praying for inner healing, it seems important to get to the root cause of emotional suffering, the initial harmful memory. Several times I have prayed for inner healing, knowing that we were praying about the right problem and yet nothing happened. It was only when we went back and found the root incident, which had been forgotten, and prayed for Jesus to enter into that moment and heal it, that the healing

finally took place. Why can't God answer our general prayer
and heal the person without our having to discover all these
specific roots? I know he can and that he does. But experience has also indicated to me (not only my experience but
that of several other people I know who pray extensively for
inner healing) that there are a few people who do not seem
to be healed until you touch specifically on the root incident
that initiated the problem.

I remember, in particular, praying for one woman in Peru
who had a rather common problem: her life was altogether
gray and dull. This boredom had nothing to do with her work;
she was a missionary and liked her work. She knew that some
kind of inner healing was necessary, for Christians should
be filled with an abiding joy and zest for life. But you can't
fake it either. So she spoke at length about all the things in
her life that had caused her sadness. Nothing, however, was
dramatic; all the events of her life seemed ordinary; there were
no great crises. Usually when you listen to a person something turns on when you get to the key to the healing; you feel
in your heart, "That's it; I know that's it." But there was nothing like that. We prayed, then, as best we could, for all the
wounding incidents of the past that she could think of. When
the prayer was over, though, nothing changed. She experienced none of the peace, the joy, the lifting of the spirit that
we have come to associate with a real inner healing.

The next day she came back and honestly admitted that
nothing had happened. So again we (Mrs. Barbara Shlemon
and I) asked if she had thought of anything more we should
pray for (often a person, out of shame, will omit the one incident that is the key to the inner healing). But she could
think of nothing further. So we turned in prayer to the Lord
for the light that would help us. While praying, Barbara
received a mental picture of a young girl, about ten years old,
holding a dog in her arms. Barbara said, "This doesn't make

sense, but let me tell you what I see. . . ." The woman said
that the picture brought something to mind that she had forgotten: as a young girl of ten her best friend was her dog. But
the dog was by then old and her parents took the dog away
from her and "put it out of its misery." As an adult she had
put this out of mind; that's what you do to old dogs. But to
a young girl it was as if her parents, the people she trusted
most in life, had taken away her best friend and killed it. If
you get hurt that painfully when you love a friend and trust
people, maybe it's better not to ever trust or love that much
again. So what she did as a little girl was to turn off, as it
were, the flow of life, so that she would never again be hurt
so deeply. What happened, though, was that she could never
again experience joy or life either. Her protection kept her
from experiencing either the joys or the sorrows of life.

So we prayed for what had happened to a ten-year-old
girl. The next day I received this beautiful note: "Life pours
in. Rejoice! I feel so happy that I want to cry. This is the
first time I have ever wanted to cry for being happy. Parts of
my being are pulling back together."

It's a mystery why God wants some of these prayers to
bring to light the precise incident that needs healing. I believe
that it is because God respects the natural process of psychological healing which requires that incidents which have been
covered up and hidden in the subconscious be *brought to
conscious light* and these be healed by him. He brings his
supernatural light to shine in the darkness so that these incidents may be brought out of the subconscious into the light;
the supernatural reinforces and accelerates the natural process
of psychological healing.

How mistaken we would have been to tell that woman,
after the first prayer, that she should accept the fact that we
had prayed in faith and that she was healed. She was not in
fact healed after the first prayer; only after the Spirit had

revealed to us the specific wound that needed our prayer was she healed.

Not getting to the specific root of sickness is also one of the reasons people do not "keep their healing." Most evangelists teach that the reason why people who have been healed and later regress is that they lack the faith to hold on to their healing. True, that is one possible reason. But another reason for the failure is not in the sick person, but in the minister of healing himself who has only prayed for the healing of symptoms. These symptoms improved as a result of prayer, but because the underlying cause remained, the symptoms later reasserted themselves. Let us not be too hasty in accusing people of lacking faith. "The fault, dear Brutus, is not in the stars but in ourselves that we are underlings."[1]

6) *Faulty diagnosis*

Just as in medicine doctors often fail in diagnosing diseases and consequently fail to prescribe the right medicine and treatment, so the minister of healing, if he lacks discernment, is bound to fail from time to time.

To be specific, the most common failures I have found are:

a) praying for *physical* healing, when *inner* healing was the basic need;

b) praying for *deliverance* from evil spirits, when *inner* healing was the real need;

c) praying for *inner healing* when *deliverance* was the real need.

For example, our team prayed for a young woman in Peru for inner healing for depression. She had known no father and had a series of traumatic sexual episodes in her childhood,

---

1. William Shakespeare, *Julius Caesar*.

so it seemed clear that inner healing was needed. But after prayer she remained as depressed as ever. Upon further inquiry we discovered that her mother had called in a witch doctor to cure her of an abdominal infection. This doctor had prayed over her and given her a potion; immediately afterwards she fell to the floor in a trance and woke up cured. We knew then that deliverance was needed, and that we had missed it. When three priests prayed for her deliverance she was freed. The inner healing was free to take place and the depression lifted. In this instance, praying for inner healing was really needed, but initially we missed the fact that deliverance was also necessary. We had failed to make the complete diagnosis, the full discernment.

At another time a leader of a prayer group decided to quit smoking. He wasn't able to do this by willpower (the first type of healing: repentance). So friends prayed for him for healing of his habit (the third type of healing) and others prayed for his deliverance (the fourth type of healing). None of these prayers seemed to help; he just kept on lighting up cigarettes. The response of the prayer group leaders was to tell him that he was failing to "claim his healing." So his next step was to claim his healing. Which he did; and still he went on smoking.

Some months later, hearing a talk on inner healing, he realized that his smoking habit was related to his teen years when smoking represented to him freedom and adulthood. In particular, it symbolized the freedom he needed from the overcontrolling authority of his father. Consequently, the key to his being freed of his smoking habit was connected with his need for inner healing and not to any of the other kinds of healing that his friends had prayed for. When they told him that he had been healed, they were simply wrong; his relation with his father needed to be healed, and God was not about to heal the surface problem (smoking) until the more basic need was taken care of. God's withholding the healing was not a punishment but, rather, a mercy—the painful embarrassment of smoking in front of people who had prayed for his deliverance gave him the motivation to search deeper until he found the deepest healing that God had in store for him.

Like good doctors we need to discern what is the cause behind those symptoms we can see. Otherwise, we simply don't know how best to pray. Often we are just guessing about the correct diagnosis. No wonder people are not always healed.

7) *Refusal to see medicine as a way God heals*

As I have made clear elsewhere I firmly believe that physicians and medicines are the instruments that God ordinarily uses to bring about healing. This is what most people believe and nothing should have to be said in defense of medicine. The book of Sirach (Ecclesiasticus) explicitly says that after we pray we should let the doctor take over and "do not let him leave you, for you need him. Sometimes success is in their hands, since they in turn will beseech the Lord to grant them the grace to relieve and to heal, that life may be saved" (38: 12-14).

In spite of God's revelation, coupled with common sense, we still keep hearing about ministers of healing who persist in setting up prayer (the "supernatural") in opposition to medicine (the "natural"). In the past year several persons are reported to have died of diabetes because parents or ministers encouraged them to stop taking their insulin as a sign of faith. Then the patients died. "By their fruits you will know them": such actions are simply false doctrine unless a given person is genuinely inspired by God to rely solely on prayer and not to see a doctor.

As we rediscover the charisms of the Spirit in our day,

there also is a tendency of some enthusiasts to misunderstand and oversimplify their operation; healing is no exception—witness the history of the Pentecostal movement:

> In the early years of the movement, pentecostals felt that it was a sin to take medicine or to visit the doctor. One Pentecostal preacher, F. M. Britton, once refused medical aid for one of his sons, and reported later that he "died without drugs." Some years later his wife also died after "refusing medicine." Although threatened with jail for refusing medical attention for his family, Britton never wavered in his views. . . . Rather than an exception, these cases were the rule for many early pentecostals. . . .[2]

> One of the first schisms caused by personality clashes occurred in the Georgia Conferences of the Pentecostal Holiness Church in 1920, resulting in the organization of the "Congregational Holiness Church." The controversy producing this schism began over the doctrine of divine healing. Two ministers, Watson Sorrow and High Bowling, held a view that varied from the generally accepted ideas of the church at the time. The faction led by Sorrow and Bowling held that it was not sinful to use remedies and medicines to aid in the healing of sickness. Another faction led by F. M. Britton and G. F. Taylor held that "the provision in the Atonement for the healing of the body was all-sufficient, and that it was unnecessary to supplement any human means to assist God in effecting a cure. . . ."

> In 1920, events came to a head in a trial which resulted in the expulsion of Sorrow and Bowling from the church.[3]

---

2. Vinson Synan, *The Holiness-Pentecostal Movement in the United States,* p. 189. Used by permission.
3. *Ibid.,* p. 192-193.

Time after time enthusiasts set into opposition the world that God has created with the "supernatural." This false opposition further damages suffering human beings and sets up a needless controversy with scientists that results in mutual suspicion between religion and science.

8) *Not using the natural means of preserving health*

Although most of us have a high estimation of the medical profession many of us neglect the ordinary means of keeping balance in our lives. If we neglect these we should not be surprised if we fall sick and prayer does not cure us. I find in my own life that if a cold or some other ailment begins when I am needed to give a retreat, prayer always seems to cure the ailment. But if I have been working too hard and an open time in my schedule is available, the cold may run its ordinary course, rather than being immediately cured by prayer. It's as if the body needs a rest and God is saying through these circumstances, "Put more balance in your life. Unless you take ordinary care of yourself do not expect to be cured of your sickness through extraordinary means. I want you to learn to keep your life in balance."

Similarly, in more serious illnesses, if there is some natural factor underlying the illness that the patient should attend to, he cannot expect prayer to cure him. He should be doing something about putting his life in order. If I have headaches, because I worry too much, or if I suffer from hypertension because I work up to my breaking point, I need to change my life before healing will take place.

9) *Now is not the time*

For whatever reason there often seems to be the right time for a healing to take place. Christ urges us, like the importunate widow, to continue on in prayer if at first nothing happens. There seem to be four basic time sequences in praying for healing:

a) Some healings are *instantaneous.*
b) In some healings there is *a delay.* (I have prayed for a person on Saturday whose healing occurred on the following Monday.)
c) Some healings occur in a process, *gradually.*
d) Others *do not seem to occur,* at least on the physical level, at all.

We need not be disappointed, then, if there appears to be no immediate answer to prayer for healing. Perhaps now is not the time.

10) *A different person is to be the instrument of healing*

Perhaps I am not the one who has the discernment to pray for this particular person. Maybe I don't relate humanly to him, maybe I don't have enough faith, maybe I don't have a ministry in this particular area of healing: these are some of the reasons why I am not the minister of healing for everyone who is sick. At times, I must be ready to let someone else take over and do the praying. This willingness to let God choose the right instrument of healing was most clearly pointed out to me several years ago when I was giving a retreat.

On that retreat I spent several hours praying for a woman's deliverance and wasn't able to get very far with it, in spite of a great expenditure of time and effort. So I long-distanced my friend, Bob Cavnar, who I felt would have a real ministry to the woman I had been praying for. He was able to give the needed help. In turn, he and his group were praying for a man and one of the group seemed to receive a vision of the man stuck full of nails with a spike through his heart. These nails and the spike were being loosened by their prayer but they were not coming out. Their discernment in prayer was that, in four days' time, the nails and spikes would be removed, as it were, by a prayer for inner healing. At the time they did not know that I would be passing through that city in four days' time. In four days' time their prophecy was fulfilled when I prayed for his healing. In the one instance then I was not the right minister to finish the healing, but Bob Cavnar was; in the other instance, I was to finish the healing that his prayer had begun.

It is only when God calls us to be his instruments of healing that our prayer will be successful. Jesus is the one who heals and he uses different people at different times. In short, I need to be humble enough to know that sometimes I am not the one; I need to pray for discernment to know where to send the sick person for help, rather than to feel guilty if I am not always able to help.

11) *The social environment prevents healing from taking place*

Since we are meant to live in a community of love, some of the healing we need will not take place until our relationships and our society are healed. Earlier in the book (Chapter 16) is Flor's testimony about how her daughter, Maria, was not healed, even after several prayers, until Flor, the mother, was herself healed. Hatred and bad relationships cause all kinds of sickness and that sickness usually remains until the root cause is removed. When a married person suffering from depression or anxiety asks for healing and it is clear that part of the problem is caused by a tense relationship in the home, prayer can only deal with part of the problem; if a disturbed child is brought by its mother for healing, you know that you are only dealing with part of the problem until the entire family is brought into a more harmonious relationship. Much sickness in our society is caused by wounded relationships and will only be healed when the larger relationships are healed, and until we have Christian communities where people can be loved into wholeness.

I do not expect that most readers will want to remember all these reasons why people are not healed. The key thing for us to know, deep down where it affects our attitudes, is that there is more than one reason why people are not healed: lack of faith is not the only reason, and ministers of healing who imply that it is are simply leading people into all kinds of false guilt. They also lead intelligent, honest people to question the whole concept of healing when they honestly question why so many people are not healed—including people who seem to have utmost faith in prayer, and yet are not healed.

The healing ministry is perhaps the most dramatic, and one of the most beautiful demonstrations of God's love for us. There is no need to overstate the case or to lead the scientific community to disparage it. If we think we have all the answers we are shut off from God's light. Healing is a mystery of God's love.

Whom does he want to heal? When? Through whom?

You should be open to being used for healing, or for not being used. Wait upon God's wisdom in all simplicity, like a child. We face the mystery of God's providence.

19

Medicine and Healing

SOMETIMES IT HAPPENS that persons asking for healing receive an inspiration to stop taking their medicine or to act as though their sickness were cured even though the symptoms and pain still remain. That was the case of the Sister (cf. Chapter 9) who asked the retreat group to pray for the cure of her endometriosis, the only medical cure for which is surgery. I have kept in touch with her, so I know that this healing has lasted for three years since the retreat took place. Her inspiration to stop taking her medication has proven out in its effect.

Such faith experiences that pass beyond ordinary medical remedies do happen often enough. They have, unfortunately, led some persons to generalize and to separate medical healing from prayer for healing, as though a patient should always abandon the ordinary human means of consulting doctors or taking medicine. "Do you have faith in this prayer or not?" is the question that some ministers of healing pose to the sick who come to them for prayer. The sequel, after praying for healing, is: "Now that we have prayed, believe that your prayer has been answered, that you are now healed. You can disregard any symptoms you may still have. And, as a sign of faith, stop taking your medicine." We have spoken about this in Chapter 8, "The Faith to Be Healed," but it should be pointed out here that an artificial opposition between medicine and prayer has been set up in this way by a few faith healers who have overgeneralized from their genuine experiences.

It is not a fair generalization to say that, because some people receive real inspirations from God either to stop taking their medication or to disregard their symptoms, this is the way God works in all cases. God not only works directly and miraculously through prayer but he is also at work in all nature and in all human intelligence, provided it is subject (even unconsciously) to him. To say that God inspires some people to stop taking their medicine, and even to disregard their symptoms, is according to my experience, true. But to say that this is the way he always works leads some people into a serious problem of faith: they are torn between believing in their doctors or in someone who claims to represent the mind of God. They are forced to make a false choice: between faith (not taking the medicine, and not accepting the appearance of disease symptoms) and science (the doctor's judgment according to what he sees before him). Such theories of healing—which, in effect, oppose faith and medicine —also lead to discrediting the entire ministry of healing, in the view of those doctors and psychiatrists who have run into problems with patients who have gotten worse after being told at healing sessions to disregard their physicians' orders. If a physician's first introduction to prayer for healing comes through patients like these who refuse his suggestions, the chances are he will write off all healing prayer as "faith healing" and quackery.

In consequence, we have almost contradictory attitudes

among Christians: some have little faith in prayer for healing, coupled with a healthy respect for the medical profession; other Christians have a newly discovered faith in God's ability to heal. But in ruling the medical profession out of God's healing plan, they, in effect, drive away those very people who have devoted their lives to healing as a profession, the doctors and nurses who could most profit by discovering the power of praying for the sick.

Since the bible is the basis of these claims for faith it is important to see the high respect the author of the Book of Sirach (Ecclesiasticus) pays to the medical profession at a time (second century B.C.) when medicine was in its infancy and was little more than the art of the apothecary:

> Hold the physician in honor, for he is essential
> to you, and God it was who established his profession.
> From God the doctor has his wisdom, and the king
>   provides for his sustenance.
> His knowledge makes the doctor distinguished,
>   and gives him access to those in authority.
> God makes the earth yield healing herbs
>   which the prudent man should not neglect;
> Was not the water sweetened by a twig
>   that men might learn his power?
> He endows men with the knowledge
>   to glory in his mighty works,
> Through which the doctor eases pain
>   and the druggist prepares his medicines;
> Thus God's creative work continues without cease
>   in its efficacy on the surface of the earth.
> My son, when you are ill, delay not,
>   but pray to God, who will heal you:
> Flee wickedness; let your hands be just,
>   cleanse your heart of every sin;

Offer your sweet-smelling oblation and petition,
    a rich offering according to your means.
Then give the doctor his place
    lest he leave; for you need him too.
There are times that give him an advantage,
    and he too beseeches God
That his diagnosis may be correct
    and his treatment bring about a cure.
He who is a sinner toward his Maker
    will be defiant toward the doctor (Sir 38:1-15).[1]

There we have it all: a belief in prayer for healing as well as a recognition that God cures likewise through the skill of the doctor and through medicine. Medicine and prayer are not opposed, but the doctor, the nurse and the person with the gift of healing prayer all together form God's healing team.

In our prayer group in St. Louis we are privileged to have several doctors who pray for their patients before, during and after operations. The beautiful thing is that they, too, have seen cures wrought through prayer when they came to the limits of their medical art.

At other times, doctors, relatives or friends have asked us to visit the hospital and pray for patients. Some then underwent successful operations; others were not even operated on, for the growth disappeared or the condition was cleared up beforehand. The very first person I remember the prayer group in St. Louis praying for was a young sister who was scheduled for an operation for nodules on her vocal chords.

1. This Book of Sirach (or Ecclesiasticus) is not contained in many Protestant versions of the bible, but is only listed among the Apocrypha. I became aware of this problem when I quoted the passage to some 500 people on a retreat in Texas; their consternation soon became evident as they kept flipping through their bibles but couldn't find the passage. Quotation from The New American Bible translation.

When the doctors examined her larynx before beginning the operation, they found that the nodules had disappeared.

The following story is typical of what we have come to see as the ordinary working together of medicine and prayer in God's providence:

> I underwent surgery on March 13, 1972. A week later, on the 20th, I was told that barium sulfate was leaking at the juncture of the parts of the colon that had been sewn together. If mother nature did not heal it within two or three days, a temporary colostomy would be required which, in effect, meant two more surgical operations. The next evening, Father F.M. and M.D.R. stopped to see me. After a quiet visit of about 20 minutes we prayed together for about 10 minutes. Later, shortly after 1 a.m., I felt that Father's request that "all channels be open" had been heard and I was certain that I would be all right. About 7 a.m. the surgeon told me that I was doing wonderfully well and that he was going to change my diet from liquid to a regular diet. (He skipped a few in-between kinds of diet.) There was no further talk of surgery. Before being dismissed, I asked one of the surgical residents how they knew I was all right. He said, "Your temperature suddenly dropped to normal. Your white count also suddenly dropped to normal. You remember we also took another X-ray which showed that the barium had been cleaned out of your system." How that barium, seen in an earlier X-ray, got back into the colon and out of my system is still a mystery to me. I praise and thank the Lord for this healing. (From Father Larry Walsh, S.J., St. Therese Church, Parkville, Mo.)

It seems, then, that to set up any opposition between prayer for healing and medicine is unscriptural as well as contrary to common sense. Sometimes God cures directly through prayer; at other times through nature, assisted by doctors who have learned how the body can be assisted to throw off the sickness that oppresses it. As Paul Tournier put it:

> Sometimes what happens is that a patient's relatives refuse, for religious reasons, to entrust him to technical medical care, claiming that if he is converted he will be healed without such treatment. It can only harm a patient to realize that instead of being properly treated, his sufferings are being made use of as a means of bringing him forcibly to accept the doctrines that someone wishes to impose upon him. Nothing is more surely calculated to turn him away from the faith. . . .
>
> We have something better to do than to enter into controversies between partisans of religion and those of science. To do so is to perpetuate the awful habit of thinking of faith as being opposed to technology. People are suffering. Medicine is a very difficult art. There are not too many of us persons of good will to work together to heal the sick.[2]

To some readers this may all seem obvious; however, it does need to be said, because there are those who pray for patients and, as a general rule, tell them to stop taking their medicine and to disregard their symptoms. If an individual person has a genuine inspiration from God to do this, fine, but if this disregard for ordinary channels of healing is set up as a general faith principle I cannot imagine its doing more than sowing confusion, self-condemnation in the patients not cured,

---

2. *The Person Reborn*, p. 10. Copyright © 1966 by Paul Tournier. Reprinted by permission of Harper & Row, Publishers, Inc.

and opposition to healing prayer on the part of the medical profession.

Since the Lord often teaches us through experience, one incident stands out especially as teaching me about the inter-relation of prayer and medical care. It happened in Houston where I was visiting the home of my good friends, Harry and Ruth. At dinner I shared with their family what I had been learning about the healing ministry. At the end of the evening, as I was about to leave they asked me if I would pray for their son, Randy, who was suffering a great deal from attacks of asthma. So, before I left we gathered the whole family around Randy and prayed for him that the Lord would cure him of his asthma. The next day I left Houston and it was a whole year before I was again in Houston and had a chance to visit Harry and Ruth again. I had forgotten all about Randy, but while we were at dinner Harry asked if he had ever written to tell me what had happened. Then the entire family began laughing—which I couldn't understand. Then they explained what happened: when I had left, after praying, Randy went through the worst asthma attack of his entire life. In fact, the attack was so severe that they had to make an emergency phone call to a doctor who lived down the street from them. This doctor, who was not Randy's regular doctor, came right over and gave him some medication to quiet the attack until morning. Then they took Randy over to their neighbor's office in the morning where they ran him through some tests and came up with a new diagnosis which, in turn, resulted in different treatment which effectively took care of his asthma.

The prayer, then, had been answered in a way helpful to my humility: Randy got worse. But the prayer was answered: his getting worse resulted in his getting another doctor, whom they wouldn't otherwise have consulted, who, in turn, dis-covered the correct diagnosis which eventually worked the cure. It was as if the effect of our prayer was to find the right doctor through whom God wanted to cure Randy.

PRAYER AND PSYCHIATRY

A similar relationship should exist between prayer for inner healing and counseling, psychology and psychiatry. I think it is probably true to say that psychiatry is longer on analysis of problems than it is on cures, but what we know through the study of psychology can be a great help in knowing precisely *what to pray for*. It is true, of course, that God can move beyond human knowledge and help people know what to pray for through the gift of discernment. Nevertheless, I have ordinarily found that the knowledge born of study and experience—knowing what to look for, say, when a person is mentally depressed—knowing what the danger signs are—can be a great help in prayer. Just as we cannot give up ordinary study in other areas of life, so we cannot expect to be used for a ministry of inner healing, if we do not cooperate by learning what we can of the workings of the human mind and the subconscious. Yet, here again, I find that some persons who pray for healing evince a real fear of psychology; they often treat it as unnecessary, if not actually dangerous. Perhaps it has been the fear of Freud and other psychological innovators who have, on occasion, attacked traditional Christian morality, which has made Christians fear their genuine discoveries. At any rate, I have found frequently an antipathy toward the study of psychology among Christians who practice a ministry of healing or deliverance (exorcism).

The kind of attitude that would scrap psychology as useless, if not harmful, is typified by such statements as:

To put the issue simply: the scriptures plainly speak of both organically based problems as well as those problems that stem from sinful attitudes and behavior; but where in all of God's Word is there so much as a trace of any third source of problems which might approximate the modern concept of "mental illness"? Clearly the burden of proof lies with those who loudly affirm the existence of mental illness or disease but fail to demonstrate biblically that it exists.[3]

Rogerianism, therefore, must be rejected *in toto*. Every remnant of this humanistic system exalting man as autonomous must be eradicated.[4]

Depressed persons whose symptoms fail to show any sign of a biochemical root should be counseled on the assumption that they are depressed by guilt.[5]

Such a completely condemnatory attitude toward the knowledge discovered about man by psychology is based upon a biblicism that holds that there is nothing worthwhile discovered about man which is not already in the bible.[6] The answer is again, I suggest, that we must learn to distinguish, as do Karl Stern (*The Third Revolution*) and Paul Tournier (*The Person Reborn*), between the true discoveries of psy-

3. Jay Adams, *Competent to Counsel* (Grand Rapids: Baker Book House, 1970), p. 29. Used by permission of Presbyterian and Reformed Publishing Co.
4. *Ibid.*, p. 103.
5. *Ibid.*, p. 126.
6. This kind of controversy is reminiscent of the biblical controversies experienced earlier in this century in the Roman Catholic Church. As early as 1893 Pope Leo XIII, in the encyclical, *Providentissimus Deus,* stated that in describing the world of physical nature, the sacred authors did not formally intend to teach natural science. God spoke to men in the way they could understand—a way to which they were accustomed. But there are many persons in the ministry of healing, deeply devoted to the bible, who base their knowledge of psychology almost solely on what they know from the bible and, with a fundamentalist interpretation, they look upon any knowledge of man not found in scripture as at best useless and, at worst, dangerous.

chology and those which are contrary to Christianity. The basic discoveries of psychology help us to understand the problems of man and often suggest how to cope with them. The gospel indicates how we can bring God's healing power to bear upon these problems. Psychology helps to bring problems to the light for what they are; then once they are brought to the light, we can use God's healing power to cure them.

Those of us who pray for inner healing should know something about the intricacies of the human mind if we are really going to help the people we pray for. If we don't know, for instance, how crucial the time of our childhood is—especially the time between eight and 18 months—we are not likely to consider the time of childhood seriously, when we counsel with a person who has come and wants to pray about some chronic emotional problem.

Paul Tournier is a prime example of a practicing psychiatrist who believes in the primacy of grace and prayer. For those interested in investigating the relationship between psychology and healing I highly recommend Dr. Tournier's book, *The Person Reborn,* in which he gives examples of the need for science and faith to work together:

> A young student comes to see me in the throes of a psychological crisis. He has lost interest in everything, is becoming unsociable, and finds it impossible to concentrate on his work. We use technical methods in order to throw light on the situation. They reveal a crisis of retarded adolescence in a young man who has remained morally dependent upon his parents. But he is soon telling me that he is conscious that in reality he is going through a religious crisis behind the screen of his psychological crisis. The reason why he has been unable to detach himself from his parents is that he had no strength of personality,

and he feels the emptiness of an impersonal religious attitude, which he had inherited from his family tradition. . . . A case such as this seems to me to illustrate clearly the necessary relationship between the technique of psychology and the cure of souls. Everybody has complexes, and comes to some sort of terms with them. When they begin to cause real suffering, this is because they are standing in the way of the realization of a person's profoundest aspirations. Such aspirations are always religious in kind—taking the word in a nonformal sense. Technical means must then be used to break up these complexes. . . .

Technology of itself is negative. "Psychoanalysis," says a letter from a patient who herself has undergone it, "reveals evil, with its hundred faces and its thousand tricks. But where is good?" . . . I do not think that analysts will contradict me if I maintain that, strictly speaking, no problem is ever resolved. We bring them out into the daylight in order to be honest about them. . . . A repressed tendency poisons the mind and disturbs its functioning. On the other hand, the always humbling process of bringing it out into the light opens the door to a real experience of God's grace, even if no word of religion has been uttered by doctor or patient.

People come to me for my help in "solving" their problems. No one knows better than I do that all human effort is powerless to solve any problem. In fact, when I try to understand their difficulties, I discover nothing but insoluble vicious circles. Faith is needed to experience God's grace, and God's grace is needed in order to find faith. . . .

Our patients often tell us how unjustly hurt they feel when they are plied with exhortations and advice: "You only have to believe. All you need is willpower. Just love others and forget yourself. It's only a matter of confidence." Psychology cures us of this oversimplified view of personal problems. It shows us that they are tenacious and terribly complicated. And these same people who, from the security of their faith and health, are so free with their "all you need is . . ." (which always means: "all you need is to do as I do") would soon discover, if they themselves were assailed by doubt and depression, that things are not so simple. . . .

I believe that problems can be dissolved by grace, like a mist is dissipated by the sunshine. . . . In the climate of faith, a life that has seemed to be nothing but a tangle of problems looks quite different. The problems disappear without anyone actually solving them. This process of dissolution is all the more definite if one does not try to find human solutions, but relies rather upon God's grace. . . .

This is the way that, in my experience, technology and faith work together. Psychoanalysis explores the problems in order to bring them out into the daylight. Grace dissolves them without our ever knowing exactly how.[7]

In an earlier chapter we have shown how, through prayer for inner healing, God's love can be brought to bear upon our problems to heal them. The arts of medicine, counseling and psychiatry are ordinary ways in which God can work to create wholeness in broken man through freeing the forces of nature (which he also has created) to move toward health. Unless there is some obstacle, nature (man's body, mind, emotions) moves toward health; the doctor or counselor works to uncover these obstacles whether they be a virus or a painful past, in order that the patient might grow toward that same health

---

7. *The Person Reborn*, pp. 34-37 *passim*.

for which we pray. The ideal, it seems to me, would be when we reach a time when doctors, counselors and psychiatrists would—as some already do—pray for the patients that God might do what they cannot do, or even that God might perform that same kind of cure that medical science can provide, but in a more perfect, more speedy, and less expensive way.

Sometimes God works through nature and the skill of doctors; sometimes he works directly through prayer and sometimes through both, but always there should be cooperation, mutual respect and an admiration for the variety of ways in which God manifests his glory.

20

Sacraments and Healing

SINCE THE SACRAMENTS are particularly chosen channels of God's saving power it is little wonder that they are channels of healing, which is Christ's power to save applied to every area of human life. Three sacraments, Anointing of the Sick, Penance, and the Eucharist are specifically directed toward healing, while a fourth, Holy Orders, empowers the priest to heal the sick. In addition, I have seen healing connected with Baptism and with prayer for the renewal of Marriage. So I have seen healing in its connection with six of the sacraments; nor would I be surprised if healing, at least in its broader aspect of healing the whole man, were connected with Confirmation. To see how the power of the sacraments is being renewed, let us first take a look at those which are most clearly ordered toward healing.

1. ANOINTING OF THE SICK

As I noted in the Preface, a startling transformation has just come about in this sacrament: with the renewal of the liturgy, the sacrament's purpose is now once again declared to be healing. The official teaching of the Roman Catholic Church is now closely related to the basic ideas proposed in this book. The new sacramental form of Anointing emphasizes healing of the whole man, rather than stressing forgiveness of sin, as it used to:

> Through this holy anointing and his great love for you may the Lord help you by the power of his Holy Spirit.
> R. Amen.

> May the Lord who freed you from sin heal you and extend his saving grace to you.
> R. Amen.[2]

The new prayer for blessing the oil to be used is even more explicit:

> Lord God, all-comforting Father, you brought healing to the sick through your Son Jesus Christ. Hear us as we pray to you in faith, and send the Holy Spirit, the Comforter, from heaven upon this oil, which nature has provided to serve the needs of men.
>
> May your blessing come upon all who are anointed with this oil, that *they may be freed from pain, illness, and disease and made well again in body, mind, and soul.*

---

1. Unless otherwise noted the source of information concerning the Anointing of the Sick is the article by J. P. McClain on "Anointing of the Sick" in the *New Catholic Encyclopedia*, Vol. I (New York: McGraw-Hill, 1967).
2. Study Text II: *Anointing and Pastoral Care of the Sick*, published by the Bishops' Committee on the Liturgy (Washington, D.C.: U.S. Catholic Conference, 1973), p. 9.

Father, may this oil, which you have blessed for our
use, produce its healing effect, in the name of our Lord
Jesus Christ.[3]

This restoration of what has been called the "most neglected of sacraments,"[4] means that a sacrament which, in
recent centuries, was used primarily to prepare a person for
death and only secondarily and conditionally, to lead to healing, has been changed so that its primary purpose is now to
heal the whole man who is suffering the special trial of sickness. As Pope Paul VI writes: "We thought fit to modify the
sacramental formula in such a way that, in view of the words
of James, the effects of the sacrament might be fully expressed."[5]

The important changes in the rite of Anointing that go to
implement its purpose of healing are:

1) No longer is it to be called *Extreme Unction* or the Last
Rites, but is to be called *Anointing of the Sick.* (This change
was effected in the Second Vatican Council *Constitution on
the Liturgy,* No. 73.)

2) The essential form of the sacrament has been changed,
as stated above, to emphasize *healing,* whereas the previous
form stressed *forgiveness of sin* ("May the Lord forgive you
by this holy anointing whatever sins you have committed").
The previous form of Anointing stressed solely the penitential
aspect, and failed to mention any healing other than forgiveness of sins.[6]

3) The sacrament is to be administered to those who are
seriously ill, rather than merely to those who are in *danger of*

---

3. *Ibid.,* p. 22.
4. *Ibid.,* p. 7.
5. *Ibid.,* p. 5, quoting Apostolic Constitution *Sacram Unctionem.*
6. *Ibid.,* p. 9. Other prayers in the rite mentioned healing, but not
the essential form itself.

death.[7] There is no longer any mention of death as a condition for the reception of Anointing. This change is specially noteworthy because according to canon law, the disciplinary law of the Latin Church, Extreme Unction could formerly be ministered only to those sick who were in danger of death—and this was binding, for licitness, under pain of serious sin (Canon 940.1).

4) Ideally the Anointing is to be a *communal* prayer, involving the patient's family, doctor, nurses and other members of the people of God.[8] This is in contrast to the way Extreme Unction was usually ministered—in private because of its connection with the confession of sin. Now anointing is a communal celebration involving the local, caring community of the Church.

There are other changes, too: the oil may be blessed by the priest, if necessary, and not just by the bishop; vegetable oil other than olive oil can be used where olive oil is hard to come by; and the forehead and hands are anointed rather than all five senses (they used to be anointed because of the sins the senses had led to). But the main change is from a sacrament for the dying, to prepare them for immediate entrance to glory, to a sacrament for the sick to fortify and to heal the person in whatever way is necessary, applying Christ's saving grace to the special human weakness and trial which is sickness.

Understanding the history of these changes will help us understand not only the sacrament of Anointing but also what has happened to the whole idea of healing in the Catholic Church, leading to its renewal in our day.

---

7. *Ibid.,* p. 8.
8. *Ibid.,* p. 11.

History of Anointing

The scriptural sources for Anointing are Mark 6:13:

> So they set off to preach repentance; and they cast out
> many devils, and anointed many sick people with oil and
> cured them.[9]

and the celebrated passage of James 5:14-15:

> If one of you is ill, he should send for the elders of the
> church and they must anoint him with oil in the name of
> the Lord and pray over him. The prayer of faith will save
> the sick man and the Lord will raise him up again; and
> if he has committed any sins, he will be forgiven.

"Will save," "will raise him up," and "will be forgiven,"
are the three key verbs here that indicate the effect of the
anointing. The first, "save," in the original Greek, is a verb
that can mean either healing of the spirit (as does our "save")
or healing in the sense of restoration to physical health. But
in the context of sickness, death, or their danger, it always, in
New Testament usage, refers to physical healing.

The second verb, "raise him up," clearly refers to healing
and is the verb often used in Mark to refer to the healings
worked by Jesus.

"Will be forgiven" is the third effect and refers to sin.
This effect is conditional ("if he has committed any sins")
and the Greek word here used for sins implies *grave* sins.

The intended effect of the anointing seems then to be healing of the man's sickness, the healing of the whole man, including his sins if need be. The direct intention is healing of
the sickness, with forgiveness of sins as the conditional effect.

9. In this brief passage three of the four kinds of healing developed
in this book are mentioned.

How then did this come to be reversed so that healing came to be regarded as the conditional, secondary effect?

The first stage took place when healing began to drop out of the ordinary experience of the Church in the third and fourth centuries. This was emphasized when the Church's official Latin translation of the bible, the Vulgate, obscured the meaning of the Epistle of James. St. Jerome in his famous translation (written c. 400 A.D.) used the Latin theological word *salvo* ("save") to translate both "save" and "raise up" in James 5:14. In this way, the Church's attention was turned away from healing itself to focus on what healing represented symbolically. Since the Vulgate was the only official translation used for some 1,500 years its effects on an understanding of the Anointing of the Sick were considerable.

In the early Christian Church there are not many clear references to the practice of anointing. But the references we have indicate that the oil was regarded as of key importance. In the early fifth century, for instance, a letter of Innocent I indicates that the oil must be blessed by a bishop. It was then taken home by the people who used it whenever anyone in the home was sick. There were two kinds of anointing: one performed by the sick person himself or by relatives or friends, and another—connected with Penance—conferred by the bishop or priests. The prayer for the blessing of oil asks God to give it a curative power so that it becomes a means of removing every sickness and disease for the soundness of soul, body and spirit, and for perfect well-being (*The Euchologian* of Serapion, d. after 362). In those days it was clear that the anointing with oil was for healing and could be administered by the laity. Even at a later date St. Genevieve used to anoint the sick for whom she cared; one day she ran out of oil and was distressed because there was no bishop around to bless it. The oil seems to have been regarded as a permanent sacrament, much like the Eucharist is today, so its preparation (by a bishop) could be separated from its ministration (sometimes by a layman).

Then, in the Carolingian reform of liturgy (c. 815) in the Frankish kingdom, lay anointing was suppressed, as part of a movement aimed at renewal of priestly ministry. A further change in the organization of the ritual (with the praiseworthy purpose of stamping out abuses) was to place the Anointing immediately after the rite of deathbed Penance. This resulted in confusing and connecting Anointing with the Last Rites.[10] As a result, in the 12th century the original order of administering sacraments had been changed from Penance, Anointing and Viaticum, to Penance, Viaticum and Anointing.[11] No one spoke of Extreme Unction until Peter Lombard first used the term in the middle of the 12th century!

It was in the 12th century, in the beginnings of the Scholastic era that the real change of emphasis in the Anointing of the Sick took place. The Scholastics took a great interest in defining the sacraments and determining how many there were. They concluded that there were seven and that they had a) a *spiritual* effect which b) was *always produced* ex opere operato. If that was the case the theologians next questioned how physical healing could be the primary effect of this sacrament, because physical healing is not primarily "spiritual," nor does it always happen when the sick person is anointed. Consequently, a dispute developed between two schools of thought:

a) the first school preserved the earlier view: Anointing

---

10. Study Text II: *Anointing and Pastoral Care of the Sick*, p. 20.
11. On Jan. 1, 1974, Pope Paul VI reversed a thousand years' trend by restoring the original order of administering these sacraments in the Apostolic Constitution *Sacram Unctionem*. Penance is now clearly to forgive sin, Anointing to strengthen and heal sickness as it affects the whole man, while Viaticum (Holy Communion) is to unite the sick person as intimately as possible with Jesus Christ.

is the sacrament of the sick. Its purpose is the cure of the body, although its more noble effect is the forgiveness of sin (Hugh of St. Victor, Pope Alexander III, and William of Auxerre espoused this traditional view);

b) the second school, stressing the definition of a sacrament, saw its purpose as mainly spiritual, one of forgiveness of sin. They saw it as the sacrament of the dying. This view was adapted by Peter Lombard (d. 1160), who was followed by St. Albert the Great (d. 1280), St. Thomas Aquinas (d. 1274), St. Bonaventure (d. 1274) and Duns Scotus (d. 1308). In consequence, the influential Dominican and Franciscan schools of theology came to hold that the sick person was only to be anointed when death was imminent and recovery was despaired of.

Problems still remained, the main one being a vital one: what is the purpose of this sacrament? If its purpose has to do with forgiveness of sins for the dying, then why isn't the sacrament of Penance appropriate and sufficient? If its purpose is immediate union with God, then the Eucharist (Viaticum) should be appropriate and sufficient. Once this school had taken away healing as the purpose of Anointing, it had to come up with a purpose that all theologians could agree upon. There were a wide range of opinions, but the purpose of Anointing that finally came to prevail was that it was to serve as preparation for immediate enjoyment of the beatific vision through removing the last effects of sin. This again reinforced the practice of putting it off until the moment of death. On the human level another reason for the ordinary man to put off receiving Extreme Unction was that one of the penances often enjoined by the confessor at the deathbed was never again to enjoy marriage should recovery happen to ensue.

By the time of the Council of Trent in the 16th century the "spiritual" view of Extreme Unction had won the field and the first draft of the document on Extreme Unction stated that it should be only administered to those "who are in their final struggle and have come to grips with death." But, the Council Fathers providentially changed this to read, "This anointing is to be used for the sick, but especially for those who are so dangerously ill as to seem at the point of departing this life" (*Denziger*, 1698). This, then, was an improvement over the prevailing medieval view, but was not the primitive one. Trent did not demand the danger of death as a condition for validity, even though this was discussed.[12]

After Trent there was a gradual relaxation in interpreting what "danger of death" meant until the time of the Second Vatican Council when it was once again titled the Anointing of the Sick and a determination was made to restudy and renew the sacrament—a renewal finally accomplished in the new rite for Anointing which went into effect January 1, 1974.

This welcome return to the original purpose of the Anointing of the Sick has come rather suddenly. Even the recent theological work *Sacramentum Mundi* states that:

This sacramental anointing of the sick today holds little pastoral appeal. Sick people send for the doctor, not for the priest. Only when medical science and skill fail, do they ask for the sacrament of the sick. This sacrament is considered as the herald of death, and people keep away from it as long as possible. Even when presented as the sacrament of the sick, if not of healing, rather than as the

---

12. As an example of different understandings of the Anointing it is significant to note that the Greek Orthodox Church, far from holding that the sacrament was only to be ministered to the dying or to the seriously ill, held that it was to be ministered to the *healthy* as a preventive against illness.

sacrament of the dying, people find it hard to appreciate
its precise role in the Christian life. . . .[13]

It seems to me that the reason the contemporary Christian
finds it so hard to understand this sacrament is precisely
because the understanding of prayer for healing has dropped
out of the experience of most Christians. The Roman Catholic
Church has now redirected our attention to the ancient tradition which sees the purpose of Anointing as being the healing of the whole person:

> . . . As a result, the inward anointing with the Holy Spirit
> will either remove the outward cause of this danger to
> salvation, namely sickness, or, as may be expected in
> every case where this sacrament is received in faith, the
> inner body-soul personal constitution of this sick Christian
> will be healed by the grace of Christ through a special
> strengthening of his entire being.[14]

It seems to me that some such understanding of healing as
I have tried to set forth in this book is needed to renew the
sacrament of the Anointing of the Sick. For the full effect of
the sacraments to take place we need to have faith that something will happen—in this case, healing. Just as we believe
that the Lord becomes present in a special way in the Eucharist, we also need to have faith that the sick person is to be
healed in some real way—whether by way of a kind of spiritual or inner healing or through a physical cure and raising
up if this is God's perfect plan for the sick person. (The chapter
on "The Faith to Be Healed" here has a special pertinence.)

---

13. Prudent de Letter: "Anointing of the Sick" in Vol. I (New York:
Herder & Herder, 1968), p. 37.
14. Study Text II: Anointing and Pastoral Care of the Sick, pp.
24-25.

The Rite of Anointing and Pastoral Care of the Sick states that the celebration of anointing consists of "the laying on of hands by the presbyters of the Church, the prayer of faith, and the anointing of the sick with oil sanctified by God's blessing" (No. 5). In this obvious allusion to *James,*

> . . . The prayer of faith looms as an important component both for the minister and for the recipient of the sacrament, as well as for the worshiping community.[15]

> Anointing of the sick, perhaps the most liturgically deprived of all the sacramental ministrations of the Church, is never to be administered in a quasi-magical, mechanistic manner but rather as a sacrament of the community of faith.[16]

I think this is certainly true—that *faith* really does enter into the effectiveness of this sacrament; if the minister, if the sick person, if the assembled group of relatives and friends have the faith to believe that healing will happen, then miracles of healing will take place through the renewed sacrament of Anointing. To renew this sacrament, we need also to renew our faith in the reality of Christ's healing power today.

2. SACRAMENT OF PENANCE (RECONCILIATION)

The sacrament of Penance, like Anointing of the Sick, has recently been renewed (February, 1974) with the publication of the first new rite of Penance in more than 400 years. This renewal likewise moves in the direction of many of the ideas suggested in this book. Among these new features some of the most important are:

---

15. *Ibid.,* p. 13.
16. *Ibid.,* p. 12.

a) *Reconciliation* is now the key word, rather than *confession* of sins. Reconciliation means that God's action of bringing man back into harmony—healing, really—is stressed more than what man does by way of repenting and confessing. Man's repentance and confession open the way for God to forgive and reconcile.

Furthermore, reconciliation emphasizes the communal nature of sin and our need to be reconciled with our brother if we have hurt him. The sins stressed in the examination of conscience recommended for the new rite have more to do than previously with sensitivity to sins against justice. This corresponds to what we have found in working with healing: the most injurious sins are those leaving resentment and bitterness—sins which militate directly against our being reconciled with our brother.

> Come to terms with your opponent in good time while you are still on the way to court with him, or he may hand you over to the judge and the judge to the officer, and you will be thrown into prison. I tell you solemnly, you will not get out till you have paid the last penny (Mt 5:25-26).

b) The new rite encourages *face-to-face* confession, deemphasizing the screen separating the penitent and confessor. This will make it far easier to incorporate the personal element that is so helpful to any kind of healing.

c) The priest—or the penitent—opens the service of reconciliation by *reading scripture* passages that stress God's mercy.

d) *Spontaneous prayer* is encouraged both for the priest and penitent. Even the prayer of contrition need no longer be a formula, but the penitent can say it in his own words.

All these elements can contribute to utilizing a prayer for healing in addition to the absolution of sins, provided the priest and penitent so wish. I think the incorporation of prayer for healing would be a wonderful contribution to the renewing of this sacrament. Here I would highly recommend reading Father Michael Scanlan's booklet, *The Power in Penance*,[17] which provides a beautiful, balanced approach to incorporating elements of healing and deliverance into the sacrament of Penance.

Healing Related to Penance

The basic reason why healing is desperately needed in order to renew Penance is precisely because *repentance is not usually sufficient to root out the evil that holds us down morally and spiritually.* The more I deal with penitents the more I see that most moral problems that people face have a large element of the involuntary in them. The alcoholic seldom has merely a problem of willpower; he may also have a deep need for inner healing and, possibly, for deliverance as well. When a person comes to confession we cannot always expect that absolving the confessed sin will solve the problem; we ordinarily need to deal with healing the whole man.

Once we offer that possibility of real healing to people, then they start flocking back to this sacrament. On the other hand, I believe that the falling off in the numbers of people who once lined up in our churches to go to confession, is a sign that the people realize that repentance alone is not enough to change their lives. I don't think that it's just a lack of faith which has led to a lessening of use of the sacrament of Penance; it's a feeling instead—shared by many priests themselves—that "I keep confessing the same thing week after week, so something is wrong: either I don't really want to change and lack a purpose of amendment; or else I want to

---

17. Notre Dame: Ave Maria Press, 1972.

change but can't—in which case my sins are not voluntary and I can't in all honesty say I'm sorry."

The answer here is, I think, that we need to add prayer for healing. Take a common example: the person who feels guilty about masturbation and has kept on confessing it for years. Perhaps none of the advice given him has proven really helpful. What is the answer for such a person—to tell him that he shouldn't worry about it anymore, because he's done the best he can? Without the possibility of healing, that might be the most honest answer. But I have seen—not just once but many times—such a problem healed by the Lord in prayer, in such a way that it has simply ceased to be a problem. It's as if God didn't simply fortify the person's will to engage in some prolonged battle with temptation (which can be an exhausting process) but actually deals with the temptation *from within* so that it ceases to occupy the center of the person's attention and becomes a nonproblem, so he can concentrate on the more important issues of life.

The chapters on inner healing and deliverance show the kind of prayer that might be wisely incorporated into Penance so that the penitent might be freed from the sins that cling to every human being. In my experience most situations of sin really need the help of healing prayer for the sinner to be truly set free.

In the Context of Traditional Penance

In the situation which we still face, where the penitent comes to the confessional, the priest could easily add a simple prayer for healing directed to that area of the penitent's life where he is having trouble. This prayer can be added either before or after giving absolution. I find that people invariably appreciate the added prayer.

The problems with trying to pray adequately for healing in

the context of Penance as it has traditionally been celebrated are fairly obvious:

a) There needs to be *time* to get down to the roots, finding out what to pray for, and then praying in an unhurried way. If the penitent is on his knees and other people are waiting in line, it is clear that the priest can't spend more than a minute or two extra. And if the need is deep, an hour might be needed to try to help the penitent.

b) If there is a screen between the penitent and priest there isn't as much opportunity for the *personal* contact that helps any prayer for healing—and prayer for deliverance is ruled out almost altogether.

c) The penitent often tends to *list a number of sins* rather than to get down to the roots of his relationship with God and with his fellowman.

The new regulations concerning Penance should be a great help in all this: if the priest arranges for people to come to the rectory for confession he can see to it that there will be *sufficient time;* he can now talk to the penitent *face to face;* and if the penitent is simply listing sins, he can get down to more fundamental questions, such as

—what do you feel about your *relationship with God*?

—what do you feel *about yourself*?

—how are you doing in your relationships *with people,* especially at home, in your community, and at work?

This then opens up the possibility of priest and penitent praying together for all the areas of life that are hurting, in addition to giving absolution and proclaiming God's forgiveness for sins. The sins represent the past, but healing is often needed to change the penitent's life in the future.

In a Counseling Context

I have found it helpful—especially on retreats—simply to be available to people who want to talk or to pray for healing, rather than just to be available to hear confessions.

In this way people come and in a very natural way open up their lives: they want to talk about their relationship—or lack of relationship—with God and with their family and friends. It's much easier for them to come at it fresh in this way, rather than to try to sort it out in a list of sins. Yet, when they talk about their lives, the question of sin sometimes comes up (for about one person out of four I would estimate) in which case, after eliciting a prayer of repentance, the priest can give absolution. But *almost always* there is a need for a prayer of inner healing or for the healing of relationships.

In short, the broader context of life is simply that, because we are human, we hurt in many ways and therefore desperately need the encouragement and prayer of others. In other words, we all need healing. When the priest or minister is available to pray for their needs the people eagerly come to him, as Christ's ambassador, seeking that help. One of those forms of healing—but it is only one—is forgiveness of sins.

I find that it seems most helpful, therefore, to make myself available as a minister of Christ's healing love in the broadest possible way and then I can let the needs of the people determine how best I can ask Jesus for help: in giving light and wisdom, in forgiving sin, in praying for inner healing, in praying for physical healing, in praying for deliverance or in simply ministering Christ's love to people.

This is ministering Christ's power to eradicate sin and evil in the fullest possible context. I would look forward to that time when we learn to minister the sacrament of Penance to all those roots of sin that weigh us down and prevent us from receiving the liberation that belongs to the children of God.

3. THE EUCHARIST

Traditionally, the Eucharist has always been regarded as a sacrament bringing healing. The prayers at Communion time reflect this ancient faith (italics added):

Deliver us, Lord, *from every evil,*
and grant us peace in our day.
In your mercy keep us *free from sin*
and protect us *from all anxiety.* . . .

Lord Jesus Christ,
with faith in your love and mercy
I eat your body and drink your blood.
Let it not bring me condemnation,
but *health in mind and body.*

Lord, I am not worthy to receive you,
but *only say the word and I shall be healed.*

Recently I was celebrating Mass with a group of about 40 priests, brothers and sisters. During a shared homily, one of the priests mentioned that the Eucharist is a sacrament of healing. I then asked if any of them had ever seen healing take place during the Mass, and none could remember having seen anything happen that was memorable enough to share. But I know of at least half a dozen healings that have taken place during the Mass without any prayers being said other than those in the liturgical form; and I think I can say I have seen hundreds of healings take place when I have added special prayers for healing after Communion or immediately after the Mass is over.

As a time for healing I would prefer praying with the community during the Mass than at any other time I know of—

at that time when Jesus Christ is most especially among us.

4. BAPTISM

Since Baptism is meant to infuse a person with new life—the life of Jesus Christ—the power of that life can drive out before it all the powers of sickness and death. Baptism is directed toward the eradication of sin—including original sin, which includes among its effects sickness and death. Baptism, then, of its very nature brings healing and life to drive out sickness and death.

Witness a portion of the blessing of salt from the rite of Baptism which, until recently, read (italics added):

> I exorcise you by the living God, the true God, the holy God, the God who brought you into being to safeguard the human race, and commanded you to be consecrated by his servants for the benefit of those who are coming into the faith, so that by the power of the Holy Trinity you might become a *health-giving* sacrament to *put the enemy to flight.*
>
> Therefore, we beg you, O Lord our God, to sanctify by your power of sanctification this salt which you have created and to bless it with your blessing, so that it *may become a perfect medicine* for all who receive it and may remain always in *every fiber of their being.* . . .[18]

This prayer for salt explicitly connects healing with the power of Baptism. Little wonder then that Agnes Sanford records that,

---

18. *Collectio Rituum*: Ritual Approved by the National Conference of Bishops of the United States of America (New York: Catholic Book Publishing Co., 1964), pp. 87, 89.

My own husband has often been called to baptize a "dying" baby. Not one of them has ever died. So he is now sure that the interposition of the sacrament of baptism together with his own person between God and the baby is sufficient to recharge any child with life.[19]

In my work I only have the chance occasionally to baptize, but one of the few times that I have, the baby (who was immersed) was healed overnight of a stubborn case of diaper rash that had resisted treatment by medication for weeks.

If we had more faith in the life-giving power of this sacrament we might see the kind of incident Agnes Sanford describes repeated more often:

There was another minister who was once called upon to baptize a dying baby, six months old. By the time he had reached the house in his buggy over the winding mountain roads, the child had been dead for half an hour. He was laid out upon the parlor table and surrounded by weeping women. When the young minister looked upon the child and its weeping mother, he had compassion on them. And the love of Christ speaking through his mind bade him baptize the child, living or dead.

As he began the baptismal service the feeling came to him that the child would live again. Therefore, he placed the women upon the far side of the room and stood between them and the baby. Shielded thus from observation, he laid his hands upon the child, dropped a little water into its mouth and stroked its tiny throat. The child's flesh began to grow warm. Toward the end of the baptismal service, the child opened its eyes.

So he restored the child to its mother, even as Elisha restored to the Shunammite woman her only son. And not

19. Agnes Sanford, *The Healing Light*, p. 73.

knowing why he did so, he had used not only the sacrament of baptism but also his own body for the conducting of God's life into the child.[20]

5. MARRIAGE

Several times, not praying for healing, but praying for an increase of love for married couples, I have seen one of the partners healed of physical ailments.

But, most important, in the past few years we have learned something about how to pray for the *healing of relationships.* The ideal situation for this is when both partners in the marriage come together, seeking to strengthen or heal their relationship. This prayer takes a leisurely amount of time— ideally, several sessions, and seems to go in four stages:

a) It begins with an ordinary *counseling* session to find out how the partners feel about themselves and about their relationship.

b) If there is need for *forgiveness,* each can ask forgiveness of the other, while affirming the beauty and goodness that the other partner has brought to the relationship.

c) This is followed by prayer for *inner healing* for each of the partners, taken singly. Often the discovery of the sorrows and hurts that the partner has brought to the marriage and seeing the effect this has had upon the relationship is in itself a revelation and a beginning of healing. Take, for example, a husband and wife who have drifted apart since their little daughter has died of a lingering illness. Enduring such a tragedy together might strengthen the love between them, but instead it has driven them apart. How did this happen? The husband came from a family where there was a lot of tragedy when he was growing up; the only way they knew how to make the suffering bearable was either to keep quiet or to joke about

20. *Ibid.,* pp. 72-73.

it—much as soldiers in war learn to harden themselves to the death of their comrades. The only way to survive is to become hardened on the outside; talk only makes the suffering worse. So when his daughter was sick he didn't want to talk about it; in fact, he even joked about it a little.

The wife came from a small family, insulated against too much suffering—a family who showed their sorrow as well as their love in demonstrative ways.

So when the baby was sick and the mother cried, the father was embarrassed by the display of emotion and retreated into silence; she interpreted this as coldness. She told him how heartless he was. In order not to further destroy the deteriorating relationship, he repressed his anger and retreated further into his shell. He wasn't around when she felt she and the baby needed his support the most.

In this way, and in so many others, people's backgrounds influence their present relationships. When a couple begins to understand the wounds of the past that need healing, the understanding that comes is in itself healing. For the wife here, for instance, to be able to see that her husband was not unfeeling, but was handling his feelings in the only way he knew how, this was in itself the beginning of healing.

Next we pray for each partner—getting the wife to pray with us for the husband, and the husband to pray with us for the wife—praying for an inner healing, so that each may be freed of past hurts in order to relate freely in the present. This is a beautiful kind of prayer.

In this kind of prayer, by the way, it often helps to have a man and woman praying together for the husband and wife.

d) The prayer can then close with the married couple praying for the *healing of the marriage relationship* itself.

As can be imagined this kind of prayer requires great honesty; it can never be forced—both partners must desire it. All those engaged in the prayer need to be sensitive. But I would look forward to a day when marriage counseling will culminate in prayer to heal all the brokenness that honest discussion has brought to the surface. In this way the grace of the sacrament empowering the couple to love each other with the love of Jesus will continually be applied to their lives together.

6. THE SACRAMENT OF ORDERS

Healing seems to be connected with priesthood—and little wonder, for the priest is ordained to continue ministering the life of Jesus Christ to the community. He carries on the work of Christ himself in a life dedicated to preaching, to healing and to exorcising; he is meant to be like Jesus. "God had anointed him with the Holy Spirit and with power, and because God was with him, Jesus went about doing good and curing all who had fallen into the power of the devil" (Acts 10:38).

In the early days of the Church it seems that the commission to heal was seen as a special charism. Consequently, the person who received it did not need to be ordained. The *Apostolic Tradition of Hippolytus* (written about 215 A.D.) states:

> If anyone says, "I have received the gift of healing," hands shall not be laid upon him; the deed itself shall make manifest if he speaks the truth.[21]

Similarly, exorcism was not a specifically priestly function, and in the third century laymen were trained for this work. The number of exorcists grew so large that one bishop in Rome complained that they outnumbered the priests.[22]

21. *Apostolic Tradition of Hippolytus,* I. 15, ed. by Burton S. Eaton (Ann Arbor: Archon Books, 1962), p. 41.
22. Morton Kelsey, *op. cit.,* p. 153.

The *Apostolic Constitutions* show that, by the fifth century, the Church had decided that healers and exorcists should be ordained. Moreover, the bishop prayed that all those being ordained would receive the power to heal:

And now, O Lord, give and forever preserve in him the spirit of thy grace so that, filled with powers of healing and words of instruction, he may teach thy people in meekness of heart and serve thee sincerely with a pure mind and a willing soul and blamelessly fulfill his sacred offices for thy people.[23]

The *Canons of Hippolytus* contain a specific prayer for a presbyter or bishop:

Grant him, O Lord, a mild spirit, and power to remit sins, and grant to him power to loose all bonds of the iniquity of demons, and to heal all diseases, and to beat down Satan under his feet quickly.[24]

This power was principally channeled through what came to be recognized as the sacrament of the Anointing of the Sick. The power to heal should be seen, however, as channeled not only through the sacrament, but also through the living instrumentality of the priest, who is ordained for the purpose of healing. As Amalarius writes (in the ninth century):

Our bishops maintain this custom: they anoint the hands of priests with oil. It is obvious why they do this, namely, that their hands may be clean for offering sacrifice to God

---

23. *Apostolic Constitutions,* ch. VIII, 17, ed. Funk, Vol. I (Paderborn, 1905).
24. *Canons,* 17, as contained in W. K. Clarke, *Liturgy and Worship* (London: S.P.C.K., 1954), p. 475 ff.

and open for the offices of piety. Both are signified by the oil—the grace of curing, and charity or love.[25]

This represents the tradition of a still earlier time when visits to the sick by a bishop were encouraged because, "He recovers from his disease when a bishop comes to him, particularly if he prays over him."[26]

It seems clear, then, that healing which was first considered as a charism given to individuals as part of the ordinary ministry of the Christian community later became a part of the priestly office, to be particularly sought and used through the sacraments.[27]

In Conclusion

I hope that this book will help contribute to that renewal of a belief both in the healing ministry in general, and, in particular, of its part in the full working of the sacraments.

I think that the churches at large are undergoing the same kind of renewal and change of attitude that St. Augustine underwent. In his early writings he held that healing was meant for the beginnings of Christianity but that Christians were not to look for a continuance of healing.[28] Then his attitude changed and he frankly admitted in his book of *Retractions* that he had been wrong. His own experience as Bishop of Hippo (c. 420 A.D.) changed his mind:

. . . once I realized how many miracles were occurring in our own day and which were so like the miracles of old and also how wrong it would be to allow the memory of

25. *Liber Officialis II,* 13, 1. J. Hanssens, S.J., editor of *Amalarii Ep., Opera Liturgica Omnia* (Vatican City, 1948-50), II, p. 227.
26. *Canons of Hippolytus,* 199.
27. Kelsey, *op. cit.,* p. 180.
28. Kelsey, *op. cit.,* p. 184.

these marvels of divine power to perish from among our people. It is only two years ago that the keeping of records was begun here in Hippo, and already, at this writing, we have nearly seventy attested miracles.[29]

Wonderful things will happen through the sacraments as we learn to believe more in their potential. The only sacrament where I have not personally seen healing take place is Confirmation—and that may only be because I haven't been present at a Confirmation since my own some 30 years ago. I look forward, therefore, to a day when God's love is manifested commonly as it was in the following instance—the healing of a sister that took place through a combination of Penance, inner healing and deliverance:

Perhaps you know how different I feel. I'm really new. I feel like I'm white as snow, pure and beautiful. I feel light as air and happier than I've ever been in all my life. Others don't make me feel hurt by what they say or do; I don't feel jealous, but happy. I need to check myself on old thought patterns, but now He's helping me do it. I had read Agnes Sanford's *Healing Light,* but all my efforts couldn't stop those mean thoughts. I could control my efforts to a point—then they would explode, and I'd feel simply miserable. I knew I couldn't do it, so I'd feel sinful and hopeless. Now He does it, and it's easy.

I had a most beautiful "re-entry" into the community (the evening before I felt incapable of being with them). My spirits and those of the community are lifted. Anyway, *I'm new.* God has simply been overpowering in his graces, and I need never cease thanking Him.

---

29. Augustine, *City of God,* XXII, 8. Tr. by G. Walsh and D. Honan. (New York: Fathers of the Church, 1954.)

21

Questions Most Often Asked

THERE ARE A NUMBER of questions people at workshops frequently ask that don't exactly fit under any of the topics that have been covered so far. In the practical order some of them are important, so I will do my best to answer them.

How do I tell if I have the gift of healing?

This is a delicate question, one that I don't feel comfortable in answering—just as I experience a mixed reaction when someone says, "I have heard you are a healer."

In the first place, it centers too much on the person. It sounds as if I can say I *have* something that I can control, that I can turn on and off at will.

What I can do is to pray—that I can decide to do. But whether or not the person is healed depends on God, not on my own powers. This is not magic or superstition. I don't change God's mind by prayer, but cooperate with God's plan for man (which includes my prayer) whose basic movement is always toward life and health. In a given instance, because of some obstacle or because of some higher positive purpose, healing may not take place. Healing, then, is more like my having a potential to be used by God than it is a gift which is under my power. The gift is not for the minister of healing, but for the sick person; he is the one who receives the gift of health.

I believe that every Christian has the potential for being used in healing. Christ is the one who does the healing and since he, the Father and the Spirit reside within each Christian they can, upon occasion, work through the prayers of any Christian: "Everything is possible for anyone who has faith," said Jesus (Mk 9:32b). We are all encouraged to pray for healing. In particular, we have a special responsibility to pray for those who are close to us in any way: parents are used by God to pray for their children, husbands and wives for each other. Friends, too, have a special bond of love that God uses for healing when they pray for one another. Ministers and priests, because of their position as leaders of the Christian community, and as counselors, have a special gift of healing connected with their office. The sacraments of Penance and Anointing of the Sick, in particular, make their healing office part of the liturgical life of sacramental churches.

Nevertheless, some persons seem specially gifted in the area of healing and develop a *ministry* of healing when others in the community recognize this gift. St. Paul says that *some* are given the gift of healing (I Cor 12:9), so it is clear that others are not given this gift. In context Paul is speaking about special ministry gifts given for the sake of the community. Clearly, that kind of remarkable gift is only given to some persons, but I believe every prayer group should have some persons who are recognized by the group as having more healing power than others.

When people ask how to tell if they have the gift of healing, this special ministry gift is what I presume they are asking about. The only real test that I know is *if people are healed* when we pray. The ones who will be the first to know are the other members of the local community, so it is not the kind of thing a person needs to worry about.

The gift of healing—like love—admits of more and less. It's not so much a question of having it or not having it. It's not that simple. Any gift of healing allows for growth; most of us have it to some extent, and so, hopefully, we can grow in that gift. There need be no hurry to prove that we have the gift. My experience leads me to believe that anyone who has an extraordinary gift in this area is spotted very quickly by other persons and very soon he, or she, will have to try to hide—as our Lord did—rather than to wonder whether or not he has the gift. If you have a real gift of healing as a ministry there will soon be no doubt about it. Those who are not sure had best wait and just continue to grow.

Some persons seem overanxious to find out if they have the gift of healing. Perhaps their motivation is not altogether pure; along with a laudable desire to help others, they may also have an excessive need to be needed. Such persons somehow manage to make their appearance at most prayer groups I know of and there announce, in one way or another, that they have a ministry of healing. They may make one of our workshops on healing and then feel they have been certified in some way. If anyone at the meeting seems to be ailing, this person proceeds to take over and lead the prayers or takes the person aside in order to minister privately. They are persons who think they have a ministry, and they are anxiously looking for someone to minister to.

No one feels comfortable in such a situation. Things are turned around. Maybe the person is helpful to some people and you hate to discourage him. I find that people with problems know intuitively to whom they should go, with whom they should pray. Ordinarily the sick should be free to seek out the minister of healing—just as in the natural order they phone the physician of their choice; the reverse, a doctor looking for patients is a sign that something is wrong. If a doctor is successful, he doesn't have to go around looking for work. Sometimes the pressure to be recognized is subtle; the person wants a special ministry of healing to be set up by the prayer community so that people can only come through certain channels to himself. At times there is a real need for a prayer group to recognize and establish a team for ministry, namely, to protect persons in the group from poor teaching and from people who think they have a ministry but who do more harm than good. In general, though, people will eventually surface in a prayer group or community who have a genuine ministry. Most of the community will recognize who they are; they won't have to push themselves forward. If time is made available for those people who wish to consult and pray with them, freedom will be preserved. The harm is caused by people who need to feel important, who need to minister more for their own sake than for that of the sick.

For all these reasons, I feel somewhat uncomfortable when people ask how they can tell if they have the gift of healing. If people were healed through their ministry, the community—the sick in particular—would be the first to recognize that gift.

Most of us can just pray for the sick when the natural opportunities present themselves. In this way that gift for healing we all have as Christians will have the chance to grow and increase as we gradually grow in faith, love and wisdom, the deep foundation of healing power.

Are there physical phenomena that accompany the healing gift?

Yes, there are. And sometimes these can be a help, but they

are only indications and effects and not the gift of healing itself. The gift is only clearly manifested when someone is actually healed.

Mrs. Agnes Sanford used to experience various sensations when praying for healing while her husband did not. Yet persons were healed through his ministry as well as through hers.

Some of these phenomena include:

—heat; this is the most common of all physical phenomena connected with healing. Often it centers upon the affected organ and sometimes remains as an indication that the body is being healed long after the prayer is over;

—a gentle trembling of power. Some people feel their hands shake as a kind of current of power moves through them. This trembling lasts as long as the healing prayer continues;

—something like an electric current or a filling of power, but without the trembling.

These sensations can be helpful. Some persons, for instance, who experience the trembling have learned to pray as long as the power seems to be there, and to stop praying when the sensation stops. This time varies, sometimes lingering for a while, as if it were like a cobalt radiation treatment. At other times, it is brief.

Other persons who have learned to associate healing with heat or a sensation of some kind of current in the hands believe that this helps them know when to pray, and when not to pray. If they feel this sensation, for instance, during a prayer meeting they know, through experience, that someone in the group needs healing and can receive it.

Those with a ministry of healing need not seek after such phenomena; yet, I find that these various sensations are frequently experienced without their being sought. When persons receive such manifestations they need not be surprised or take pride in them but should simply regard them in a matter-of-fact way. They should see if they can find any factors that give these manifestations some kind of practical meaning. Do they, for example, help us to know when to pray? Do they help to build up our confidence that God can use our prayers for healing? The emphasis should not be upon these phenomena in themselves, but upon any significance they may have. They should neither be feared nor scorned—nor should they be overprized. They can be a real help in assisting us to understand our own healing ministry. On the other hand, I know of some friends who experience a slight trembling when they pray for healing and who come to believe that this is simply a weakness of the human body, not acclimated to the power of God. They incline to the opinion that for those who are more accustomed to the presence of God these physical phenomena are almost nonperceptible.

Is it best to pray for healing in community?

At times, there are advantages to praying in community; at other times it is best to seek individual prayer. There is no definite answer that will suit every individual or every occasion.

Individuals with a gift of healing include some who have special gifts of discernment that help in difficult cases. But there is a power in group prayer: "wherever two or three are gathered together. . . ." In general I think we can say:

1) In praying for *physical healing* it helps to pray in community.

2) In praying for *inner healing* and for *deliverance,* it is usually best to provide for individual prayer, either one-to-one or with a small team. The kind of confidence that is often shared, the revelation of deep hurts, requires the greatest possible respect for privacy. The reason for a small *team* is:

a) to make use of the special gifts such as discernment that are given to different individuals; b) to have a man and woman praying together for a healing of past hurts, and c) to avoid any kind of compromising situation that might develop in a one-and-one situation.

In praying for physical healing, why not combine the advantages of both group and individual prayer, by having persons *with the gift of healing lead the entire group in praying* for the sick?

What about praying at a distance?

Distance seems to be little problem when praying for *physical* sickness. I have heard of many instances when, at the very time a group prayed for someone in a distant hospital, the sick person experienced the presence of Christ and was healed.

In praying for *conversion* and *inner healing* of any sort (or a fortiori, *deliverance*) where the person's own active part in the healing is important, it is usually helpful for the person to be present. Prayer is not magic and God does not bypass the person's own part in the healing if it is needed—as it is in inner healing. Ordinarily, if a person comes up and asks for prayer (for instance, for a relative suffering from emotional problems), I usually suggest that it would be better to have the sick person himself, if he really wants help, to come and ask for prayer. Yet there are exceptions:

I know of conversion and inner healing being occasioned through distant prayer (with the suffering person's subsequent inner cooperation). In the gospels we read about the Canaanite woman who came pleading for her daughter to be freed from the torments of evil spirits—and the daughter was freed from the moment that Jesus prayed (Mt 15:21-28). In November, 1972, I prayed with Pastor Jose Fajardo and his wife at a retreat in Bogota, Colombia, for the conversion of his

son, who at the time was at home in the city of Cali. At that
precise time, about 1:00 a.m., his son was waked from sleep
and underwent a tremendous conversion experience in which
he committed his life to Christ and came off drugs—without
any apparent external influence (but still with the cooperation
of his own will).

Are other gifts involved with healing?

Among those gifts mentioned by St. Paul in I Corinthians 12,
the following have a clear connection with healing: the discerning of spirits, the gift of faith, the word of knowledge, and
the working of miracles. Although the purpose of each of
these gifts is not altogether clear there seems to be a common
consensus among ministers of healing that the gifts have these
uses:
    —The discerning of spirits enables us to ascertain whether
or not healing is needed—or a deliverance. And what kind
of deliverance.
    —The gift of faith, as was said earlier, enables us to know
whether or not the sick person is to experience healing at this
particular time. It also imparts the confidence needed to act
upon that knowledge and to pray the prayer of faith.
    —The word of knowledge[1] enables us to discern the roots,
the causes of sickness for which we should pray, even when
sometimes the person himself doesn't understand fully what
is wrong. This gift is especially helpful with inner healing or
when physical sickness is somehow hooked up with a deeper
wound.

---

1. The *Jerusalem Bible* translates this as the gift of "preaching instruction"—which is, of course, a different meaning. Without trying
to decide which is St. Paul's intended meaning, we find that God
does help us diagnose the root cause of problems—whether or not this
is in this particular list of Paul's.

—The gift of miracles differs, I believe, from the gift of healing in that it creates where something was missing, while healing hastens or changes what would ordinarily be accomplished by the healing processes of nature.

All these gifts clearly are a great help working toward the full and perfect working of the gift of healing. The gifts of healing and miracles have to do with God's *love and power* in curing sickness, while the gifts of discernment, knowledge and faith enable us *to know* when and how to minister God's healing love.

Can you pray more than once for healing?

For some reason many people who believe in healing also believe that they can only pray once; to pray again indicates to them that they lack faith in their first prayer. (Some evangelists apparently give this kind of advice, too.) So far as I can judge this kind of absolutism goes contrary to the clear teaching of Our Lord in the parables of the Importunate Friend (Lk 11:5-8) and the Importunate Widow (Lk 18:1-8). "I tell you, if the man does not get up and give it to him for friendship's sake, persistence will be enough to make him get up and give his friend all he wants. So, I say to you: Ask, and it will be given to you . . ." (Lk 11:8-9b).

Nevertheless, there are those times when a person prays once and then seems called upon to accept the fact that he has been healed. But, to raise any one factor here to the status of an absolute—"We can only pray once and then we must claim healing"—is to create a new legalism and to make an idol out of a method. Each person should pray and then make a decision as to how best God wants him to pray: once, or several times, or many times.

Praying for chronic ailments of long standing is, for example, usually a matter of continuing prayer over a long period of time. Ordinarily (again, not always) ailments such as arthritis are gradually healed. When parents ask prayer for a mentally retarded child, I teach them how to pray every day, with the whole family, for the child. What usually seems to happen is that the child improves gradually—and much faster than the medical prognosis would call for. For long-term, deep-seated ailments a kind of "soaking prayer," repeated often, seems to bring the best results.

What about leg-lengthening?

For those who have never seen this kind of prayer—and for some who have seen it—"leg-lengthening" may sound somewhat bizarre. It simply means that the patient, suffering from some such ailment as a lower back injury, sits in a chair, and then holds his legs straight out in front of him, where their length can be compared by putting one heel against the other. Since most people have an imbalance in leg length, some difference usually shows up. The group gathers around and prays while one or more persons hold the feet, watching one leg move out until it is the same length as the other.

To many people the whole process seems ridiculous, something like a sideshow. Friends of mine, whom I respect highly and who have a real ministry of healing, want to have nothing to do with this practice which they feel lends a circus atmosphere to prayer groups. They feel it leads people to seek after the spectacular, instead of keeping their mind on God.

Since I have tried to remain open to whatever is genuine, no matter how unpromising it seems at first, I have to admit that my own experience (as does that of so serious a minded person as Rev. Derek Prince) convinces me that it is a valid way of praying. I have seen extraordinary healings take place, especially of back problems, through praying in this way.

To put this peculiar ministry in focus several things need to be said:

Actually, "leg-lengthening" is a misnomer. If anything is wrong with the alignment of the spine or hips, it affects the alignment of the legs. What goes on is not really a lengthening of the legs; the change in length is more likely caused by changes going on in the spine or hips.

As any doctor will tell us, measuring leg length accurately requires more than the kind of rough measurement that goes on with this "leg-lengthening" prayer. To claim an accuracy that does not exist only holds this kind of prayer up to medical ridicule.

Nevertheless, rough measurements or not, misnomer or not, something seems to happen almost every time we pray for someone with a spinal or hip problem. This particular method helps, too, in that the people in the prayer group can actually *see* something happen as an effect of the healing that is going on. Remarkably, the persons prayed for usually report that they actually feel a shifting and a healing in the spine as if things were moving into place. A dramatic instance of prayer of this sort that I experienced was in praying for a man who had been diagnosed at Mayo Clinic as suffering from a deterioration of the hip that would eventually require an operation to install an artificial hip socket. When we measured his legs there was a big difference—about three inches. As we prayed, in the course of five minutes, the shorter leg gradually extended until both legs seemed the same length. He then stood up and for the first time in two years was able to walk using his heel. The following morning he told us that he had been able to sleep on his back for the first time in six years, and that he was now able to walk without a limp.

Exactly why this kind of prayer seems to work so well, I don't understand. All I know is that it serves as a powerful visual help for people who are skeptical about the healing ministry and that—at least in my estimate—some 90 percent of the people I have seen prayed for in this way for back ailments seem to be cured or notably improved.

How do you know this isn't just suggestion?

Some of it may be. God works in many ways through the various facets of his creation. But, as far as I am concerned, the great mass of evidence points in the direction of a power far greater than unaided human powers.

What do you make of psychic healers?

I believe that, in general, three forces can be at work in healing:

First, there is the divine power of healing: "Ask for anything in my name and you will receive it."

Then there seems to be a natural force of healing, based on love, which is given to some people. Various experiments are presently being conducted, such as by Dr. Thelma Moss at U.C.L.A., regarding this phenomenon. There is some evidence, shown through special photography, that people with a strong life energy are able to transmit some of this to other people through the laying on of hands. If this is shown to be true, I see no reason to fear it any more than any other natural force that we discover, for it ultimately reflects glory to God, its creator.

Last, I believe there are demonic forces which can work toward healing anything they themselves have inflicted. Such persons as witch doctors work with this kind of healing force. To seek healing from anyone whose powers are connected with the demonic is ultimately to invite far greater evils, even if a true cure should take place in some subsidiary area of a person's life. Real discernment sometimes needs to be exercised as to the source of the healing power. If the power is not of God, directly or indirectly, we should stay away from it, no matter what the claims of the healer, nor how great the need for healing may be.

In regard to this, Mrs. Agnes Sanford has learned not to pray for anyone who has been involved in spiritualism. At one time she had prayed for four people in a short period of time—each of whom had been involved in spiritualism. Not only were they not cured, but death struck each one's family a short time after the prayer.

> Four times in a row! That was enough for me. Whatever the explanation of this phenomenon might be, I was evidently not a good person to pray with for anyone involved in spiritualism. This troubled me greatly, for there were times when with all my determination I could not help it. I might find myself involved with a group and find out later that there was a spiritualist among us. The results were not so drastic in a group, the mind of the group overshadowing and to some extent protecting the participants. But even when thus shielded, I have known undesirable aftereffects of praying in such a group, and as far as I know, no healings have resulted. . . .

> The reader may bring forth all kinds of reasons as to why this ought not to be. But, praise God, this book is not a series of lectures, but is merely an autobiography, and I do not have to argue about the reasons! I am merely stating facts.

> However, I myself greatly desired to understand, and, if possible, to be set free from this hampering restriction concerning those for whom I might pray. Therefore, when a chance came to me, I consulted a woman whom I consider a final authority upon all matters of the occult; her innate wisdom and acquired knowledge are great and so

is her real devotion to Jesus Christ.

"What can I do to prevent these things from happening?" I asked her.

She replied, "You can do nothing except to abstain. You may meet socially with these people interested in spiritualism, but you must not pray for them. This is for their own protection."

"Why?"

"Because they do actually conduct a current of supernatural power from the lower regions, and you happen to conduct a particularly pure current of supernatural power directly from heaven. Now these two currents are inimical. They cannot mix together, as direct-current electricity cannot mix with alternating current. One must choose one or the other. When you do mix the two, there comes an explosion of a destructive nature. You are surrounded with protection, and it cannot touch you, so it rebounds upon the other person. . . ."

"But many good people are involved in spiritualism!" you may cry.

Yes, it horrifies me to go to Christian conferences and see books about Edgar Cayce, and other spiritualistic literature, for sale along with my books. They do not belong together. This confusion between the power of the Holy Spirit and the danger of spiritualism is the greatest menace to the Christian church today. It is our duty to combat it however we can.[2]

Regardless of whether you can accept her friend's theory about why the problem exists, there is a serious problem here and a Christian has no business confusing Christian healing with any healing coming from spiritualistic sources. On the other hand, I find some Christians too ready to condemn any

---

2. Agnes Sanford, *Sealed Orders,* pp. 153-154.

form of healing that is not explicitly Christian, but which might be a natural power—putting it on a par with witchcraft. I think the wisest course is for us to learn to experience the beauty and power of Christian healing, to *abstain* from, while not condemning, any forms of healing prayers that are not Christian, while clearly *warning* people to stay away from any healing connected with spiritualism or witchcraft.

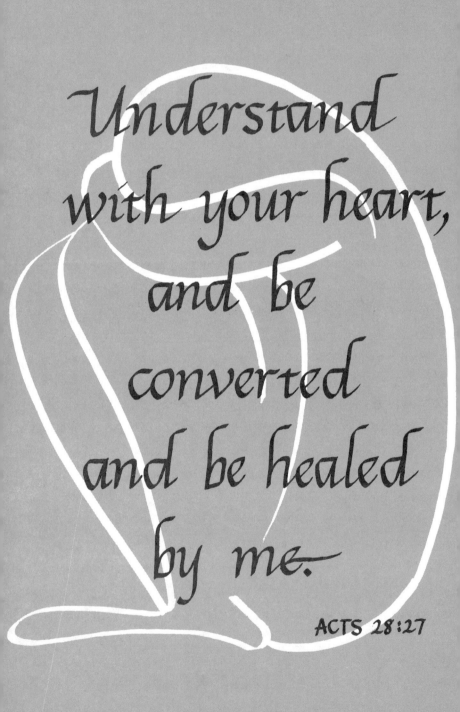

Understand with your heart, and be converted and be healed by me.

ACTS 28:27

A Talk to Priests:
Healing and the Incarnation

by Rev. Tommy Tyson

(This is taken from a talk given at a healing seminar in February, 1973, in Mexico City, at San Jose del Altillo. Tommy Tyson is a Methodist evangelist from North Carolina who has traveled extensively giving retreats. The following is a rendition I transcribed and edited from a tape recording of his talk, given to an audience made up primarily of priests.)

THE MINISTRY OF HEALING means that we take the Incarnation seriously. The Incarnation means that God is here. Not only is God with man, but God has become man. Jesus is God, as it were, coming down; it is not a humanitarian reach for heaven. A humanitarian understanding leaves you with a psychological approach to healing. Your ministry will be a diagnostician's approach; you will be problem and symptom centered. The Incarnation is not man reaching up, but God becoming man and perfecting within himself that which concerns man. It is simply Jesus giving himself.

This is what I understand about healing! We are not ministering salve to sores; we are ministering love to suffering people. It is *Jesus Christ living within us,* who has perfected

317

our humanity, who is ministering to suffering people. He is not simply a spiritual being, but he has become flesh. He is now spirit and body: this is the Incarnation. Jesus does not reveal a compartmentalized life. Rather, he reveals the marriage of opposites, with spirit and matter becoming one. God and man becoming one—heaven and earth becoming one. Heaven coming to earth, and earth being caught up into heaven. In this way we have the supernatural made manifest through the natural, and the natural lifted up to the level of the supernatural. That's what we are talking about when we talk about healing.

This means that all methods are ours. For instance, we use natural methods: we build hospitals, we train doctors, and we train nurses—all in God's image. Yet we believe in the supernatural. So we pray and utilize the sacraments. In me they all come together. It is not either/or; it is both/and. All things are ours, for God has married all these elements in Jesus. As one of the early Church Fathers put it, "Jesus became what we were that we might become what he is."

Our Father now shares with us what he has achieved in Jesus Christ, and this achievement includes the redeeming of humanity—a new kind of humanity. Jesus comes into the all of us, becomes mind of our mind, becomes spirit of our spirit, becomes bone of our bone and flesh of our flesh. God's purpose is to conform us to the image of Jesus Christ; God intends for us to be like Jesus—not in the abstract, but in the concrete here and now. He accomplishes this by the power of his Spirit working within us. This is what we are talking about when we are talking about healing: we are talking about being conformed to the image of Jesus. That's wonderful, isn't it? Jesus ministers to us from the realm of the Resurrection, and shares with us his own achievements. There are limitless ways in which he accomplishes this.

Nevertheless, there are some specific issues involved. For

example, Jesus Christ reveals himself, sharing our humanity, for our instruction, in several basic ways. Most important of all, he accepts himself in terms of his union with the Father. He never tries to minister what he has not worked out within himself. He does not heal in order to prove that he is the Christ; he heals *because he is* the Christ. His healing power comes from his very being. That reverses the usual order; in the natural order we are judged by what we do: this man is a priest, this one an attorney, and this one a banker. But in the kingdom of the Father our doing comes out of our being. Jesus Christ manifests himself from within.

For instance, here comes the man with the withered arm. Jesus Christ does not begin by diagnosing the cause of the man's problem, but he goes within himself to his Father. Through his union with the Father he sees the creative power of God: he sees this man *as whole* before God. And from that inner level of union with the Father he speaks, "Stretch forth thy hand."

The same thing with St. Peter. His name is Simon, which means "a reed"—a reed blown about by every wind. At Caesarea Philippi, Jesus asks his disciples, "Who do men say that I am?"

"Some say you are Elijah, some say you are John the Baptist, some say you are another great prophet." Then Jesus looks at his disciples and says, "Who do you say that I am?" And Simon says, "Thou art the Christ, the son of the living God."

Jesus says (I'm going to paraphrase at this point), "You did not discover this by natural means, but you have been before my Father, and my Father revealed to you who I am. Now, Simon Peter, I've been before the Father about you. So while those around you call you a reed, I see you before the Father's throne, and I see a rock. You're not a reed, you're a rock."

Who told Jesus that? How did he know it? It was revelation that came from his union with his Father; in that
union he saw Peter as the rock on which the Church was to be
built. That is the way the healing ministry of Jesus works—
yesterday, today and forever: he sees people before the Father.
He manifests outwardly what he sees by the Spirit. That is
glorious! You really glimpse the glory of God when you see
the heart of Jesus. He looks at people and he sees them not as
trees, not as goats, but he sees them as sheep without a shepherd. That is glorious, isn't it?—that before the Father people
are sheep; that is healing.

How do you see people? How do you see people in your
heart? That is the very key to your healing ministry. How do
you see *yourself* before the Father? Do you let Jesus Christ
establish in your heart who you are in the light of his love?
This is what the Holy Spirit does. He shows us who we are
separated from God, and then he shows us who we are in relationship to God. Then we simply make that exchange; that
is what confession is all about. (Please don't do away with it.)
We come to confession because of a conviction of our sin. We
are saying, "Apart from God, this is what I am. I neglect my
husband; I get mad at my children; I ignore my Church.
Apart from God I am all these things and more." When the
priest hears our confession he says, "You are right: and the
truth is you are a lot worse. But where sin did abound, grace
does much more abound. And so, here is who you are before
God. And here is how you go about appropriating that grace."
These ways of appropriating grace are simply a bridge to
where people ought to be in Jesus. That is healing. That is
what Penance is supposed to do for people; it gives them a
bridge to move from where they are to where they ought to be
in Jesus.

One basic element of healing is helping persons to accept
themselves in relationship to God even while they still have

the sickness. Now, this is basic, and yet so often we don't do it. We give people the impression that they are sick because of their meanness: "If you do not get right you are going to get sicker. There is not much hope for you anyway; God makes you sick in order to make your spirit sweet." That is the impression we give. But that isn't the gospel; that isn't our ministry. That doesn't bring anyone into union with Jesus. The gospel says that God loves us as we are—that while we were still sinners Christ died for us. When Christ was crucified there wasn't a single Christian—not a single Christian in the world.

There wasn't even a Catholic.

Just one Baptist.

By the grace that is in Jesus we belong to God. By his healing power we belong to God. Don't you know that most sickness is rooted in the people's sense of not belonging? They are sheep without a shepherd. They don't know the shepherd; they don't know they belong. So we come in Jesus' stead and tell the precious people, "You belong to Jesus, and I've come to tell you this." That is the real power of our healing ministry. If we don't know this much about people, our ministry of healing will be greatly limited. Our healing ministry should come out of a conviction that we have been sent by God to lay his claims on people, and God's claim is, "You are mine!" Haven't you seen miracles happen through that kind of commitment, through people who know that they belong to Jesus?

You priests know this. You are ministering to hungry, starving people. You know it, not just intellectually, but experientially. But they will come to know God's love as you manifest it in your relationship with them. For if you believe you belong to God, they will know that they belong to him, too, because you are in God's healing ministry. This will really get you involved with people through the compassion of God. If you are afraid of getting your hands dirty, stay out of the healing ministry.

In that story about Peter and John at the Gate Beautiful, Peter reached out and touched the man. He had perhaps been lying there nearly 40 years—no salve, no Band-Aid, no penicillin. He was a stinking mess and, yet, Peter reached out and touched him. Are you afraid of touching people? Stay away from the healing ministry if you think you are too good to get involved with people's mess. Stay out of the healing ministry because you will have to minister with the compassion of God —you belong to God and you have come to tell people, "I've come to love you! I've come to transmit to you what I've experienced of the love of God."

So, we get people to accept themselves in relationship to God in the midst of the sickness, *but* we don't stop there. I think often the Church has stopped there—that we have let people know they belong to God even if they are sick and we tell them that God can give them the grace to bear the sickness. So often we have left the impression that grace is the power to bear, the power to endure suffering. Now, grace *is* the power to endure, but, more than that, grace is the power to overcome. As we help people to accept themselves in relation to God, we also have a teaching ministry to let them know what their inheritance is in God. You see, very few people have difficulty believing God *can* heal, but, so often, people do not know he *wants* to heal them. This is where we are in the healing ministry: really helping people to know that their inheritance is health and healing. Jesus called it the "children's bread." That's a wonderful descriptive phrase for healing—the children's bread. Every child deserves bread from his father. No father makes a child pay for its own meals. "Thank you, Father. Thank you, Mother." "You're welcome," is their response.

This is true of our ministry to people—we are ministering to them their inheritance: "God loves you—God wants to heal you." This is not only true of healing for the body but also for the mind and spirit. I used to hear people testify of the healing grace of God and I knew it was real—I knew it was real for them, but I felt my case was different—I didn't deserve it! I had no right to ask for it, so all I could say to God was, "God, have mercy!" and ask him to help me endure the pain.

But, on the contrary, the Word of God comes and says, "I love you. I've taken your sins into my body and by my stripes you are healed. This is your bread; it's your inheritance." "Father, you mean I have a right to the saving grace of God, a right to the healing love of Jesus? You mean that Jesus loves me in this way?" Yes, this is what people need to know: that Jesus loves them in this way, that they have a high priest who is touched by their infirmities. And by the sacrament of priesthood you are touched by their infirmities. God forgive us if we try to have a ministry separated from the suffering of those whom we love. Our priesthood means being touched by their infirmities, so that I rejoice with those who rejoice, mourn with those who mourn, and suffer with those who suffer. I stand in the gap so that the grace of God may be transmitted through me. This is our ministry: letting people know what their inheritance is.

Of course, this means step-by-step teaching. It means going into the deep areas of the subconscious. It means walking where there are mental blocks with a sense of assurance. This calls for a corporate sense of the Body of Christ, knowing that we are baptized by one Spirit into one Body. Out of that fellowship the person and ministry of Jesus are made manifest. We do not give Jesus Christ to others without his giving himself to us.

This means our healing ministry is committed to those to whom we minister. Otherwise, it is just so much academic procedure. We want involvement with life, which means coming into a real awareness of the love of Jesus as we begin to see what our inheritance is and to learn ways of appropriating the grace of God. In this regard the Catholic Church has a responsibility before God that is greater than you can imagine; it means that, instead of lessening the emphasis on the sacraments, you must rediscover the power of the sacraments—not merely of the sacrament of the Eucharist, but of the total sacramental ministry of the Church. You need to realize, for instance, that Holy Unction is not merely meant to prepare the spirit to go to heaven—that's not the purpose of the sacrament. The purpose of Holy Unction is to minister health and healing. Yet, when the average layman sees the priest coming with a vial of oil, he calls the funeral home. We need to rediscover that the sacrament is special—the Church is saying that through this sacrament you have been given a means of transmitting the grace of God.

You stand before the Holy Table and you break that wafer. You say these words, "This is my body," and you say, "Take and eat." Do you mean that I can eat the body of Jesus without appropriating health? What could be a greater healing ministry than the sacraments? "This is my blood which is shed for you." Does it just go into my digestive tract and that's the end of it? Isn't there some way for the average laymen to appropriate that healing grace which goes through his entire body, mind and spirit? Did God simply give you a liturgy, or did he give you a way of bringing people life?

Are you just a priest in robes carrying on a beautiful liturgy, or are you ordained of God as a minister of life?

We are ministers of life! We must be! So we take all of these sacraments—of Marriage, of Holy Unction, of the Eucharist, as well as the sacrament of our own Priesthood—and we affirm that all these sacraments are ways by which God's grace is transmitted to people.

And God's grace is the life that is in Jesus Christ.

The
bruised
reed
will not
be broken.

ISAIAH 42:3

Epilogue
The Story of the Three Indians

IN AN EARLIER VERSION of this book the first chapter was called *The Story of the Three Indians.* I put the story there as a kind of test of our belief: can we really believe that such a healing as the Indians told about actually happened? After reading that story, the editors and readers all agreed that it was a bit much to expect the average reader to believe—that we might lose most of the readers, say, before they got past the first chapter.

Agreeing to the wisdom of their observation, we relocate the story here. Test it out with your own reactions. Do you think that what these Indians relate could possibly have happened?

Appropriately enough, I heard the story of the Indians at Blue Cloud Abbey (Marvin, South Dakota). I had been invited there as one of six priests who composed a team which was conducting a nationwide series of workshops on prayer for priests. These workshops, held in seven areas of the country, were sponsored by the National Federation of Priests' Councils.

This particular workshop was attended by a bishop and 45 other priests from the upper Midwest. My part in these workshops, as part of the team, was to give a talk on charismatic prayer.

On the way to this workshop our team, led by Father Frank Callahan of Baltimore, met at the airport in Minneapolis, from where we were to catch a plane to Watertown, South Dakota. There, at the airport bookshop we bought copies of *Bury My Heart at Wounded Knee,* which had just come out in paperback. It seemed especially appropriate to read this book as background for the land we were to visit, for the Battle of Wounded Knee had taken place in South Dakota, the heart of Sioux Indian territory.

We were met at Watertown by the Benedictine fathers, who drove us to Blue Cloud Abbey. On the way we were joking about the isolation of the spot where we were headed; all the previous workshops had been held in large cities where I could bring in local people to amplify my talks by illustrating points from their own experience. In Houston, for instance, members of the Church of the Redeemer community were invited to share with the priests what the Spirit had done in helping them build up their remarkable parish community. Marvin, South Dakota, would be a real test; it would be a real challenge to discover a charismatic prayer group in the midst of that prairie land.

When we got there, sure enough, the prior, Father Odilo Burkhardt, O.S.B., told us that there was a prayer group of Indians that met right there at the Abbey. But when I asked if members of the group could share their experiences with the priests, Father Odilo said that, no, he was afraid of embarrassing these people who might be too shy to address a large group of priests. So we gave up that idea.

After my talk Wednesday afternoon, April 26, Father Callahan asked me to give still another talk that evening, a free evening, since there was no place for the priests to go for recreation out **there** on the prairie. So I gave them an additional talk about the healing ministry as it pertains to the life of a priest. As I neared the finish of my talk, Father Odilo's call bell rang, so he got up and left. A short time later, he returned, came up to the lectern and whispered that three Indians had just arrived at the Abbey, looking for the key to the library to borrow a book on Sitting Bull. He said they had recently experienced healing and might be willing to talk about it in spite of their habitual reticence. Would I want them to speak, if they were willing? I said yes, so he went out again.

Just as I finished speaking these three Sioux Indians suddenly appeared from behind the movie screen at my rear. Father Odilo introduced the unexpected visitors: Simon Keeble, his wife, Lucy, and Nancy, a young woman about 20 years old.

In the following transcription from the tape recording, I have not changed the style or the grammar. (The rhythm and the way of speaking are hauntingly reminiscent of the statements of the Indians themselves which preface each chapter of *Bury My Heart at Wounded Knee*.) The first to speak was Mrs. Lucy Keeble:

> I like to praise my Lord every day for what he has done for me. I used to be a wicked woman: I liked to gossip, and go around telling peoples, hate peoples, and talk about them and do things like that. But one time I needed prayer, and the people, they come and they prayed for me. And Jesus set me free from all the things, all the bad things I was going through, especially the Indian dances, all the witchcraft and everything I've done. He set me free when I opened my heart and dedicated my life to the Lord. He healed me from many things; he healed me from my

sickness. Everytime I get sick I pray and then he heals me.

Last Sunday we was up to Minneapolis and we went to a healing service. And just when we got there—my boy was with me—he said, "Mom, I got a toothache. They are having a healing service over there. Why don't we go over there?"

So we went over there. He went up and this man prayed for him. And right there Jesus filled seven of his tooth that had cavities. He filled them with silver. This is really so. That's how powerful Jesus is. He can set you free from all your troubles, all your miseries. I never read a bible when I was out in the world. (I'm in the world, but, you know, when I was out there having a good time and things.) But when I'm closer to walking with Jesus, that's when he showed me many things—all the miracles he could do. Really have faith in Jesus!

And this is what he has done Sunday for my son. He healed my son, filled his cavities, and he come home. There are some other things he has done; you can't believe it! How Jesus could work—how he was healing those persons.

I was setting there watching them—how the peoples are going in line, and they get healed. And how powerful Jesus is, because I have that touch from him. When that man touch me like that, I just went out of myself.

So he can fill you if you have faith in him and give yourself to him and open your heart to him. He'll come in. He'll fill you with the Holy Spirit.

Next to speak was Nancy, the young woman, dressed in the slacks in which she had been working all day. What was most convincing about her testimony was the fact that she was shy and didn't like to talk: she was just saying it because that's the way it was.

I didn't believe that Jesus can heal anybody. I didn't believe, because I have never seen anything happen like that, but these people from Minneapolis took me up there. We went to the prayer meeting, and we walked in the door. I sat down.

I was sitting there, and the man that was standing up there come up to me and told me to come up front. He said, "You don't believe: you never did really accept Jesus. I want to pray for you." I didn't say nothing. I just stood there. He said, "Do you have any fillings?" I said, "No," and he said, "Do you have gold fillings?" I said, "No." He said, "Do you have any cavities?" I said, "Yes, but I am going to go to a dentist." He said, "Well, I'm going to pray for you. I want you to put your mind on Jesus. Forget everything else." I did what he said, and he started praying for me. I started feeling funny—you know, shaking inside and getting hot. Then he looked in my mouth and said, "You have never had any gold filling or silver filling?" I said, "No," so he called a lady up there and told her to look in my mouth. She say the top part of my mouth had gold in it and the bottom had silver fillings. I still didn't believe him. He knew that, so he told me to go home and look in the mirror.

I went back home that night, and I looked in the mirror. I could see the gold and the silver.

I went to the dentist; the dentist said, "You sure have some unusual fillings."

That's when I started believing.

I know it takes a lot from a person to really try to follow the way of the Lord. And it takes a lot to stand up and tell you people about him.

Father Odilo had just said a prayer for the Indians of the Dakotas and was about to conclude the meeting, when Mr.

Simon Keeble asked to speak. He began:

> You read Acts 1:1-9.
> Jesus goes out 40 days,
> And nobody knows what he does—
> How many prayers he uses,
> How many faiths and loves he got.
> You read that; you will see.
> But you in your own heart
> You really believe in him.
> He will show you right off,
> God can heal you!
>
> But it is the person—you—who will heal.
> You have to forgive the sick man yourself,
>   and to give him time:
> You ask him, "Do you have faith?"
>   "Do you love God?"
> And he answers, "Yes, yes, sure!" You
>   question him. You tell him he must
>   leave all his sins at the bottom.
> You ask him again, "Do you believe him?"
> He says, "Yes."
> Then you go touch him and you heal him right
>   now. Powerful how Jesus acts!
>
> I found that out.
> It comes through here (pointing to his heart).
> I can feel it—just like you get hold of
>   electricity.
> Is all in your body—makes you sweat.
> Then gets you warm and touch you.
> And you can heal.

We heal quite a few people in Sisseton.
They sometimes backslide and that's bad.
Jesus don't like that.
But Jesus forgives;
He likes the sinner.
He don't want nobody die.
He wants to be good to everybody.

Now, who likes Jesus? Raise your hand!
(Here the priests didn't know what to expect.
They all raise their hands hesitantly.)
How many of you ever heal anybody? (Here only
about two hands went up.)
How come? How come you know Jesus and you
no heal nobody? (Dead silence.)

The question, can it be true? confronts us all, as it did
those 45 priests that evening. With most cures that we hear
about we can imagine a natural process being speeded up;
we often harbor a deep-down suspicion that perhaps a natural
explanation can be found for what happens. But the filling of
teeth? How can we visualize that?

The call for a practical decision: "How come you know
Jesus and no heal nobody?" was taken seriously by at least one
priest who began from that day to pray for the sick, and now
has seen for himself: "Now we no longer believe because of
what you told us; we have heard him ourselves and we know
that he really is the savior of the world" (Jn 4:42).